CULTS

CULTS

FAITH, HEALING, AND COERCION

SECOND EDITION

MARC GALANTER

New York   Oxford
OXFORD UNIVERSITY PRESS
1999

Oxford University Press

Oxford   New York
Athens   Auckland   Bangkok   Bogotá   Buenos Aires   Calcutta
Cape Town   Chennai   Dar es Salaam   Delhi   Florence   Hong Kong   Istanbul
Karachi   Kuala Lumpur   Madrid   Melbourne   Mexico City   Mumbai
Nairobi   Paris   São Paulo   Singapore   Taipei   Tokyo   Toronto   Warsaw

and associated companies in
Berlin   Ibadan

Library of Congress Cataloging-in-Publication Data
Galanter, Marc.
Cults : faith, healing, and coercion / Marc Galanter. — 2nd ed.
p. cm.
Includes bibliographical references and index.
ISBN 0–19–512369–7 (hardcover). — ISBN 0–19–512370–0
1. Cults.   2. Sects.   3. Psychology, Religious.   4. Spiritual
healing.   I. Title.
BP603.G35   1999
200'.1'9—dc21   98–33532

2 4 6 8 10 9 7 5 3 1

Printed in the United States of America
on acid-free paper

In memory of my father

And the Spirit of the Lord will
come upon thee, and thou shalt prophesy with them,
and shalt be turned into another man.

I Samuel 10:6

CONTENTS

PREFACE TO THE SECOND EDITION

The term *cult* used to refer to a minor religious sect that practices its own peculiar rituals. Nowadays it suggests a secretive and dangerous group, one led by a madman or a charlatan. We regularly hear of bizarre behaviors in cults, but the glare of media attention belies the fact that there are lawful psychological processes that underlie their operation. I wrote the first edition of this book a decade ago to describe these processes, based on fifteen years' research, and did not expect it to attract much interest, since more startling perspectives were presented on television and in the press. So it was surprising to find that the book was successful with the general public as well as with the academics and students for whom it was intended. On reflection, it is clear that there was a broad base of interest in an objective look at the psychology behind this troubling phenomenon. With the Millennium now impending, and with the unfolding of the tragic episodes of the Branch Davidians, Aum Shinrikyo, and Heaven's Gate, further clarification is needed on what gives cults their power to wreak havoc. Suicide, immolation, and even mass murder have occurred in these groups.

Another important issue has emerged recently. The intense psychological forces found in the more harmful cults apparently operate in a modified form in a number of spiritually oriented groups directed at relieving the burden of illness. They range from the constructive movements like Alcoholics Anonymous to some dubious approaches at the periphery of "alternative medicine," like the misplaced use of untested Eastern healing rituals and New Age treatments. One might ask where alternative medicine ends and cultic healing movements, potentially harmful, begin. Because of this pressing question I chose to examine these healing movements as well.

There are many ways to study the influence brought to bear by all these zealous groups. Some approaches emerge from psychiatric hospitals, others from university laboratories or from behind the analytic couch. But most models fall short in describing how these groups engage their adherents, and moralistic interpretations add little to an objective understanding of the influence of cults. In this book, I hope to provide an integrated perspective on how we can approach these diverse groups and lend clarity to their potent appeal.

My own research this last decade included studies on a number of groups that were described colloquially as cults, and extended as well to spiritually oriented healing movements and other ideologically oriented self-help groups. We have also developed and evaluated some approaches to the treatment of substance abuse in my academic program that employ techniques observed in the healing groups. Over the past decade, I carried these studies out at New York University Medical Center while I was head of an academic division of research and teaching on addictive illness. These efforts were given valuable support by Saul Farber, past Dean of the Medical School, Robert Cancro, Chairman of the Department of Psychiatry, and Manuel Trujillo, the Head of Psychiatry at Bellevue Hospital. Appreciation is also due the faculty of the Division of Alcoholism and Drug Abuse, which I direct, and to our staff, particularly Kristin Frillmann. Grant funding was provided by the National Institute of Drug Abuse, the Substance Abuse and Mental Health Services Administration, the Scaife Family Foundation, the J. M. and Achelis and Bodman Foundations, and the New York Community Trust. As with the first edition of this book, this effort could not have been carried out without the wise counsel of my wife Wynne, and some inspiration from my daughters Cathryn and Margit.

New York   M. G.
January 1999

ACKNOWLEDGMENTS
TO THE FIRST EDITION

This book was written after fifteen years of studying the psychology of contemporary charismatic groups. Although this is an unusual subject for today's psychiatric research, I found it compelling because of the remarkable ability of these groups to exert influence on the thought and behavior of their members, often greater than our most potent treatments. An understanding of the "cult" phenomenon might offer valuable insights in areas as diverse as the treatment of mental illness and the understanding of group violence.

Inspiration for this quest lay in the work of observers who had succeeded in defining the nature of group behavior without being distracted by the particulars of ritual or circumstance. Max Weber, a sociologist, drew a perspective on charismatic leadership that could be employed in the most varied cultures. Wilfred Bion, a psychoanalyst, used the psychodynamic approach to understand small groups, and thereby afforded an understanding that went beyond the specific concerns of individual members to the innate forces governing group process. The contemporary sociobiologic paradigm recently articulated by Edward O. Wilson provided the foundation for the approach I developed in empirical biology, a reassuring opportunity for a physician researcher. Ideally, this approach will do justice to its antecedents.

I was fortunate to have skilled and understanding support in securing agreements with the groups I studied. Richard Erlich, Bonnie Blair, Kathy Lowrie, and Nora Spurgin were extremely helpful in this endeavor. Leaders of the groups themselves must certainly be credited for their willingness to undergo independent evaluation, particularly Neil Salonen and Mose Durst, presidents in their respective terms of the Unification Church in America.

Unfortunately, some members of these groups will question having their movements likened to others mentioned here. Conversely, detractors will likely take issue that criticism or even condemnation was not given. To proponents of both views I can only say that this book's purpose is to convey a psychological understanding of the charismatic group. Early on I realized it was necessary to avoid passing judgment on the merit of the groups' pursuits in order to study their operating principles. Very different groups could thus be compared with regard to their psychological and organizational processes but not for the inherent worth of their ideologies or tactics.

I am grateful to my colleagues and collaborators for their support and collaboration, both on conceptual issues and statistical analysis, and especially thank Robert Plutchik, Hope Conte, Mark Mizruchi, Peter Buckley, Alexander Deutsch, and Richard and Judith Rabkin. Assistance with data analysis was also given by my research assistants, Mary Tramontin, Denise Cancellare, Charles Flavio, Virginia Privitar, and Luiza Diamond.

The Department of Psychiatry at Albert Einstein College of Medicine in New York served as a home base for this work, where support was provided by Wagner Bridger, Herman van Praag, and Byram Karasu. I completed this book while at New York University, under the leadership of Robert Cancro. Grants and funding for this and related endeavors were given by the National Institute of Mental Health, the National Institute on Alcohol Abuse and Alcoholism, the National Institute on Drug Abuse, the Commonwealth Fund, and the J. M. Foundation.

My wife, Wynne, was patient and most helpful in offering valuable advice. She, along with Cathryn and Margit, gave inspiration.

New York   M. G.
September 1988

CULTS

1

THE CHARISMATIC GROUP

We tend to think of cults as anomalies, as if alien forces had swept their members—people who once seemed normal—into a netherworld beyond reason or understanding. When a cult is first discussed on the news, it is often described as if it were a new illness, different from the ones that came before. Even so, there is a way of understanding these groups not by their external trappings but by the psychology and social structure they hold in common. Once viewed in this way, their beliefs and behavior become more understandable, and the patterns underlying their idiosyncrasies emerge. We may even see that they have some things in common with movements and groups regarded as socially beneficial, and that the people who join them are not so different from ourselves. Some are looking to belong, others for emotional or physical healing. The purpose of this book is to clarify the puzzling transformations of human nature that take place in cultic groups and to explain how people can become engaged in them, adopt their beliefs, and follow their rules. We will look at spiritually oriented healing groups in this respect, as well, in an effort to shed light on contemporary alternative medicine.

Individuals who become involved in a religious cult or radical political group may do things that puzzle and dismay their friends and family. They may shave their heads, give away their family legacies, or even commit suicide on their way to heaven. Some turn to exotic healing practices. They may accept strangers 10,000 miles away as prospective mates, dedicate their lives to panhandling, or simply disappear. Their families may ask, "How could this happen? Nothing would have led us to expect it."

Strange as these transformations in attitude and action are, they can be understood in terms of psychological principles. These principles in turn can be explained and illustrated by recent research findings from seemingly diverse

1

groups that share a "charismatic" quality. Charismatic groups are highly co-hesive. They impute transcendent powers to the group's leader or its mission, and they strictly control members' behavior by means of a shared system of beliefs. Among these groups are cults and zealous religious sects; some highly cohesive self-improvement groups; and certain political action movements, among them some terrorist groups.

Three examples of individual members' experiences illustrate the impact of such cult-like groups. The first involves a young woman whom I interviewed some time ago.

> After breaking up with her boyfriend, Debbie left home on the East Coast to start summer school at a college in California. She was optimistic, if also a bit apprehensive, about her upcoming adventure. Her parents expected her to do well in the school environment, as she had dealt quite successfully with high school and the first year in a local college. Before summer school began, though, she was befriended by a group of youths who suggested that she get to know members of their informal organization, dedicated to promoting "social ecology and world peace." Within a month, she was spending all her spare time with the group. Only at this point was she told by them that the group was associated with a small religious cult with an elaborate and arcane theology. She was soon asked by the group's leader to adopt its idiosyncratic beliefs and leave school. Interestingly, she agreed to all this without hesitation, and began to devote herself full time to raising funds to support the cult. For the next three months her parents could not locate her. In the midst of their anxiety, they could offer no explanation as to why she "threw away" the family's values and her own stake in her future. Five years later Debbie described the period as a difficult but meaningful time, and the friends she made there as among the best she ever had.

In recent years, many such young people have had similar experiences. In most cases, neither a psychiatric disorder nor overriding social pressure explains the profound changes in their lives. Was this young woman's mind "captured" by the group? There was no evidence that physical restraint or even psychological coercion was used. Was she only superficial in her previous relationships? Neither her family nor her friends thought so. There was apparently something extrinsic to her in the group experience that exerted an unusual, overriding influence.

Consider another example:

> After increasingly heavy drinking that began in his teens, Ted became addicted to alcohol in his mid-thirties. His work performance passed from adequate to irregular, and he eventually lost the sales job he had held since college. Within the next year, his wife left him, taking their child with her (he had recently begun to beat her when he was drinking). Within five years he was hospitalized twice for gastrointestinal bleeding caused by his drinking. Despite frequent exposure to medical advice and the exhortation of his extended family, he expressed no interest in so-

briety and had refused to attend meetings of Alcoholics Anonymous. On one occasion, though, he accompanied a recovering alcoholic friend to an AA meeting and found himself agreeing to stay after the meeting to speak with some other members. When I talked with him two years later, he remarked that by this point no one seemed to care whether he lived or died, but he couldn't admit that it might be within his power to change this. He could give no clear reason for agreeing to attend the AA meetings at this point, but he continued to do so. Within two months of regular meetings, he had acquired the resolve to remain abstinent, although he himself still wondered how he had fended off for even sixty days the alcohol that had controlled his life for over two decades. Later contacts would reveal that AA helped him maintain abstinence thereafter.

We have come to view alcoholism as a disease, one reflecting both compulsive behavior and physical incapacity. How can social influence, through a self-help fellowship, so dramatically change this syndrome? How can it achieve such impressive results when family, friends, and professionals have been so limited in their ability to aid alcoholics alter their behavior, even when their illness seems likely to be fatal? As we will see, the mutual support by members of Alcoholics Anonymous serves to engage alcoholics and promote their acceptance of the group's values. The combination of intense social cohesiveness and strongly held, shared belief (in abstinence, in this case) allows for such striking behavioral change.

Consider a different issue. Here is a case of group influence leading to murder and international threat.

In March 1995, the nerve gas sarin was used in an attack on the Tokyo subway system, killing twelve and leaving a thousand injured. Members of the Aum Shinrikyo cult were later found to be responsible. Their leader, Shoko Asahara, was a self-proclaimed Buddhist guru who had predicted that the world would erupt into a war, and that only members of his cult could survive. The "medical director" of the cult, a respected cardiologist before he joined, testified later that a similar attack in the United States had been planned in detail the year before but was called off. The violent history of the movement was reflected in the murder by strangulation of a dissident member along with his wife and infant child several years before, and in a sarin gas attack in a small town the previous year, where seven people were killed. Evidence of responsibility for these crimes, which led to members of the cult, had been largely ignored by authorities. Even after the Tokyo subway poisonings, and the revelation of the responsibility of the cult and its leader, many of the group's members who were active in the Japanese cultural mainstream continued to avow fidelity to Asahara and his ill-defined philosophy.

How does such a network emerge and what keeps it together in the face of frightful criminality? How does it instill highly deviant norms of behavior in its members, for whom the act of murder was unimaginable before they joined? In psychology, social background, and education, these cult members were no different from their well-educated friends who moved on to conventional lives of family, work, and politics. How does an all-encompassing philosophy compel religious and political activists to give up their most deeply rooted standards of behavior, sacrifice the lives of others, and risk their own? Are there common mechanisms of group influence at work in these various examples, different as their personal, social, and political aims and outcomes may be?

What Is a Charismatic Group?

A charismatic group consists of a dozen or more members, even hundreds or thousands. It is characterized by the following psychological elements: members (1) have a *shared belief system*, (2) sustain a high level of *social cohesiveness*, (3) are strongly influenced by the group's *behavioral norms,* and (4) impute *charismatic* (or sometimes *divine) power* to the group or its leadership.

In a charismatic group, commitments can be elicited by relative strangers in a way rarely seen in other groups. Even Freud, who championed the compelling nature of individual motives, addressed this impressive capacity at length in his book *Group Psychology and the Analysis of the Ego.*[1] He discussed these forces in terms of the "primitive sympathetic response of the group," and said that "something is unmistakably at work in the nature of a compulsion to do the same as others, to remain in harmony with the many."

We will see that the cognitive basis for this conformity is a *shared belief system*. When these groups are religious in nature, their beliefs are often codified, but some groups have no more than an ill-defined ideologic orientation. In some religious cults, as shown in Debbie's experience, converts are introduced to the group's ideology only after they have affiliated. Once they have identified with the group's general orientation, though, they accept the particulars of belief quite readily when these are spelled out.

Members of these groups tend to be intensely concerned about each other's well-being, and are deeply committed to joint activities. Their *social cohesiveness,* essential to the group's integrity, is reflected in the close intertwining of the individual's life circumstances with those of all group members. Meetings are frequent; they serve as a focus for group functions and articulate their cohesiveness. Members often express their need to associate regularly with each other by developing joint activities such as minor group tasks and rituals, which in turn justify such meetings. Both cult and self-help group members are always well aware of when their next group meetings will be held, and look to them as a means of instilling commitment and a sense of purpose. A member's emotional state may be highly vulnerable to disruptions of this routine, and a group gathering missed can become a source of distress. As one longtime AA member noted while describing his despair over everyday problems, "It always feels good to go to a meeting."

The *norms for behavior* in a charismatic group play an inordinate role in determining how its members conduct themselves. Marital practices, for example, may be changed profoundly when the group itself adopts a certain style of betrothal. This emerged strikingly among the American-born members of the Unification Church (the "Moonies"). Although coming mainly from ordinary backgrounds, they agreed to get engaged in mass ceremonies to marriage partners whom they had never met before, selected for them on the spot by Reverend Moon.

Members also look to group norms for ways to behave in new situations. They may respond in a similar fashion to strangers perceived as threatening—in some groups, with a blunted and distant stare. Often they are implicitly aware of their style of behavior in an unexpected situation since it is based on previous instruction to the group. At other times it emerges without conscious appreciation of how they act. I found it intriguing to visit the headquarters of cult members overseas where even the style of socializing, the way food is served, and the response to strangers are the same as in countries several thousand miles away.

Behavioral change may also extend to mimicking the symptoms of mental illness. In these groups, transcendental experiences, often hallucinatory, are quite common. A deceased comrade "literally" stands by a member or a historical figure brings divinely inspired advice. Intense emotional experiences are reported, such as profound euphoria or malaise. Such phenomena, which are often seen among the mentally ill, occur among individuals who give no other evidence of psychiatric disorder.

Charismatic powers are typically imputed to leaders but can also be ascribed to the group or its mission. Some contemporary terrorist groups, for example, are viewed by their members as heralding an inevitable new world order—a remarkable belief, since the general acceptance of their peculiar philosophy is so unlikely.

These traits of charismatic groups are often best illustrated by the way they bring about changes in the thinking and behavior of individual members in single episodes. One example comes from my own research experience with the Divine Light Mission, a Hindu-oriented new religious movement. Janice, an eighteen-year-old American-born high-school senior, had described her problems to a counselor from this group at one of the group's religious festivals. I was studying the group while visiting the festival site, and was able to interview members at the counseling center.

The atmosphere at that center was highly cohesive; strong feelings of camaraderie and a sense of shared belief were evident as members arrived to discuss a variety of psychological problems. Janice came to the unit looking quite distressed. The counselor she encountered was not a health professional, but was contributing her time for Service, as religiously motivated good deeds were called. She allowed me to sit in as she spoke with the girl.

As the counselor approached her, Janice immediately burst into tears, explaining her misery and feelings of helplessness. She concentrated on her difficulty in meditating properly, saying of their Guru, "Maharaj Ji has given me Knowledge but I cannot see his light." This was very important to her, she said, because she could not be a premie, or a member of the sect, without this transcendental experience, achieved through proper meditation. She was further troubled because she felt obliged to do more Service for the Guru to compensate for her inability to meditate properly. This was best done by engaging new converts, but, she reported tearfully, she was too frightened to approach potential members.

The counselor listened to these expressions of distress, implicitly conveying support by her presence and demeanor. Her actions were in keeping with the atmosphere of the counseling center; she was empathic, even affectionate, and alluded to similar problems with meditation other members might experience from time to time. She expressed her perspective from the vantage point of the group's transcendent beliefs, and did not minimize the need for proper meditation or Service. She did, however, give Janice some examples of how problems like hers may be overcome in time with full devotion to the Guru, and reassured her that it was not necessary to perform an undue amount of Service at present. She said that the resolution of this distress might come through a ritual called *darshan,* meeting with the Guru in person, where such difficulties are often remitted. The following exchange ensued.

> COUNSELOR: Now tell me how you feel toward the premies you meditate with.
>
> JANICE: Of course, I am very close to them. They mean so much to me, like brothers and sisters.
>
> COUNSELOR: So you know now that when you are with them you confirm Maharaj Ji's Knowledge. You attend *satsang* [religious sermons] with them, and you will be going to *darshan,* too. You know that Maharaj Ji will see that you are faithful, and this will soon lead to your relief.
>
> JANICE: Yes I do. You *are* right.

By now the girl, like many others healed by faith, was composed and visibly reassured, even serene. I asked her counselor how she understood the girl's distress. She tried to explain, searching for a simple response, as a professional would speak to a layperson. "She had somehow lost the Knowledge. This happens often. She did not know how to rejoin Maharaj Ji's path." This was stated more as literal fact than metaphor, an expression of the charismatic role of their leader.

I was then able to speak with Janice. She had been having an affair with an older married man around the time she became affiliated with the group. When he ended their relationship two months before her arrival for counseling, she became acutely depressed, withdrew from social relations, and was unable to concentrate on her school work. At this point she also began having difficulty meditating, clearly due to the anxiety associated with her depressed state. This only compounded her sense of guilt and probably prolonged the depressive reaction that might otherwise have abated. She began to feel the need to do more Service for the group, in part to atone for the sexual liaison and also because she saw herself as an inadequate sect member. She had not discussed these matters with anyone. She felt her conduct had run contrary to the group's principles, and she was ashamed.

The genesis of Janice's difficulties in meditating seemed fairly clear to me, but she had not really put the pieces together herself. Significantly, this issue of her disrupted affair did not have to be broached with her Divine Light counselor because the cohesiveness of the group and the explanatory nature of its dogma (Maharaj Ji's Knowledge) were implicitly available without fuller exploration. These group forces were mobilized to relieve her feelings of guilt.

I spoke with Janice the next day after a protracted KNOWLEDGE session, a religious experience conducted for a large group of members by a principal of the Guru, and asked her how she was feeling. She said that the counselor

> was right to say that Maharaj Ji could offer me other ways to serve him. I could tell that when I was with all the premies today, Maharaj Ji's wisdom was touching me and that what I was doing was right. . . . it's clear that everything will work out; I have the Knowledge in me again.

This young woman had been wrenched into anguish compounded by her *feelings of distance* from the group, and apparently relieved and then healed through a renewed closeness. The norms for behavior set by the group were used to construct her "treatment," and the resolution of her problem was sealed by her commitment to the group's charismatic goal of "Knowledge," or divine enlightenment.

A Research Perspective

The psychology of zealous groups has not been a popular area of research. In recent years, however, scientific interest in such groups, and our ability to investigate their emotional impact, has advanced dramatically. To appreciate this newer perspective, we need to review previous studies.

Although Freud wrote about the infectious nature of cohesive groups, the fate of that work stands in contrast to his contributions to individual psychology. His concepts of the unconscious and the importance of early childhood experiences have been studied in great depth, but his views on group experiences were not extended by psychologists and psychiatrists. William James was aware of the absence of scientific attention to the impact of such experiences even two decades before Freud wrote on group influence. In 1902, this founder of modern psychology wrote an acerbic critique of the profession's ignorance of the psychology of religious affiliation.

> Medical materialism finishes up St. Paul by calling his vision on the road to Damascus a discharging lesion of the occipital cortex, he being an epileptic. It snuffs out St. Teresa as a hysteric, St. Francis of Assisi as an hereditary degenerate.[2]

Why wasn't James' call for attention to the psychological side of such religious phenomena more actively heeded? This can be put another way relative to our thesis. If the charismatic group is a discrete phenomenon governed by psychological principles, why has it attracted so little systematic study? Why have we not developed a coherent body of observation and explanatory principles to make sense of its members' experiences? The reasons for this reflect contemporary attitudes toward psychological research and limitations in our understanding and study of the biologic basis of social behavior. First let us consider "styles" of scientific investigation.

That scientific investigation is shaped by social bias goes without saying. In its extreme such bias was enforced by a trip to the stake. More commonly, it is reflected by inattention to alternative perspectives. The contemporary paradigm of psychological research is based on carefully controlled measurement of observable behavior. It is closely allied to a philosophy of science articulated by the natural philosopher and historian David Hume some two hundred years ago.

> If we take in our hand any volume of divinity or school metaphysics, for instance, let us ask, does it contain any abstract reasoning concerning quantity and number? No. Does it contain any experimental reasoning concerning matter of fact and existence? No. Commit it then to the flames: for it can contain nothing but sophistry and illusion.[3]

From this attitude toward empirical science comes the value we attach to quantifiable observation of measurable natural phenomena. In psychology it fosters an inclination to study psychological phenomena that can be reproduced and measured in a controlled setting, not necessarily those that are most intensely compelling. This general approach has indeed borne fruit in the field of psychology, as in the works of Pavlov, Watson, and Skinner. Needless to say, these investigators did not study charismatic group experiences in their laboratories.

Indeed, the laboratory-based scientific community has long been suspicious of the subjective nature of inference in such areas, where formal, controlled studies are not easily conducted. What scientific approach can consequently apply to charismatic groups? One perspective, derived from evolutionary theory[4] and popularized by Edward Wilson, is sociobiology,[5] which applies the principles of evolution, ethology (the study of animal behavior), and genetics to the study of social interactions.

Population geneticists have pointed out that the survival of biologically grounded behavior traits over generations depends on the traits themselves more than on the person who manifests them. A behavioral trait can persist if it promotes the survival of *relatives* of that person who carry the same genes for that trait.[6] Social affiliation and altruism therefore become important aspects of evolution. In my own studies, I attempted to investigate the nature of affiliative behavior[7] and then relate it to behaviors observed by anthropologists[8] and ethologists[9] to understand how patterns of group affiliation evolved and continued.

My first study of charismatic sects was the Divine Light Mission, a Hindu-oriented group, followers of a child guru. I found among the high membership an intense social cohesiveness, as well as a decline in the level of neurotic distress symptoms on joining the group. There was a relationship between these two observations: a high correlation existed between the degree to which a member felt affiliated with the group and the relief in distress that person experienced on joining.

I later studied induction and membership in the Moonies, and found that potential recruits acquire a high degree of social cohesiveness very quickly during initial phases of the introductory workshops. Furthermore, the psychological well-being of active members was directly proportional to how closely affiliated with the group they felt, in terms of both social ties to other members and acceptance of the group's beliefs.

One might therefore conclude that members of charismatic groups experience a relief in neurotic distress on joining, and that maintaining that relief (i.e., a sense of psychological well-being) depends on the intensity of their relationship with the group: if they disaffiliate somewhat, they experience distress; if they remain close, they keep their psychological well-being. This "relief effect" serves to reinforce members' involvement in the group and also continually reinforces their acceptance of the group's beliefs by rewarding them for their conformity and acceptance. As we will see, both anthropologic and ethologic evidence suggest that such affiliative behaviors and biologically grounded drives improve the ability of a group to adapt and survive.

A different scientific perspective—*a systems approach*—can be used to analyze a group's structure and functioning.[10] In looking at a system, we do not first ask what motivates an individual member to act. Instead we say, "How are the *group's* needs met by the overall behavior observed in its membership?"

From this viewpoint many observations of individual behavior can be synthesized into a model that can help us to better understand motivations. We may consider these individuals' behavior as it is generated by the needs of the social group, even when it seems to run contrary to their interests and personalities. This enables us to see how strongly they can be influenced to conform to the system's need to stabilize and carry out broader objectives.

Many years ago I saw a striking example of how this influence filters the impact of events within one group on another. On a Sunday in November 1978 a banner headline in *The New York Times* read, "GUYANA TOLL IS RAISED TO AT LEAST 900 BY U. S., WITH 260 CHILDREN AMONG THE VICTIMS AT COLONY." It was rapidly becoming clear that a bizarre and frightening situation of historic proportions had arisen in the past week among the followers of the cult leader Jim Jones. A mass suicide of American citizens had occurred in an isolated South American encampment where members of this group had sequestered themselves. Ironically, Jones was a Protestant minister who had been an esteemed member of the San Francisco Bay Area religious community only months before.

I was unsure how to relate this tragedy to the Moonies, whose recruitment techniques I was studying. The Moonies themselves had just been the subject of a critical congressional inquiry, and were quite vulnerable to the anxieties that fueled public opinion on the issue of cults. They had been compared to every deviant movement that congressional witnesses might suggest.

Only a few days before, when interviewed about the events in Guyana by a national newsmagazine,[11] I was reluctant to tar the vulnerable and less ominous new religious movements inadvertently by association with these bizarre events, since it seemed to me that unique circumstances surrounded the Peoples Temple. (Particularly important was the prolonged isolation of Jones's followers in a jungle setting, with no feedback from outside the group to contradict the paranoid views that Jones himself had come to espouse.)

The vulnerability of the Moonies to public opinion at this juncture was corroborated that morning when I telephoned their workshop center in the San Bernardino mountains of California, where my study of recruitment practices was soon to begin. The workshop coordinator reported with concern that parents of five of the participants had driven up from Los Angeles to wrest their children away from what they feared might be an ominous fate. One family brought the local police to remove them, and the workshop leaders had felt it wise under the circumstances to accede to the parents' demands, even though they recognized no legal ground for removing these members, who were neither minors, nor coerced, nor mentally incompetent.

Later that day, as I entered the Unification Church's U.S. Headquarters in Manhattan, to make final administrative arrangements for the study, I wondered whether some shock wave might have struck the group by now. Were they rushing to prepare for public attacks on their sect? I knew the young man at the reception desk, and remarked how unfortunate it was that events in Jonestown might be used against his church. He said, "It's sad it happened to them. But no one would compare us to that terrible group."

I went upstairs wondering why he would think that, and found an air of calm. It soon became clear that they saw the events in Jonestown as not related to them in any way. It was further clear from discussions with members at large, as well as directors of church departments, that no statement had been promulgated by the leadership about what views the members might adopt toward the Jonestown affair. The Moonie members, functioning as an integrated social system, had somehow developed a psychologically defensive perspective. Their denial of the implications of the Jonestown affair apparently protected the group from being confronted by the similarities that might be drawn between their own cult-like structure and that of the Peoples Temple. One member gave me his view of the group's detractors while rationalizing what criticisms might be raised.

> We don't really need to deal with them on this. They would pick up on any little matter they can dig up to criticize us. Anyway, if there's one thing we can do here [in the church] it's to do what each of us wants. Reverend Moon would never lead us astray anyway, because of his own Divine Principle.

I soon concluded that the issue was better avoided. Members of this social system had obviously arrived at a consensus that, above all, assured the system's equilibrium by quashing potentially threatening self-examination.

On this basis, we may consider the operation of a religiously oriented charismatic group in relation to one aspect of systems theory—the role of feedback among system components. The group must struggle to preserve its integrity and gain acceptance or tolerance from society at large, since it typically constitutes a small and deviant minority. With the Jonestown events, the Moonies with whom I spoke were clearly moved to suppress any threatening implications. As if by plan, the system "unconsciously" assumed a posture that assured its own stability. It needed to avoid the feedback implied in any acknowledgment that the Unification Church might be similar to the Peoples Temple. In similar ways charismatic groups may operate to effect their goals. By incorporating members' needs for affiliation into the group's social system, they create a strong social unit capable of exerting much influence over the members' thoughts and actions.

Decades passed, and Guru Maharaj Ji, leader of the Divine Light Mission, married an American airline stewardess and settled down; Reverend Moon married off 1,410 of his followers in New York, couples that he himself had paired three years before. The Moonies and the members of Divine Light Mission bore children and took jobs to support themselves. These charismatic groups seemed to evolve into small but peaceable religious groups, as many such sects had done earlier in American history.

But new groups and new events, headlined in the press, now shocked us, each erupting like a small volcano in one's backyard. One such event occurred in Waco, Texas fifteen years after the cataclysm in Guyana. Under FBI command, federal tanks stormed the compound of the Branch Davidian cult to flush out members with tear gas after a long siege. David Koresh, the group's leader, apparently ordered the torching of the group's interconnected buildings, which caused the incineration of more than eighty of his followers, both adults and children, and himself. The government assault on Koresh's Branch Davidians in Waco led to another tragedy in another unremarkable American city. Two years later to the day, in 1995, Timothy McVeigh, an unemployed army veteran enamored of right-wing cultic literature, sought revenge for the government's actions in Waco. He detonated a truck bomb at a federal office building in Oklahoma City, killing 168 people—again, adults and children. A cult's potential for generating overreaction by organized authorities helped spawn this tragedy.

Also in 1995, in Tokyo's central Kasumigaseki subway station, a sarin poisoned gas attack was ordered by Shoko Asahara, the Japanese leader of a large cultic group called Aum Shinrikyo. Twelve people died and hundreds were injured. Two years after this Tokyo assault, thirty-nine bodies of members of the Heaven's Gate cult were found in a suburb of San Diego, California, after they had poisoned themselves, expecting to leave their "earthly vessels," their mortal bodies, and be transported to heaven. Their act had been signaled by the Hale-Bopp comet's appearance in the sky.

How do some charismatic groups evolve from idiosyncrasy to seeming normalcy, while others move on to suicide or murder? All engage the emotional needs of their members in an intensely cohesive social system, legitimated by ideologies drawn from an indigenous cultural base. On the other hand, their ideologies are sufficiently idiosyncratic to define a psychological border around the group. Several factors come into play in the transformation of these movements, and we will see how such closed systems, spearheaded by leaders with imputed divine powers, even allegedly divine identities, draw their members deeply into a vortex of social controls that require absolute fidelity and the dissolution of ordinary social norms.

Paradoxically, there is an entirely different aspect to the phenomenon of charismatic and zealous groups, and we will explore this as well. As medical care has become increasingly oriented toward technology and impersonal in nature, spiritual movements oriented toward recovery from illness have become popular in recent years and have established a healing mainstream of their own. They draw on the strengths of the cultic psychology we have considered here: strongly held ideologies that are idiosyncratic in nature and social cohesiveness that creates a movement tied to the image of a leader whose flock reveres him. The engagement of people in such groups are driven by their distress. In the case of spiritual healing movements, it is the fear of death or emotional or physical pain, more than loneliness and social displacement, that underlies cult recruitment.

Some of these healing movements have become well-structured over time and are clearly beneficial, like Alcoholics Anonymous—"Friends of Bill," the charismatic founder of the movement, as they sometimes call themselves. Some adhere to Ayurvedic medicine or one of a number of other Eastern healing techniques, or oddities like creative visualization. These may offer little physiologic benefit but can provide important emotional support in the face of illness. We shall see how these movements emerge, evolve, and often provide considerable benefit.

I

FORCES IN THE CHARISMATIC GROUP

Few of us are expert in understanding the behavior of people in groups. We arrive at a practical "expertise" in human nature by relying on everyday social exchanges, but such exchanges are mainly with individuals rather than groups. A child begins to learn about human relations as she turns to her mother to elicit a favor, and a youth follows his teacher's behavior, trying to assess how he is expected to behave. As adults, we deal primarily with individuals: a woman studies a co-worker to gain his cooperation, then returns home to puzzle over why her husband seems troubled.

We develop working models of human behavior based on the way individuals are motivated, solve problems, react in anger, expect appreciation. This cognitive set is hard to break when the focus shifts from the individual to the group.

Attempts to influence large groups of people illustrate this point. Only the most practiced actors have developed the facility of standing on stage and reading the shifting moods of an audience so as to tap the forces operating in the group setting. It is an unusual public speaker who can motivate a large group, just as it is an unusual psychiatrist who can develop a strategy for generating a therapeutic response in a group of fifty patients, or for turning a large group's interest away from issues that create conflict. To acquire these skills requires repeated exposure to uncommon situations that give people the opportunity to practice and learn.

Few people have the opportunity to learn firsthand the principles governing the motivations of a charismatic group. And those who do are more likely to operate intuitively than to study these groups in a controlled, scientific setting. Thus, it is not surprising that our understanding of the psychological forces operating in such groups has been slow to develop, certainly slower than a comparable understanding of individuals. We lack means for "reading" these forces, for anticipating the group's motivations.

The psychological forces that mold the intensely affiliated charismatic group cannot be examined adequately through the prism of individual psychology, whether that of the citizen-in-the-street, the clinician, or the researcher. Instead, they must be understood from the perspective of the group as a whole; when properly understood, these forces have a compelling, almost palpable quality. They include group cohesiveness, shared beliefs, and altered consciousness.

2

GROUP
COHESIVENESS

Group cohesiveness may be defined as the result of all the forces acting on members to keep them engaged in the group.[1] When cohesiveness is strong, participants work to retain the commitment of their fellow members, protect them from threat, and ensure the safety of shared resources. With weak cohesiveness, there is less concern over the group's potential dissolution or the loss of its distinctive identity, and joint action is less likely.

Group cohesiveness[2] is seen in informally structured groups, such as a clique of teenagers who make every effort to get together, even when forcibly separated by their elders. It also exists in formally structured groups, such as professional sports teams or military platoons, whose members undergo great sacrifice to assist each other in their common mission, particularly when confronted by adversaries. In most organized groups, however, it is characterized by neither adversity nor great drama; in a fraternal organization, for example, members meet regularly to share experiences and give each other practical assistance.

A Clinical Model

Two group settings in particular attract the attention of clinicians: families and therapy groups. In both settings a body of empirical observation highlights the impact of a group's cohesiveness on the psychological function of members, and although both family and therapy groups are smaller than charismatic groups, they demonstrate the potent role this psychological force can play in shaping feelings, attitudes, and behavior.

We will begin looking at the issue of cohesiveness with a review of some studies on the relationships in families that are intensely close-knit, and for this we must rely largely on clinical observations. The concept of the "differentiation of self," developed by family theorists such as Murray Bowen and Lyman Wynne,[3] helps explain the interaction between the individual and his or her family, and can be assessed independently of a person's diagnosis, social class, and cultural background. At one end of this scale lies the highly differentiated individual, characterized by autonomy and even rugged individualism. At the other end family relationships exhibit emotional fusion and an inability to make critical judgments because of a need to assure harmony with others.

Emotional fusion in families is akin to group cohesiveness in its merging of identity and decision-making functions. It occurs in large charismatic groups as well as in families because members of both may be highly dependent on each other and rely excessively on their compatriots for emotional support and decision making.[4] This is also seen among certain disturbed families unable to tolerate disruptions in the balance of their members' relationships. For example, if a psychiatrist attempts to change an apparently harmful pattern of interaction with a family, one way or another that pattern will soon reestablish itself; this takes place without any formal understanding among family members, as if a governing structure existed outside their awareness.

Take, for example, Ann, an unemployed, twenty-two-year-old living with her divorced mother, who was admitted to the hospital during an acute psychotic episode. Her case illustrates the intense mutuality and lack of differentiation seen in a pathologically cohesive family. Her mother had brought her to the emergency room after a battle between them, during which Ann had become uncontrollable, demanding that she be allowed to seal the windows of their apartment to protect them from poison gas. Ann herself was hallucinating the voices of threatening figures who warned her about her neighbors' plans to kill her and her mother.

Ann and her brother, one year younger, had both been involved since childhood in intense, ambivalent relationships with their mother, but the brother had enlisted in the army three years before, hoping to escape. Mother and daughter now spent almost all their time alone together and were, for each other, their only sources of social support. Soon after the brother left, they began to develop a delusion that was remarkable because it was shared in its entirety by both mother and daughter. This *folie à deux* was the belief that their neighbors were plotting to kill them by injecting poison gas into their apartment. Both women devoted considerable time to averting this eventuality by plugging up spaces in the walls and carefully observing the neighbors' comings and goings.

The current crisis had been precipitated by the brother's return from military service. Ann's closeness to her mother was threatened, and she fell into an unmanageable state. Her involvement with her mother had become so intense that a disruption in the relationship threatened her very sanity, and Ann's perception of the world around her had become grounded in that very relationship. She now began to hallucinate and to assault her mother physically, thereby assuring herself a greater measure of maternal attention since her mother would attempt to restrain her.

The hospitalization precipitated by these events was characterized by a rivalry between the mother and the medical staff, each vying, as it were, to secure Ann's fidelity by providing their respective cures. The staff's medication did indeed stop the hallucinations, although Ann's persecutory delusion abated more slowly. Her mother sustained Ann's attachment to her by bringing in countless packages of preserved fruit, meat, and beverages, which caused difficulty with the nursing staff.

Ann's condition soon stabilized, and the medical staff, with no alternative to offer, planned to return her to her mother's care. It was presumed that Ann's persecutory delusion, like her hallucinations, had resolved in response to the medication since both symptoms had abated. When interviewed with her mother before discharge, however, Ann began once more to speak of the dangers present in the household, subtly abetted by her mother, and one month later mother and daughter again shared the same delusional perspective, although Ann was no longer hallucinating and violent. Their close tie apparently served to reinstate their distorted perspective.

A family like this, albeit pathologic, illustrates how a group's equilibrium can be reestablished in the face of an external threat. In this case, the threat was the brother's return and then intervention by supportive outsiders, the hospital staff.

Preserving intense interrelatedness is also essential to a religious cult. A cult can react similarly to the potential disruption of its social stability when, for example, its leader becomes manifestly deranged. A good example was provided by Alexander Deutsch in his study of thirty followers of Baba, an American-born, self-proclaimed guru.[5] The cult had coalesced in the early 1970s not long after Baba returned from a spiritual voyage to India and began sitting each day on a park bench in Manhattan's Central Park. His followers—"The Family," as they called themselves—ate, sang, meditated, and worshiped their leader at this spot. They also spoke of deep ties to him and to each other. Essential to Baba's philosophy was the concept of "letting go," which required that his followers detach themselves from worldly desire, ambition, and guilt to achieve unity with God. However, Baba did not speak at all; instead he communicated in sign language, a personal system understandable only through his interpreter.

Within a few years, at Baba's urging, the group relocated to a rural setting. Although their successful transition reflected commitment to the group, Baba soon began to show evidence of psychiatric deterioration. His muteness became increasingly autistic, and the sign language he developed became fragmented, to the point that his devotees could no longer follow it. He began to act strangely. For example, he used a large sum from the group's modest resources to buy himself a Jacuzzi, even though there was no electricity where they lived. He also beat some cult members repeatedly and subjected some of the women to sexual abuse.

All this should have put considerable stress on the group's stability, but throughout this period Baba's "Family" remained relatively intact and sustained its close-knit relationship. The members shared their resources; some contributed considerable personal assets to their guru. Neither the move to the rural commune, their privation, nor Baba's derangement and abusive behavior succeeded in separating them.

They adapted to the situation, compromising their sense of reality but sustaining their dependency on the leader and their cohesiveness in this small cult. They continued to insist that Baba's leadership was benign and his path merely a "hard trip," requiring much faith and fortitude. Paradoxically, they even maintained that he was a model of freedom and his bizarre behavior was a reflection of not being trammeled by socially imposed constraints. They did not deny that Baba might be "crazy" but insisted that this simply brought him closer to the expression of a "divine energy" and that, in his behavior, he was "teaching them a lesson." When a woman was sexually abused by Baba, the group concluded that she had been holding on too tightly to her chastity. The purchase of the Jacuzzi was said to illustrate the importance of letting go of money.

Both Baba's "Family" and Ann's family reflect the dynamics of excessive mutuality in family pathology. Both needed to preserve their cohesiveness and interdependency, to remain stable in the face of internal or external threat. This led to a distorted consensus, a mutually held point of view, that allowed equilibrium to be maintained. The consensus was achieved by denying reality and rationalizing their shared perspective. Reality becomes less important to certain groups than the preservation of their ties.

The aberrant manifestation of social cohesiveness found in pathologic families (and to a lesser degree in normal ones) has its parallels in psychotherapy groups. Contemporary models of group therapy owe much to Wilfred Bion, a British psychoanalyst who pointed out that a group may be moved by latent forces, usually unknown to its members. As a leader of early experimental therapy groups, Bion chose to remain silent, making only occasional interpretive comments. He provided little if any leadership so that he might observe the psychological forces operating within the group. Central among these forces was the desire of the members to be dependent on the leader and remain close to each other. By not acting to fulfill this need and avoiding an active leadership role, Bion allowed the groups' unmet needs to become increasingly apparent as the level of anxiety mounted,[6] reflecting the force of social cohesion.

Bion observed that a group operates on two levels simultaneously: "tasks"—matter-of-fact functions such as, "When will the next meeting be held?" or "Who will arrange for proper heating in the room?"; and "basic assumptions"—unconscious drives such as the dependency that places pressure on the leader to meet the group's expectation of being held together and led. At any given time the basic assumptions can influence the nature of the group interactions and its task-oriented behavior. Thus, a practical group decision to reorganize its schedule may be compromised by members' fears of having their security in the group threatened.

For the clinical training of group therapists, A. K. Rice at the Tavistock Clinic developed participatory group exercises that shed light on the dynamics of large groups led by trainer-"consultants." By providing little or no structured leadership within these training groups, trainers elicited surprising behavior. For example, members would sometimes become extremely hostile over petty group concerns. Rice commented on the need for a cohesive structure.

> Without an abstract ideal or external enemy its boundaries are difficult to define; without boundaries, and hence without even an elemental structure, action is impulsive and hence potentially dangerous. . . . In this emotional climate the members turn to the consultants for reassurance that they, at least, can control the violence; the fear, and it is shared by the consultants, is that they too will be unable to act quickly or wisely enough to avert disaster.[7]

In charismatic groups, leaders express no such fear. Instead, they channel these inchoate forces into forming, in Coser's words, "a greedy institution." Such "institutions" seek exclusive and undivided loyalty. They reduce the social roles available to members to those provided by the group. They form "social cocoons" that help transform members' identities by forcing the group into social, ideological, or physical isolation.[8]

Freud's observation about group psychology and the pressures that draw individuals into consensual and irrational response is particularly apt here. The evolution of a crowd, he noted, is based on a compulsion in people to do the same as others, "to remain in harmony with the many."[9] This presents both a promise and a threat.

A Charismatic Religious Sect: The Divine Light Mission

A friendship led to my first encounter with contemporary sects or new religious movements[10] and served to highlight the influential role of group cohesiveness in shaping the behavior of charismatic groups. I had known Beth[11] for ten years, and we had kept in touch while living in different cities. Her personal life had been disrupted by a divorce and a move to a new university teaching job. Soon after she gave up a promising academic career to devote herself to the philosophy of a teenage guru who had arrived in the United States the year before; eventually she moved into a commune of the guru's followers. How could she have adopted such a deviant lifestyle after spending her adult years at liberal universities?

The group she joined, the Divine Light Mission, was introduced to the United States in 1971 by a thirteen-year-old boy from India, scion of a family of Hindu holy men; members believed in the lad's messianic role. Divine Light was not unlike a number of Eastern-oriented sects that emerged in the United States around this time. Along with others having a neo-Christian orientation, these groups constituted the bulk of the emerging cult phenomenon, or, depending on one's view, new religious movements. The introduction Beth gave me to the Divine Light Mission led to a series of studies of these movements.

A History of the Sect

Like many groups of Hindu orientation, the Divine Light Mission originated as religious practice in India. It was founded in 1960 by Sri Hans Ji Maharaj, father of the Guru Maharaj Ji and a former member of the Radhasoami Satsang Beas, one of several Sikh religious movements in northern India. Each of those movements operated independently and was headed by a leader regarded by members as a satguru, or perfect master, whose task was to lead his followers along a path to God.[12]

Maharaj Ji was the youngest of four sons of Sri Hans Ji, and even as a young child participated with his family in their public religious programs. Given this status, he was accorded a great deal of attention by his father's devotees and lived in luxury.[13] When his father died, eight-year-old Maharaj Ji was selected to lead the sect instead of his older brothers because of his unusual talent at delivering religious homilies.

Within a few years, the sect began to send mahatmas, or apostles, overseas to preach the young guru's inspired mission, and by the time he was eleven, Maharaj Ji himself had traveled to London. Two years later he came to the United States at the invitation of several American premies (followers) who had received Knowledge (enlightenment) in India. The young guru visited several cities and was accorded a favorable reception by many young people who were experiencing the uprooting of the late counterculture era with its rebellions against established authority. As he traveled, he began to attract a following.

Maharaj Ji returned to India to tend to the members of the Mission there, but came back to the United States a year later and established a national headquarters in Denver. Within months, hundreds of American youths accepted the guru's invitation to receive Knowledge and flew with him to India in several chartered jumbo jets for a festival called Hans Jayanti. On their arrival, his followers were taken to the family's ashram, or religious commune, for several weeks.

By this time, about a thousand members had moved into a dozen Divine Light communes in Denver,[14] and soon there were several thousand members nationwide. Commune residents devoted their full time to the group, and took an active role in developing a national organization for the guru. The study I carried out then provided a profile of sect members,[15] revealing that they were typically single (82%) whites (97%) in their twenties (73%). The distribution of Catholics (32%) and Protestants (44%) was not very different from the general population (38% and 57%, respectively), but there was a greater proportion of Jews (21% vs. 2%).[16] The members' middle-class background was reflected in the large majority that had attended college (76%), as had one or both parents (71%). Typical group members were middle-class young adults, many of whom had interrupted higher education to join the sect.

What were some of the trappings of religious practice in this emerging movement? Potential initiates were usually introduced to the Divine Light Mission at a session of religious discourse called a satsang, where experienced members presented the philosophy of the sect to the assembled group. The satsang could be delivered to active members or to those with only a casual interest. It was something of a polemic interspersed with parables, and because members were bright and sophisticated, these discourses tended to be engaging, making use of both Hindu mythology and Western philosophy.

After a period of acquaintance with the group, a potential member might approach a mahatma from the sect. These were longtime Indian devotees designated by the guru to initiate new members. Although their pronouncements were often obscure, they lent an aura of transcendence to the initiation. In the initiation ceremony the mahatma rubbed the eyes of the newly initiated members, producing a sensation of flashes that were perceived as a divine light. Initiates wee thereafter called premies, or followers of the guru.

The premies undertook four types of meditative experience during daily periods of silent repose, spent with eyes closed. In the first meditation they visualized a light, described as real and intense. In the second they heard music, and this too was reported not to be metaphoric but rather an essential sound of the universe. In the third meditation they tasted "nectar," supposedly a purifying fluid flowing from the brain to the throat,[17] and finally they spoke the "word," said to be a primordial vibration that underlies all existence. These meditations were recounted with great zeal.

Performing Service, or good works, for the sect was a requirement, and giving satsang was one type of Service, as it led others to hear that the knowledge was available. Other Service included helping with the arrangement of speaking tours for the mahatmas and drawing new converts into the group. Premies could live in the ashrams to devote themselves more fully to Service. These premies often worked part- or full-time outside the ashram and gave a sizable portion—sometimes all—of their income to the movement. They also practiced celibacy, vegetarianism, and frequent meditation. The focus of this ascetic existence was their religious mission rather than personal pleasure or gain.

In 1973, the sect rented the Houston Astrodome for a celebration of world peace and religious rejuvenation, "Millennium '73," billed as "the most significant event in human history." Devotees were flown from overseas, and the event was promoted with considerable advance publicity and a good deal of media coverage. A highlight of the celebration was the participation of Rennie Davis, one of the Chicago Seven anti–Vietnam War protestors who had recently become a premie. The event, however, fell far short of expectations. The stadium was only partially filled; a variety of millennial expectations, such as the arrival of world peace, failed to materialize, and the whole undertaking left members of the movement disillusioned and in debt.

The guru himself, however, was increasingly taken by the enticements of American society. He was, after all, still a teenager, not above spraying his coterie with shaving cream for fun. Such pranks led them to speak of his "heavenly playfulness." He began dressing in Western clothes and adopted a luxurious lifestyle that included setting up residence in a mansion and being ferried about in a limousine.

Soon he married his secretary, an attractive American woman several years older. This he did against his mother's wishes, and the event precipitated a schism in the family, ultimately leading to the estrangement of the American branch of the religious sect from its main body in India, where his mother and brothers remained. His mother revoked his title of satguru, an action he refused to accept. Maharaj Ji now began to preach against the betrayal he felt he experienced at the hands of his family, couching his arguments in parables drawn from Hindu mythology. In America too, the marriage caused dismay, particularly among the premies living in ashrams who had followed the strict path of celibacy dictated by the guru himself. Perhaps half of these members left the sect over this issue.[18]

Maharaj Ji now moved his headquarters from Denver to Miami without explanation. This caused a major dislocation among his remaining followers, most of whom did accompany him. In Miami, he moved further away from the sect's traditional Hindu flavor and gave less active direction to sect members. At first, he led religious meetings about once a month in a hired auditorium, where as many as 500 to 600 followers would assemble, but after a while he appeared less often, and rarely visited the ashrams in the community. Maharaj Ji nonetheless was still regarded as a divine figure by his followers.

The movement had apparently reached its peak of expansion and popularity, and in the next few years many members drifted away, although they still retained an attentuated fidelity to their spiritual leader. Some who had interrupted their education or their careers began to look for a more stable identity within the Miami community. As they settled down, they increasingly adopted more traditional roles as young working adults and parents, while maintaining their reverence for the guru and their affection for other premies.

In 1984 Maharaj Ji moved again, with his wife, four children, and considerable assets. This time he went to the affluent beach community of Malibu in West Los Angeles but did not ask his followers to join him. Although he continued to make occasional spiritual tours, he did not appear at most of the religious gatherings held in his name. The diminishing numbers of his faithful, most of them still in Miami, did not appear to be disappointed in the sect's lack of coherence, and often explained it as paradoxically showing the strength of their leader's spiritual message. They continued in their meditations, although these became more of a personal matter and were practiced less frequently and in isolation.

Initial Encounters

My first encounter with the Divine Light Mission came when Beth invited me to visit an ashram at the time the group was expanding. She thought the sect would be interesting for a psychiatrist to observe because some members had experienced a relief from serious emotional problems when they joined. She felt her group had tapped a large area of mental function psychiatry was unaware of.

The atmosphere in the ashram was indeed quite striking. On entering a large apartment on the Upper West Side of Manhattan, I was greeted in a friendly, even intimate fashion by people who were complete strangers. The intense communality of the members was immediately apparent, a quality that was clearly an important aspect of the group's function. One could sense a closeness among those present, and an absence of the minor tensions that would be expected in a setting where two dozen people were living in tight quarters. A college dormitory, a military barracks, or a summer camp soon reveal a certain amount of hostile banter or argument. These appeared to be absent in the ashram. Caring and intimacy, reflective of the group's cohesiveness, seemed to mute any expression of animosity.

There were kind words, offers of food, expressions of interest, and warm smiles, all from people I'd never met before. Any question was soon answered, sometimes even anticipated. Having been invited by one of their members and defined temporarily as one of their own, I was made to feel as if I were entering a supportive envelope, to be protected from the rough edges of relationships in the outside world.

To illustrate the healing offered by her newfound religious experience, Beth told me about Janet, a twenty-six-year-old premie whose case showed the vital role that social bonds within this group play in stabilizing the members' subjective state and behavior. I later corroborated the details in interviews with the woman herself and her relatives and friends. Over the course of several hospitalizations dating back to her mid-teens, Janet had been diagnosed as schizophrenic. She had been placed on a variety of medications, usually major tranquilizers in modest to large doses. Despite this treatment, the intermittent hallucinatory periods, episodes of rage, and inappropriate behavior were not effectively brought under control. When Janet was not in the hospital, she lived with her hapless parents, and was apparently quite demanding and easily upset by their presence. The parents, unable to move her into an independent living situation, were pleased that she at least retained a few friends, some of whom she had met while in the hospital. Occasionally her tenuous equilibrium broke down at home, whereupon florid psychotic symptoms appeared, including delusions of persecution, and her unpredictable behavior often led to a return to the hospital. In the most tragic periods of her illness, fearing that her eyes were the source of demonic visitations, Janet actually blinded herself with her own hands.

The sight of her sunken eyelids confirmed this, as did a later physical examination; here was even more convincing evidence of unmanageable behavior than the hospitalizations and trials of psychotropic medication. But Janet was now behaving appropriately, even though she had taken no medication in the three years since joining the group. During my first visit she conversed with companions, apparently in good spirits, and was able to tell her story to me. She said she felt relaxed with other premies and had experienced no psychotic symptoms since joining the group, although she had seen the "divine light" during her meditation, an experience common to other members.

It became apparent from observing her and speaking with other members that the group not only displayed affection and support, but also set clear standards for her social behavior. This was something her parents had tried but failed to do. While engaged within the cohesive structure of the group, she felt compelled to comply with the expectations of her fellow members, a process that aborted the downward spiral of regressive behavior regularly ending in a psychotic state at home. This dynamic was illustrated by the comment of a friend and fellow member: "When she gets irritable or complains, I let her know that it's not the way premies should behave. She knows that we care for her, and that our scolding is done with love." Indeed, other members did not leave her alone for extended periods, even if she did not approach them.

This supportive atmosphere and sense of closeness apparently had a strong impact on the mental state of certain members, especially individuals like Janet. Somehow the sect was reaching some disturbed persons in a way that conventional psychiatry could not. Through intense togetherness and support, it seemed to have turned around their thinking and behavior.

But this was also true for members who had been well adjusted. Beth, for example, was profoundly changed by the sect. She had previously demonstrated herself to be highly intelligent and competent, and excelled academically without great effort. With independent-mindedness, she had assumed a leadership role in the antiwar movement of the late 1960s, yet only a few days before my visit to the ashram she sat with me at the dinner table and seemed transfixed, removed from all worldly cares. Only when she spoke of her newfound commitment did she become animated. She talked of the divine light she could literally see, the sacred nectar she could taste, and the divine music she heard. Under the group's influence Beth had somehow acquired a mental set entirely at variance with her previous attitudes. This development seemed no less surprising than Janet's; both women had apparently been transformed in their behavior, feelings, and perceptions.

Within a few months, I began to study this compelling phenomenon. I enlisted the help of Peter Buckley, a colleague at the Albert Einstein college of Medicine, and we conducted interviews and designed a questionnaire to evaluate two issues: first, the relief of psychological distress experienced on joining, and, second, the degree of social cohesiveness felt by these members toward the group. I hypothesized that a relationship existed between the perceived emotional relief and fidelity to the group.

The study was conducted on the outskirts of Orlando, Florida, at a national festival held by the Divine Light Mission, one of the conclaves regularly organized to allow members the opportunity for personal contact, or darshan, with the guru. A field had been rented for the weeklong event. Events there showed how the group's cohesiveness could be mobilized as a potent social force and how nonmembers could be excluded.

The atmosphere of belonging was pervasive, as some 5,000 young adults gathered to make preparations. They interacted in a congenial and open manner, even when they had struck up acquaintance only moments before. To say the least, this was not an impersonal work site. It represented a network of people who hastened to assist each other and sought ways to further their common cause of making the festival a shared experience, something valuable to all.

As a group, the members looked as though they had been drawn from the graduate campus of a large university—bright, not too carefully groomed, casually dressed. They were lively, good-tempered, and committed to their mutual effort. Some set up tents; others sold religious tracts and pins with pictures of the guru, his American wife, and their baby. Some handled food; others moved about with an air of eager expectancy. There was no idleness, brashness, marijuana, beer, loud music, or flirtation—all hallmarks of a more typical assembly of people in their twenties.

The administrative structure for the event appeared informal, but no sense of disorganization pervaded. The speakers addressed the group from a large floating stage on a lake. The program moved along smoothly from one event to the next, whether singing for the guru ("He's Got the Whole World in His Hands") or listening to various leaders deliver satsang.

The group's congeniality apparently extended to anyone designated as acceptable, as long as the proper signal was made. Thus, because Beth, who held a position of respect in the group, had labeled my colleague and me "okay," we were acceptable. After being introduced to the appropriate parties, we were greeted warmly and made to feel a part of the group. Help was offered as I began to query various organizers on strategy. Was it possible to pick out people at random from the registration lines to administer the questionnaire? There surely was a way, once I deliberated with them over the options available. Was space necessary for subjects to sit quietly and fill out research forms? Something would be worked out for every need. Soon we were all sitting around and talking about experiences of mutual interest, even of a few remote common acquaintances.

We also saw the other side of the coin—how the group defined and protected its boundary between members and the outside world. The demarcation could be drawn tightly, much as a droplet of quicksilver coalesces and separates from its surroundings, or as family members draw together and limit access of outsiders to their personal affairs. Our own status suddenly changed from inside to outside when a more suspicious member of the administrative group asked me if the project had been "approved" by senior figures from the Mission. In the absence of a definite response, our legitimacy was now open to question. Although it was not entirely clear what this approval entailed, a request was quickly relayed to the upper reaches of the Divine Light hierarchy and was then—to my surprise and distress—peremptorily turned down.

The members I had met quickly withdrew their offers of friendship, providing an object lesson on exclusion from a cohesive group. I soon felt myself to be a nonperson, treated civilly but coolly, having become an outsider as rapidly as I had been made an insider. The very people who had hovered around us to help with our plans now found making conversation uncomfortable. People seemed to be looking *through* my colleague and me rather than at us.

Toward the end of the day approval came as suddenly as it had been withdrawn, with the information that a decision had been made at the "highest" level, presumably in consultation with the guru himself. Acceptance and offers of help came with rekindled warmth. As if automatically triggered, a renewed air of intimacy suffused our exchanges.

This experience illustrates the considerable mobilization of support that such a cohesive group can generate, either informally or with formal sanction, as well as the strength of its controls over actions. The sect's ideology lends the control structure a legitimacy that penetrates the layers of the individual members' own decision making, eliciting group-sanctioned behavior. At no point in the Orlando sequence was there any significant diversity in attitudes expressed toward us. Each group member adhered to the consensus and thereby assured unanimity. As in Ann's family, this intense mutuality reflected the need both for security in the face of an outside world that is perceived as threatening and to prevent internal conflict. Agreement in attitude and views serves to protect the integrity of the group as a social system.

Later in the festival I asked to interview people who had experienced psychiatric or drug problems, hoping that they might help clarify the sect's impact on psychiatric symptoms in individual members, as well as the function of its intense social influence in mediating psychological change. One member brought forward was Ellen, a thirty-four-year-old divorced, part-time clerk whose five children had been remanded to her mother's care by the court because they had been neglected during her protracted bouts of psychiatric and drug problems. These problems had apparently come under control when she joined the Divine Light Mission. Her story illustrates two points. First, like many other initiates, she was attracted to a charismatic group at a time of psychological crisis, as if seeking aid to cope with extreme distress. Second, the support and structure offered by the sect allowed her to pull her psychological resources together. She used the strength of the group as an auxiliary ego to help regain her emotional stability.

Seven years before, Ellen had begun using drugs and was taking ten to fifteen barbiturate capsules a day. When psychedelics became popular, she began using LSD and later became addicted to a variety of opiates: morphine, Demerol, heroin, and illicit methadone. Her opiate habit became very expensive, and for four years she survived through prostitution. While on her roller coaster of drug abuse, she was hospitalized on several occasions for psychiatric problems, typically for a few days or weeks, during which she often smuggled a supply of heroin into the hospital.

The despair that precipitated these hospitalizations led to several suicide attempts. Ellen denied any history of hallucinations and gave no evidence of formal delusional thinking. Significantly, she reported that her mood improved by the time she left the hospital, often without any antidepressant medication. This history, along with her somewhat histrionic presentation of it, left the impression that she did not have a major despressive disorder. I thought she might have a borderline personality disorder, reflecting impulsive and self-destructive behavior and poor coping skills, and that the episodes requiring hospitalization were precipitated by drug use and environmental stress.

At one point, despairing of any escape from heroin addiction and the consequent need for prostitution, Ellen applied for methadone maintenance, which allowed her to stay away from illicit drugs and out of the hospital for over a year. She thought of herself as independent, though, and did not like the regimen of frequent visits to the clinic required by the program. Like a number of patients on methadone maintenance, Ellen mistook her newfound stability for a genuine ability to withstand the pressures of daily life. Wanting to "take control of her life," she withdrew from the methadone program and soon began using marijuana heavily and taking barbiturates again. As she said, "I used anything I could to stay off the heroin."

Her drug use rapidly increased, and she began to shoot heroin again. Feeling panicky over a likely full-fledged relapse, she fled to Colorado from her native Philadelphia, in the hope that life in a rural setting would save her from further deterioration. It did not, and she continued to use drugs, setting into life as a street person.

After a month in Colorado, Ellen met some members of the Divine Light Mission. She immediately felt comfortable with them and soon began to appreciate the merit of their religious devotion. She wanted to become part of the group to salvage herself from a profound sense of desolation. Each day she went to their ashram where she was accepted warmly, began to cut down her use of drugs, and attempted to meditate. Though living alone, she felt herself to be part of a "close, loving community." Now, ten months later, she reported only occasionally using half a marijuana cigarette.

Part of my exchange with Ellen was revealing of the role played by the group's cohesiveness.

M.G.: How did you feel when you were shooting heroin in Colorado?

ELLEN: I was terrified, but I also felt that I had returned to a friend, one who would heal my wounded feelings but then hold me in its claws. I knew I couldn't control it . . .

M.G.: And the premies, how did they help you?

ELLEN: Once I got to know them, I realized they loved me. They took me up, and it was as if they were holding me in their arms. I was like a baby whose mother guides its moves and cares for it. When I wanted to take heroin, or even to smoke [marijuana], I knew they were with me to help me stay away from it, even if I was alone. And their strength was there for me, even before I could hardly meditate at all. I could rely on their invisible hand, moved by Maharaj Ji's wisdom, to help me gain control.

M.G.: What was it that they did?

ELLEN: After a while it was *everything* they did that made me know I belonged. Just feeling their love was all I needed.

The drug abuse syndrome that Ellen confronted when she arrived in Colorado was serious, and the likelihood of her aborting a decline into full-blown heroin addiction was small. A geographic escape generally is of little value. Few patients in the throes of an addiction such as hers, combining opiates and other drugs, are able to establish control over drug abuse on their own. Her description of the intense support she felt from other Divine Light members suggested an alternative dependency. Her reliance on the group for the strength to face the stress of everyday life paralleled the reliance she had placed on drugs. Both aided her in coping with conflict, but at the cost of independent action.

The sect had exerted a remarkable influence on this woman's addictive problem, affecting her in a way that our usual psychological therapies do not. What produces such influence? We can begin to answer this question by recalling the discussions of the family and the therapy group earlier in the chapter. Further insights came from our studies of Divine Light members in Orlando.

A Study of Group Cohesiveness

The objective study of behavior in charismatic groups is not a simple undertaking, and two issues complicating this research are relevant here: investigator bias and limitations in available methodologies. The problem of investigator bias reflects the very nature of charismatic groups. Such groups maintain their views even in the face of contrary evidence, and, as we just saw, do this with a mutuality that stands independent of contrary evidence. They also tend to elicit contrary views and animosity from the surrounding community, which itself may be no less biased regarding an alien sect. As a result, the investigator is almost always pressed to adopt a position that either favors or opposes the stands taken by the charismatic group. For example, at times my studies on charismatic sects were attacked as a reflection of my being "duped" by the Moonies; at other times the same studies were seen just the opposite, as evidence of the use of my "professional credentials to discredit" these groups.[19] A dispassionate middle ground is not easily defined.

A second problem in carrying out this research lies in designing a valid methodology. We had to adapt approaches and techniques from a variety of disciplines, including psychiatry, social psychology, anthropology, and sociology. In addition, questions often had to be framed so as to make use of the methodology available, rather than what might be the most interesting to study. For example, my principal interest in initiating the Orlando study was to examine the major psychopathology found among some Divine Light members. Practically speaking, this could not be studied in a controlled fashion because reliable self-report measurements for the relevant diagnostic categories were not available. Instead we had to use a more general psychological adjustment scale.

Even more broadly, the choice of a proper context in which to study the interrelatedness of group members in a charismatic group also presents a major paradox. The group phenomena observed among its members—their intense closeness, feelings, and beliefs—can hardly be re-created in a laboratory. Yet so many real-world variables impinge on the phenomena to be studied that to observe them outside the laboratory setting, without ample controls, would leave researchers vulnerable to a circus of external issues, let alone their own subjectivity.

This paradox is illustrated by my previous research on the influence of social context on drug use and abuse. Volunteers in a laboratory setting smoked either active marijuana, placebo marijuana, or no drug at the outset of each of a series of professionally led encounter-group meetings.[20] The controlled setting was too artificial, however, to create the degree of cohesiveness usually associated with drug use. The question remained as to how such a controlled evaluation of group interrelatedness could be undertaken effectively.[21]

Outside the laboratory, studies on the peyote rituals of the Native American Indian Church in the Southwest United States[22] show that the tribe's cohesive social structure was closely integrated into this religious experience when the hallucinogen is taken in the context of a close-knit community. This religious context clearly cannot be reproduced in an ad hoc fashion, but one can surmise that these close ties are an effective vehicle for transforming a potentially disruptive hallucinogenic experience into a constructive and therapeutic one.[23]

In what setting can the role of the naturally emerging social ties of a religious sect be best studied? My access to the Divine Light Mission appeared to offer an opportunity for analyzing group cohesiveness in a systematic, controlled way within its natural setting. Specifically, a statistical assessment could be made of the relationship between such variables as group cohesiveness and other measures of the members' emotional status. In this respect, the sect presented an "experiment of nature."

To conduct such an analysis, a fairly large sample of subjects was needed, and consequently it was not feasible to rely primarily on interviews, since personnel were not available. We developed a seven-page multiple-choice questionnaire and gave copies to 119 subjects who were active members of the Divine Light Mission, selected at random from the festival registration lines.*

In framing the questionnaire, we had to address certain technical problems. One was the need to choose symptoms of mental illness or health that could be queried within this format. Some scales for evaluating major mental illness, such as the SCL-90,[24] have limited specificity and are fairly lengthy. It was

---

*Members of charismatic groups are remarkably compliant in filling out long questionnaires, so long as it is sanctioned by their leadership. I have found, however, that more independent sorts in less zealous groups can give an investigator no end of trouble.

best to use a scale that drew on symptoms experienced by a large portion of the population, such as anxiety, depression, and suicidal thoughts. Since we needed to ascertain the subjects' perception of their psychological state both before and after joining the group, the scale had to be short and easy to fill out relative to the subjects' experience during more than one period in their life.

For a brief ad hoc scale, it also seemed best to develop items that would have face validity, that is, they would clearly reflect the symptoms of psychological distress. This approach contrasts with self-report psychological scales such as the Minnesota Multi-Phasic Personality Inventory (the MMPI), a widely used but quite long schedule whose validity has been tested by standardizing items on large groups of people with different psychiatric diagnoses. Each of the MMPI questions in itself (comparable to "I like to collect stamps"), however, does not have an obvious relationship to the symptoms measured by the test.

Table 2-1 gives the items developed for this Psychological Distress Scale, each rated from 1 ("not at all") to 5 ("very much") by the respondent.[25] The total points for the eight symptoms indicated the psychological distress score. Subjects evaluated each symptom during four two-month periods: the worst they had felt; right before their first contact with the Divine Light Mission; immediately after joining; and at present. This made it possible to compare their estimation of the psychological distress they had experienced before and after joining.

In addition to psychological distress, a second "outcome" variable, drug use, was studied. Each of six common drugs of abuse was listed, and subjects were asked to rate how often they used each drug during the same four two-month periods on a scale from 1 ("none at all") to 5 ("more than once on most days").

Table 2-1. *Psychological Distress Items (and Implied Symptoms)*

Subjects indicated how much they felt this way, on a scale of 1 ("not at all") to 5 ("very much").

1. I felt nervous and tense. [anxiety]   ( )
2. I felt depressed and glum. [depression]   ( )
3. I had thoughts of ending my life. [suicidal ideation]   ( )
4. I had the feeling that I was being watched or talked about by
   others. [referential thinking]   ( )
5. I was unclear about how to lead my life. [anomie]   ( )
6. I got into trouble with my job, at school, or with the law.
   [behavioral]   ( )
7. I heard voices that other people did not hear. [hearing
   voices]   ( )
8. Emotional problems interfere with my adjustment in life.
   [general emotional maladaptation]   ( )

Responses were then related to specific aspects of the group membership to find out how group membership might have led to any psychological and drug use changes. Group cohesiveness as a predictor of change, as well as other group issues such as meditation practice, to be discussed later, were also considered.

Group cohesiveness was measured on the scale given in Table 2-2, adapted from the earlier study on marijuana use and social interaction. A member's cohesive feelings about three different groups were recorded: the ten members of the sect whom the subject knew best, all the sect members, and the ten nonmembers the subject knew best. This offered a contrast between the subjects' feelings of affiliation toward people inside and outside the group.

Results of the Study

The survey produced revealing findings regarding the psychology of the charismatic group. First, the members' reports reflected a relief of distress on joining. Second, the members' cohesiveness toward the group was closely associated with this relief. From these findings emerged a beginning sense of what motivated members to comply with the group.

Members who had joined the sect roughly two years before reported a considerable decline in psychological distress and drug use after joining. Many had a history of psychological problems and several had sought professional help (38%) or had been hospitalized for emotional disorders (9%). These findings formed the first objective evidence of the role psychological distress plays in recruitment to such groups. Furthermore, members' level of distress symptoms decline over the course of conversion. The average incidence for the items on the Distress Scale is given in Table 2-3, as are the figures for marijuana and heroin use, which reflect the all-around decline in both psycho-

Table 2-2. *Social Cohesiveness Scale*

Subjects rated their feelings toward the group on each item, on a scale of 1 ("not at all") to 5 ("very much").

1. How much do these descriptions apply to the group?
   a. They care for me   ( )
   b. They are happy   ( )
   c. They are suspicious of me [scored in reverse]   ( )

2. How would you describe your feelings for them?
   a. I care for them   ( )
   b. They make me happy   ( )
   c. I am suspicious of them [scored in reverse]   ( )

3. Do they have the qualities a *premie* [member] should have? ( )
4. Do you like being part of their activities?   ( )

Table 2-3. *Outcome of Initiation into the Divine Light Mission*

These figures indicate the percentage of subjects who reported the presence of symptoms during each of four two-month periods.

	The Four Periods			
Three Sample Items	*The Worst Ever*	*Right Before Joining*	*Right After Joining*	*Now*
Psychological Distress Scale, average for the 8 items	80	71	45	37
Daily marijuana use	65	45	0	7
Any heroin use	14	7	1	0

logical distress and drug use.[26] This observation revealed an apparent overall improvement in psychiatric state derived from conversion and its retention through continued membership. These findings were confirmed in later research on the Unification Church where it was possible to study recruits as well as disaffiliated members.

The cohesiveness scores showed that respondents felt considerably closer toward members of their sect than toward nonmembers whom they knew best.[27] Almost all of the respondents (99%) said they cared a lot for the ten members they knew best, and most (56%) felt similarly toward the membership overall. Only the minority of members (39%) responded this way in relation to the nonmembers they knew best. If valid, this would mean that most members felt closer toward the sect overall (few of whose members they had actually met) than toward the ten people outside the sect they knew best. Their connection to the group far outweighed their attachments to outsiders.

To examine the relationship, if any, between the feeling of cohesiveness and the symptom changes reported, we statistically analyzed the average decline in symptom scores.[28] Social cohesion accounted for 37% of the overall decline in psychological distress that occurred after subjects joined the group. That is, a large part of the enhanced well-being derived from joining this sect could be attributed to the members' feelings of relatedness with fellow members.

Such findings were notable since the degree of neurotic distress experienced by individuals is determined by many factors, including differences in temperament, quality of life, and how people see themselves in relation to the rest of the world. But for the young adults in our study, the decline in feelings of psychological distress was directly proportional to the degree of cohesiveness they felt toward the group.

One might have thought that members like Ellen, who were most emotionally troubled before entering the sect, would have benefited the most from joining. Yet the survey indicated that serious emotional problems before joining were not specifically correlated with either a greater or lesser decline in psychological distress. Nor were serious emotional problems correlated with a higher social cohesiveness score.[29] All members, whether seriously distressed or not, reported an improved emotional state after joining.

These findings naturally raise the question of whether subjects over-estimated the degree of distress before joining and the amount of improvement after. While this may well have occurred, a later study on the Unification Church (see Chapter 8) supported the view that the effect on psychological well-being of joining the group was real.

Such emotional gains reinforce members' involvement in the group by effectively "rewarding" them for their fealty to it. The reward, specifically, is enhanced well-being when the members feel closer to each other. And this reward may help explain the members' remarkable conformity to the group's expectations, since acceptance and conformity bring relief from distress.

3

SHARED
BELIEFS

The beliefs held in common by members of cults are a vital force in the group's operation. They bind members together, shape their attitudes, and motivate them to act in self-sacrifice. I began to appreciate the importance of such beliefs in following the career of my friend who had joined the Divine Light Mission. At first it seemed certain that Beth's involvement would be ephemeral; surely this sensible and successful young woman would soon turn back to her roots in the Western mainstream. But this assumption proved wrong. Beth moved her home across country more than once to follow her youthful guru, and took a number of trips to India along with his followers. Several years later she married a fellow premie. After having a child, she obtained a university position and returned to teaching, but remained deeply committed to her belief in the guru.

A few years after Beth joined the Divine Light Mission, it was obvious that she believed very strongly in something the group offered and that her involvement reflected an abiding faith, not easy to fathom but quite telling in its implications for the psychology of charismatic groups. Consider a letter in which she spoke of her belief in the guru, whose actual contact with thousands of followers must have been limited.

> His revelation of the Kingdom of Heaven within us all is a completely practical experience for each and every individual. . . . The gift of Knowledge that Maharaj Ji has given me is so deeply satisfying and joyfully constant that I can't imagine another being conveying the truth as he has revealed it.

Beth accepted the guru's transcendent message in a way that others before her might have embraced the prophets and messiahs of old. This literal faith was hard to understand since it came from a woman whom I had known some years before as agnostic and even cynical, and was clearly at variance with the underlying attitudes one would expect in a person with her background and pluralistic views. To understand the role such strong beliefs play in charismatic groups, we will examine a related historical example.

Communities of Shared Belief

A Utopian Commune

In the mid–nineteenth century several Utopian communities, each rooted in its particular interpretations of Christian dogma, were established in northeastern United States. Most were limited in both size and duration. They included the Oneida Community, the Shakers, the Harmony Society, and— transplanted from Central Europe—the Hutterites. Though short-lived these communities had a high degree of social cohesiveness and shared belief, were typically led by a charismatic leader, and exacted conformity to their unusual norms of behavior. Particularly striking is the important role that religious creeds played in sustaining these groups. Rosabeth Kanter[1] studied thirty sects and found that those with the greatest social stability and longevity were all founded on the basis of shared religious beliefs: their respective systems of belief and ritual were essential to the groups' stability, allowing members to sacrifice their own needs in rejecting the material world. In addition, the groups' transcendent moral code serves to support the primacy of their leaders.

Among the more successful of these groups was the Oneida Community, which was established in 1847 in upstate New York and dissolved thirty-two years later after the departure of its leader.[2] It was part of a widespread religious renewal that began in the early 1830s. Around this time, John Humphrey Noyes graduated from Dartmouth College and served unsuccessfully as an apprentice in a New Hampshire law firm. During his subsequent disillusionment, he attended a four-day camp meeting in his native Vermont and underwent a religious conversion. Noyes declared himself to be without sin, drawing this position from his own interpretation of Christ's redemption, and began to seek followers for his emerging system of idiosyncratic beliefs. Within a decade, he developed a following of a few dozen people who adopted the practices of economic communism and spouse sharing that were remarkably deviant for the time. Under threat of indictment for adultery, Noyes had to remove his group to an isolated location in upstate New York. The commune Noyes established there grew to over a hundred members within a few years and nearly three hundred before its decline. The intensely held beliefs of these Perfectionists, as they were called, were striking. They espoused a utopian goal of "creating heaven on earth," a pursuit centered for the sect's duration in a large communal residence called the Mansion House. Here their society was organized around group-oriented facilities, such as a community dining room, a library, and common recreation areas. Even three generations after the commune dissolved, descendants still lived near this house, reflecting their lingering fidelity.[3]

The members' strong belief in the principles of communal ownership is seen even in the activities of its children. At one point the principle of shared property was reinterpreted so that each little girl might possess a doll of her own, rather than share in the community's dolls, as was done with all other possessions. When the adults observed that the youngsters spent too much time with these dolls and not enough on household chores, all were summoned together and told to destroy them, each girl throwing her own doll into a fire. Noyes's son later wrote that "throughout my childhood the private ownership of anything seemed to me a crude artificiality to which an unenlightened Outside still clung. . . . it never occurred to me that I could possess a sled to the exclusion of other boys."[4]

In a charismatic group, shared beliefs are best established by a close-knit communications system in which acceptable views are directly or implicitly encouraged and dissenting ones suppressed. Control is most effectively exerted through social pressure rather than forcible prohibition of dissent, which would only generate disillusionment and passive conformity. In the Oneida Community this was evident in the group's daily communal meetings. Every night the Oneidians met in the Big Hall of the Mansion House to combine religious rituals with secular functions and discussion. Hymn singing and Bible reading were part of the evening fare. Noyes himself would speak, relating the group's religious practice to the behavior and attitudes of the members. Members could also bring up personal concerns, so that issues not usually voiced in public settings were discussed by the group and then resolved by recourse to Noyes's religious ideals. This enabled the community to establish norms in all areas of social interaction and promote social conformity. Meetings were referred to by one member as "the most cherished part of our daily lives,"[5] reflecting the way in which the group's influence on a shared set of values was accepted by members, and not seen as intrusive.

In rural isolation, the group developed an ideology and related rituals deviant from those of the general population. It became known for the nature of its sexual relationships in particular, and these eventually led to widespread public criticism that contributed to its dissolution.

Noyes believed that monogamous marriage among commune members was harmful to the communist principles of his sect because it excluded others from sharing in a vital affectional tie. Although this view may have arisen from his own personal disappointments, he cited the Bible for his rationale: "In the Kingdom of Heaven, the institution of marriage—which assigns the exclusive possession of one woman to one man—does not exist" (Mt. 22:23). The system he implemented in Oneida allowed a man who wanted to have sexual intercourse with a particular woman simply to ask her. If she agreed, he would spend the night in her room. Contraception was achieved by terminating intercourse before ejaculation, a procedure practiced with apparent success. Some years later, the use of a "go-between" became conventional. This person judged the acceptability of any given liaison and discouraged "amatory" relationships, which were seen to run contrary to the group's communal ideology.

Management of marital and affectional ties by means of the belief system of a charismatic group can be a powerful component of social controls, and the go-between system clearly served this purpose. Indeed, later in its history the system was organized so that decisions on couplings were made by Noyes himself, thereby centralizing his control over the group.

The Oneida Community is an interesting historical illustration of how a group's beliefs can be integrated into its system of social controls. It also demonstrates the central role a charismatic religious leader can play in their implementation. These techniques stand in sharp contrast to the crude, coercive ones described by Lifton and others in their studies of brainwashing by the Communist Chinese.[6]

Faith and Healing

Assumptive beliefs, communication patterns, and, ultimately, norms for behavior were all determined within the confines of the Oneida Community. A step removed from this is the less clearly defined entity of a subculture, which does not exist in physical isolation from the broader social environment but nonetheless shapes communication among its members by means of consensually held beliefs.

Most often, we apply the term faith healing to treatments used in cultures whose fundamental beliefs are alien to the contemporary values of scientific medicine. In their classic studies of Navajo healing, Alexander and Dorothy Leighton[7] emphasized the role of belief, group support, shared emotional experience, and the paraphernalia of communal rituals, such as eagle and owl feathers. A disruption of the members' usual psychological and physical state (discussed later under altered consciousness) further intensified the way the group called on its shared belief system. For example, emetics were frequently consumed by participants in these rituals, and hot pokers were often applied by shamans both to the patient and others present at the healing ceremony. Syndromes treated by the Navajo have been classified in accordance with that culture's own subtypes of mental illness, and some may also be described in terms of contemporary diagnostic criteria as major psychiatric illness, including schizophrenia, agitated depression, hysteria, and pathologic intoxication.[8]

An upsurge in religious commitment in the United States in recent decades, particularly in fundamentalist religion, has brought faith healing closer to the cultural mainstream. Church attendance has increased dramatically in the past half-century. Currently, for example, about half of all married couples attend church regularly, compared to only one-quarter fifty years ago, and the ratio of church buildings to the population has gone up by almost two-thirds.[9]

Mansell Pattison and his associates[10] have studied contemporary American faith healing by evaluating psychological traits of individuals who underwent Pentecostal healing. Those who had been "healed" avowed that they could place their full faith in God and so there was consequently little reason to be concerned or upset about their problems. A systematic assessment of their mental status by psychiatric interviews showed scant evidence of major mental illness, but their responses to the MMPI indicated that these people relied heavily on the psychological defense mechanism of denial. Using this defense, an individual who is unable to tolerate an objective reality or its implications literally thinks and acts as if that reality did not exist; this occurs even though the person may be regularly confronted by unpalatable facts. Pattison's subjects perceived their faith-healing experience as a definitive treatment *regardless* of the presence or absence of physical symptoms afterward. He and his colleagues concluded that the primary function of faith healing was not necessarily to resolve symptoms, but to reinforce the group's religious perspective and thereby provide sick people with a means of avoiding harsh realities. Although healing was the declared purpose of the ritual, in actuality it functioned to integrate members into the group.

The ability to blind oneself to reality through religious ritual may serve as a solution to certain psychological problems. This is evident in research on the plasticity of people's responses to the physiologic changes underlying their emotions. In a study conducted by Stanley Schacter and Jerome Singer,[11] subjects were given a dose of adrenaline, a naturally occurring stimulant, and were then led to experience either euphoria or anger, depending on the sham setting into which they were introduced. Those who were exposed to an actor who feigned anger tended to feel anger. Those exposed to a giddy, silly actor tended to become euphoric themselves. The study was important because it suggested that people's emotional responses to drugs can be determined to a large degree by the social context. Hence, it is not surprising that a zealous religious service could prime individuals to accept a group's own interpretation of how they *should* be feeling and how they should perceive their physical state.

Another interesting study by Pattison[12] concerned a group with longstanding histories of overt homosexuality. After joining a Pentecostal Church group and adopting its belief systems, these men eventually became exclusively practicing heterosexuals. Did religious commitment lead to a genuine change (healing, as it were) in sexual orientation, or was the tendency toward homosexuality only suppressed? This is difficult to answer definitively, but the men reported the emergence of satisfactory heterosexual relationships with women, both as newfound friends and spouses, and in time homosexual fantasies among these converts became quite limited or nonexistent, essentially at the level of the heterosexual population.

How could these men have changed their sexual orientation through religion? Within the belief system of the Pentecostal Church, homosexuality was defined as an immoral attitude that the individual himself can expunge, and members were expected to refrain from all homosexual practices. By virtue of their personal experience in the group, and the behavior expected of them, they apparently relinquished what is thought by many to be an almost irreversible trait.

The Pentecostals did not regard homosexuality as a deviation from an innate characteristic or a physically grounded condition. Thus, the afflicted person could take an active role in changing his own attitudes and behavior, in collaboration with the church. Interestingly, investigators found that these "converted" homosexuals, committed to their Pentecostal beliefs and actively complying with them, experienced much less emotional distress than a comparable sample of practicing homosexual men in the general population.

A Psychiatric Hospital

Systems of belief sometimes clash in psychiatric wards. Physicians committed to the values of science and rationality often do not make allowances for alternative perspectives with patients whose cultic views have brought them to the hospital or seem intertwined with psychopathology.

A few years ago, I was asked to help evaluate Carol, a twenty-nine-year-old black woman from a disadvantaged background, shortly after she was transferred to our psychiatry service. She had just undergone exploratory abdominal surgery because of a life-threatening and self-inflicted gunshot wound. During the course of her hospitalization, I was able to trace Carol's encounters with three systems of shared belief, each exerting its influence over her behavior. The first was a delusional belief system that brought her to the hospital; the second was the worldview espoused by her physicians; and the third consisted of the Pentecostal religious beliefs she later adopted.

Though Carol was at first reluctant to provide details, her mother reported that she and another woman had shared the same lover who had driven them to a variety of bizarre behaviors. Bobby, the lover, once paraded the two women naked into the street. He occasionally boasted of having special powers, of being a "genius" who would "change the course of history and bring on the Black kingdom." Carol often parroted his words and ideas, saying, "White devils are going to leech the color out of the world." Other informants also reported that both women sometimes seemed to go into a "trance" while with Bobby, and would tell of seeing images on the television screen placed there by him. Once Carol told her mother that Bobby literally controlled her feelings from day to day.

The episode that precipitated Carol's hospitalization occurred a day after Bobby had shown her a picture of a gun, along with a book entitled *The Power of Decision*, leading her to conclude that he wanted her to shoot herself. After doing just that the next day, she telephoned him, and he suggested she call an ambulance and get to a hospital.

The staff was puzzled when Carol was transferred to the psychiatry service. They felt they were confronted by a phenomenon at the interface of a shared delusion (therefore "crazy") and a cult (presumably cultural). Psychiatry does have trouble dealing with pathology shared by groups, for it is primarily a discipline that addresses individual disorders rather than social phenomena. The staff's inclination was to treat Carol as a "routine" psychotic.

I interviewed Carol at the request of the staff and found that she had no thought disorder and no overt symptoms of delusional thinking, although it was possible she was keeping bizarre thoughts to herself. She did not appear to be suffering from a schizophrenic psychosis. Nor was she particularly depressed, although she was fairly anxious and confused about her motivations when confronted with the tale told by her mother. I suggested her psychiatric symptoms would abate now that she was removed from Bobby.

In several days, a shift in Carol's thinking was indeed apparent. She made the following statement, reflecting the distance she had begun to place between herself and the beliefs she shared with Bobby.

> I used to think that Bobby could explain everything, but what he said didn't always make sense. I think I should forget the Kingdom he promised; it was just his own crazy idea. I hate to blame him for the shooting, but maybe he had a bad influence on me.

Carol had been affected by the rational worldview of the hospital staff, who explained to her how she had developed delusional ideas under Bobby's influence. In casting out her devil, however, her doctors had not offered Carol an alternative set of beliefs that was compelling to her, unlike persons engaged in religious ritual. Explanations about delusions and mental function meant little to this young woman who had ended her formal education at age fifteen.

During her hospital stay, Carol herself stumbled on a solution. She was given a Bible tract by a fellow patient involved in a Pentecostal sect, and quickly developed a strong interest in reading Scriptures. A commitment to Pentecostalism, which she had encountered as a child in her grandmother's house, soon followed, and she began to explain both the events of the shooting and a clear-cut relief in her malaise in terms of her growing belief in Jesus.

Three weeks after admission, Carol stated that she planned to move to her grandmother's house when she left the hospital. She explained:

> When I used to go to bed at night in the old days, I felt the devils coming onto me before I could fall asleep. . . . There was no way to escape them, so I stayed awake till dawn to protect myself. Bobby told me that the devils would always follow me, and that I was going to act out their sins. Sometimes he said I had to run out into the street without my clothes on so they would be shamed into leaving me, but now the devils are gone forever, and it was Jesus who made them go. They left when I returned to Him, and that's why I'll be safe with my grandmother and with the Church.

Carol had now adopted the perspective of Pentecostalism, which seemed more comfortable for her than any offered by the medical staff. She made this clear on the fourth week after her admission to our service.

> Look, I'll tell you this. Jesus says it's evil to shoot yourself, but He'll forgive me, and I'm ready to plead for His mercy, and start again. You folks should take a lesson from Him. He's the one with the answers. . . . Bobby? The Devil must have sent him; that's for sure.

She looked forward to going home, and the edge of anxiety in her earlier manner was gone, replaced by an appearance of certitude. She was experiencing no delusions or hallucinations and was soon discharged to her grandmother's custody.

Carol had begun to move from one system of shared beliefs, Bobby's delusions, to a second one, the psychological perspective of the hospital staff, but she finally accepted a third that was more viable for her: Pentecostal Christianity. That her first set of bizarre beliefs had been validated by two other persons may reflect a bit less poorly on the integrity of Carol's mental function. Nonetheless, she was clearly disturbed. The Pentecostal beliefs provided Carol with an explanation of her illness she could accept, ascribing it to satanic influences external to herself and allowing her to feel intact once she renounced those influences.

In Carol's case, we have seen how a very small charismatic group can generate a delusional belief system. These vigorously defended views can then lead a member to pathologic thought and behavior, even to self-destructiveness. In the end, acceptance of such bizarre beliefs may be difficult to distinguish from true mental illness.

A second case of conflict between belief systems in a psychiatric ward involved a member of a well-organized charismatic sect. When I was asked to evaluate Tom, a single twenty-six-year-old at a nearby hospital, conflict was apparent from the outset: the hospital staff had become agents of Tom's family, who suggested his admission.

On arrival, I saw from the hospital's Tudor-style buildings and commodious rooms that it catered to a class of patients with access to whatever services the mental health professional might offer. The resident psychiatrist who had treated the patient in the hospital presented the case and explained that Tom had been admitted to this hospital by his private psychiatrist. He came from an affluent background, and his family was prepared to provide whatever was necessary to assure his return to a "normal" existence. He was judged to have two problems. One was the depression precipitating his hospitalization; the other was his commitment to Shri Rajneesh, an Eastern guru. The second problem concerned Tom's family most. After three months with the sect, Tom had all but severed his ties to his family, much to their anger and distress, and after four years moved to a remote spot in Oregon where the guru's followers had recently relocated.

The resident psychiatrist emphasized a conflict that, in her estimation, had developed in Tom's family. The depression began, she explained, when Tom was confronted by his father, whom he had visited in the hospital shortly after the man had been in a serious auto accident. The father insisted that Tom was pursuing a senseless course and that it was time for him to abandon his foolish ideas and return home, where he could enter into their business and have a proper future. As on previous occasions, Tom refused to accept this offer. The resident surmised that Tom felt guilty about his father's condition but was unable to express his resentment over the man's demands, given his precarious medical condition.

After the confrontation Tom spent a few weeks with followers of Rajneesh in another city but then returned home. He was apparently feeling depressed now, and over the next few weeks became more withdrawn. Eventually he agreed to be hospitalized, since he was not motivated for any activities other than meeting with local followers of the guru.

To protect Tom from further tension in the hospital, the resident psychiatrist had prohibited members of his sect from visiting him, although he was allowed to see his family. Tom resented this at first, but later accepted his isolation from his co-religionists, and soon developed a comfortable relationship with his doctor. While being treated with psychotherapy and antidepressant medications, he began to improve. When he was ready to be discharged, Tom was referred back to his skilled private psychiatrist, who continued his therapy on an outpatient basis.

The whole process served to isolate him from his fellow cult members. Since his adherence to the group's unusual beliefs depended on sustaining a mental barrier against the common culture, his psychiatrist's therapeutic regimen effectively undermined the stability of his religious worldview.

Tom's private psychiatrist had also come to the resident's presentation to discuss the case. He remarked on his own distaste for the "cult," and was pleased to say that in time Tom was able to put aside preoccupations with the group and attend to the matters at hand, which revolved around the need to consider an appropriate role for himself in the family's business and reestablish a secure identity in the general community.

I was a bit suspicious of the history presented, having encountered many young sect members who had shed commitments to their families when their parents opposed their involvement in a zealous sect. Indeed, in many such groups, parents were regularly eschewed when they intruded on sect activities. Why did Tom turn away from the sect at this time and return to his family? In addition, it was routine practice for any member in trouble to turn to fellow sect members, however far away they might be.

When I spoke with Tom, it became clear why he hadn't contacted other Rajneeshees. Apparently he experienced conflicts with senior figures in the Rajneesh movement while living in their religious community in Oregon and was beginning to question his ability to achieve the religious goals they had outlined for him, although he did not doubt the merits of the goals themselves. Tom insisted that he had otherwise been content during the previous years in the group, and had established close relations with other members. He had been involved for a while with a young woman in the group and was considering returning to her, but was not prepared to face his fellow members because of the difficulty in resolving his spiritual impasse.

Three months before his hospitalization, Tom had volunteered to organize a regional center for the Rajneeshees on the West Coast, hoping to work out his conflicts in this setting, but he apparently ran into difficulties with some members in that task too, difficulties that mirrored his prior trouble in relating to the group's hierarchy. Because of all these events, he was becoming increasingly disenchanted with himself when the call came from his family about his father's accident.

As Tom described the situation, his problems with the sect were mainly responsible for his feelings of failure. His decision to remain with his family was primarily an attempt to create a setting where he might resolve these conflicts and then return to the sect since his commitment had not wavered. His sense of failure depressed him and he was uncertain whether he would be acceptable to sect members should he turn to them for help. When the option of hospitalization was offered by his parents, he saw little alternative but to accept, even though he feared they were using this to wean him from the movement.

By preventing Tom's continued contact with the sect, his resident physician was implicitly pressing him to give up an identity and the related beliefs that had been most important to him. Both psychiatrists in effect worked to move him further from the group, identifying a "healthy" outcome as a return to the beliefs and values of the broader culture. Whether he would be better off adopting his doctors' and family's perspective was a question that troubled him, for Tom still spoke of the option of returning to the sect. He was no longer suffering from depression but was clearly unhappy, as he now felt unable to accept either option. He was torn between two belief systems.

In its attempt to provide assistance, the medical community was clearly promoting a set of beliefs in conflict with those Tom had espoused on entering the hospital. Perhaps he would be happier with the advantages and values of his family or maybe he would be better off returning to the sect where he had lived for the previous five years. But this value judgment was being made for him, at least implicitly, by his physicians.

Also troubling was that the doctors, because they shared the family's values, were unaware of making a subjective judgment and hence misconstrued some of Tom's conflicts. Specifically, they presumed that Tom's depression stemmed from guilt over his response to his father, rather than his feelings of having failed as a member of the sect. They saw his affinity for the sect as pathologic in contrast to entering the family's business and social world, whereas in Tom's mind it was a reasonable choice that he had not yet made.

In the end, Tom chose to stay with his family, and was closely monitored by them for several months after his release. During that time he held an office job in the family business and gradually reestablished contact with the friends he had made before becoming a follower of Rajneesh.

This case may convey the way in which subjective judgments can enter our assessment of the shared beliefs of members of charismatic groups, and how difficult it is to stand apart from one's own beliefs in making such judgments. It becomes even more difficult to decide on a proper course of treatment for sect members when psychiatric disorders occur. After all, Tom's parents brought him in. Unlike Tom, many individuals have resisted reacculturation at the hands of mental health professionals.

The Treatment of Schizophrenia

The issue of zealous beliefs in the treatment of mental illness is relevant not just to a small minority. Hope for the future, based on commitment and belief, is one of the vital components of all psychological treatments. Patients must accept an assumptive system (such as psychoanalysis or self-help) that implicitly explains how they will get well.

Jerome Frank[13] pointed out that a central aspect of the psychotherapeutic process is the instillation of hope. Sadly, this is lacking in the treatment of many seriously ill psychiatric patients because it usually focuses on acute symptoms, after relying on the use of psychotropic medications. All too commonly, acute schizophrenic patients are successfully medicated for relief of hallucinations and delusional thinking and are then seen ready for discharge, without serious attention to their attitude toward future readjustment.

It is also true that schizophrenics admitted to psychiatric hospitals are often unable to face their own disillusionment with themselves and their lives— only chemicals can suppress their disturbing thoughts—and they have no beliefs relevant to their illness around which they can build a positive view of the future. To maintain a measure of hope, they sometimes deny the very reality of their past problem, and may even be unable to acknowledge the immediate circumstances that brought them to seek help.

In an attempt to address the problem of disillusionment in recovering schizophrenics, a compelling experiment was conducted by Loren Mosher and Alma Menn under the auspices of the National Institute of Mental Health. They established a psychiatric treatment center called Soteria House in a modest residential building, and tried to instill a different perspective in their patients. Mosher and Menn applied many of the psychological principles we have observed at work in charismatic groups in an explicitly therapeutic context. Specifically, they created a cohesive group setting that provided an explanation for the patients' illness and also gave them a reason to feel optimistic about their return to a healthy mental state.

The experimental Soteria Program was not hospital based to avoid the feeling of a large, impersonal institution. Also missing were psychotropic medications, which were used only as a last resort for uncontrollable residents; the overwhelming majority (92%) of Soteria residents received no drugs. They were cared for by a nonprofessional staff that worked closely with them in 48-to 60-hour shifts, allowing for continuous and intense interactions.

What did this experimental treatment actually offer its patients? Caregivers did not have a professional or scientific rationale for viewing schizophrenia as an innate disease; rather, they regarded Soteria residents as having reacted in an unusual but *meaningful* way to their problems of living, and were able now, with the aid of those around them, to rebuild their lives by using their unique experiences.[14] This attitude is far removed from the biological view of schizophrenia most psychiatrists hold today. Mosher and Menn used the term *belief* to characterize the way in which the Soteria staff framed its conception of the psychotic experience.[15] Indeed, a shared belief in the value of the schizophrenic's personal experiences is conveyed to the Soteria residents, thereby affording them a basically optimistic viewpoint to which they may be "converted."

This gives the endeavor a transcendent quality. It falls within a tradition in which madness is associated with sacred quasidivine attributes; residents and staff alike take a philosophic position broadly applicable to the altered consciousness everyone may potentially experience.[16] From this derives a behavioral norm: patients, to move on to the next level of personality integration, must now adopt a constructive and positive set of behaviors. They do this with hope of moving toward this next stage rather than from a sense of needing to suppress some innate failing. That is the ideal at Soteria, and there is evidence that schizophrenic patients can develop active control over symptoms of their illness when properly motivated by their social milieu.[17] Sadly, this perspective is still alien to most established caregivers.[18]

Shared Beliefs in the Unification Church

The Unification Church, or the Moonies, was one of the best known of the charismatic sects to appear on the American scene in the 1970s. The mistrust that arose between members and the surrounding culture received extensive media coverage; it pitted proponents of different belief systems against each other in a society that had worked hard to achieve religious tolerance.

The sect gained considerable notoriety for the way it acquired youthful converts, since conversion represented a major disruption in family ties and religious beliefs. New members moved into communal residences, and for weeks, even months, refused to associate with their families. Distraught parents felt they had lost their children forever; some resorted to deprogrammers who would forcibly abduct and sequester their children, pressing them to recant their newfound beliefs. Most of those treated this way (who were, in fact, not minors) escaped their captors and returned to their co-religionists, where they were usually sent to remote church centers and protected from further abduction.

Initial Encounters

My first contact with the Moonies came through Dr. Richard Rabkin, a psychiatrist at New York University, who had heard about the Divine Light Mission project. After giving a talk on the psychology of contemporary religious sects at a nearby university, he had been approached by representatives of the Moonies, who asked whether he would be interested in learning more about this group. He felt that I might be able to organize a systematic study of it.

The opportunity was appealing because I had already begun to experiment with a treatment approach for alcoholism modeled on the psychology of charismatic groups and I now wanted a better understanding of how such groups operated. I was particularly interested in learning how dissemination of the group's beliefs and concomitant control over communication in the sect affected members' psychological states. A project on the Moonies might shed light on the remarkable beliefs these zealous groups could engender and how they motivated their members to such high levels of commitment.

Rabkin and I were soon joined in the study by Drs. Judith Rabkin of Columbia University and Alexander Deutsch of New York University. Our principal liaison with the sect's hierarchy was a likable and frank woman in her late twenties, who served as the Director of Public Affairs for the U.S. church. The necessary arrangements were made in a lengthy meeting with Neil Salonen, the president of the Unification Church of America. No doubt he too felt it necessary to have a firsthand sense of the researchers' attitude and chose to be directly involved in any final understanding. Salonen was an affable and outgoing Caucasian in his late thirties, who seemed more like the regional manager of a Middle American corporation than a religious zealot or scion of subversive aliens. He had worked in hospital administration before joining the church, and had only reluctantly left that position after an extended period of membership, when he decided to contribute more actively to the work of his newfound religion. He and his wife, both members for ten years, had borne and raised two children since joining.

The rationale I presented Salonen for supporting his members' participation in this study was the same offered for subsequent projects. I pointed out that the sect often received poor press, as he well knew. Participation would offer the opportunity to have the nature of their sect brought forth objectively and would further show they had nothing to hide on the issues of brainwashing and coercion, since they were willing to have outside observers evaluate the membership experience. I felt their openness to these studies did indeed reflect well on the group's credibility.

Conversion and Belief

Interviews with members of the Unification Church revealed several different routes of induction into this charismatic group. Some converts did not actively seek out any new order, and were only introduced to the sect's beliefs by means of *subterfuge*. Others became engaged only after their own protracted journey as *seekers* of an acceptable creed. Some were initially attracted to a group whose idealistic commitments allowed for their *identification* with an admired figure or ideal, while others felt compelled to accept church dogma they had initially *opposed*. We will now examine more closely these four ways of engagement.

My first chance to speak in depth with a church member, whose mental competency I was asked to evaluate, was with Jerry, a twenty-year-old, who had become involved in litigation over his parents' attempt to remove him from the sect. His case shed light on how new members were sometimes converted by subterfuge, often in surprising ways.

SUBTERFUGE

Three weeks before I met Jerry, his parents had been designated by a local court to serve as his legal guardians. He was alleged to be mentally incompetent, based on two pieces of evidence. The first was the statement of a family physician who had last seen Jerry when he was fifteen, when he became anxious during a family crisis; the second was Jerry's current involvement in a putative cult. The doctor now wrote that Jerry had "schizophrenic tendencies and was unstable, depending on the environment."

I spoke with an attorney assigned to the case by the American Civil Liberties Union. This organization had long defended the rights of people espousing unpopular causes, and recently provided attorneys for members of new religious movements such as the Unification Church. The attorney emphasized the overriding importance of the First and Fourteenth Amendments to the Constitution—freedom of religion and due process. New York State, for example, required that for someone in Jerry's situation to be placed under conservatorship, he must appear to be mentally ill and likely to cause serious harm to himself or others. I was well acquainted with this rule since it was also used as a criterion for the involuntary commitment of psychotic patients.

On interviewing Jerry, I found that a conservatorship on these grounds was unjustified because he was lucid, content with his circumstances, and without signs of mental illness, by any standard diagnostic criteria. His discussion concerning the nature of his beliefs was similar to those of members of other organized zealous religious groups. From Jerry I learned one way converts can come to accept a highly deviant belief system. The sect's members had introduced him to a set of nonspecific beliefs, which later served as a bridge to his involvement in the church's specific dogma. Jerry effectively joined before he even realized the group's identity, but throughout the conversion process had been fully mentally competent and able to query his hosts at will. Like many others he did not do so, and instead became entrained first in a more popular cause that later led to acceptance of the church and its dogma. Induction into the sect's beliefs, in effect, was carried out by subterfuge.

Although he had adapted well in high school, Jerry ran into difficulty when he left home for college. From what he said, he had become very distressed over his father's alcoholism, which had just recently reached a crisis. Also on his mind were uncertainties about choosing a career, accentuated by his father's own failing prospects.

After his first year, Jerry decided to take a leave of absence for one semester to work in an anti-poverty program, hoping to resolve these feelings of inner turmoil. He returned to college the next spring, but did poorly and felt isolated, even among the friends he had made the year before. He told his parents that he missed the previous semester's sense of commitment, which he had found fulfilling, and was considering leaving school again. This troubled his father, who was now expressing undue expectations for Jerry, perhaps hoping to compensate for his own recent reverses.

While visiting a friend at a nearby college, Jerry was approached by a young Japanese-born woman who engaged him in a discussion on "the future of the world's poor," and then, after an animated exchange, invited him to a daylong workshop for the One-World Crusade, which he agreed to attend. The workshop dealt with a variety of general issues related to the welfare of the poor in America and abroad. The young woman telephoned the following week to ask Jerry if he would be interested in going to a second, weekend-long workshop on the issues they had discussed, but at first he declined. When she offered to pick him up, he agreed, and was then taken to a nearby workshop center. During a weekend of group discussions, sports, and singing at the workshop, Jerry became increasingly attracted to the group's ideals of universal brotherhood and its commitment to a Divine Principle. Among the workshop guests, though, few if any appreciated that the Divine Principle was actually the basis of the religious belief system of the Unification Church. Jerry acknowledged that if had he known this at the outset, he would not have chosen to participate.

Before the weekend workshop was over, the sponsors asked the eight people in attendance if they would like to spend the rest of the week in a retreat. For Jerry, this did not entail a major disruption since he had no classes during the upcoming spring break. In addition, he said, "I found in the group some principles I could believe in, and a true concern for people." Along with two other workshop members, Jerry decided to continue with the weeklong program, and these three, along with four members participating in the One-World Crusade, embarked by van for the retreat. He did not yet realize that they were heading toward the Unification Church Seminary in Barrytown, New York, a facility recently purchased from a monastic order.

In the van, Jerry heard another recruit mention the Moonies while speaking with the driver. He recalled turning to the young Japanese woman who had originally invited him to the workshop, and reconstructed the following dialogue.

> JERRY: Say, does the Divine Principle have something to do with the Moonies?
>
> SHE: You mean the Unification Church?
>
> JERRY: I don't know. Are they related?
>
> SHE: Reverend Moon wrote the Divine Principle.
>
> JERRY: Oh? Is he that Korean guy who spoke at Yankee Stadium?
>
> SHE: Yes, he's a very wise man who gave us the ideas we've been talking about the last few days.
>
> JERRY: Oh, I see. How come you didn't mention it?
>
> SHE: People criticize Reverend Moon unfairly; they would turn you away from joining the workshop, and you would lose the chance to hear his words. We just want you to have the chance to find out what he has to say.

Jerry did not remember being very surprised or distressed at this point. In fact, he gave surprisingly little thought to his growing involvement with a system of beliefs likely to have a profound influence on his life. The transition from views tenable to the population at large to ones that were clearly deviant took place through such casual subterfuge that it provided little cognitive dissonance in the convert. Jerry made the transition from a general support for the poor of the world to engagement in the church's unusual beliefs without even noticing—a telling reflection on the plasticity of belief when those vested with authority promote such a change.

The day after he arrived at the seminary, Jerry telephoned his father, describing in general terms where he was. He recalled subtly trying to avoid identifying the Moonie movement itself, as he knew his father would not approve. Within a few days his family heard from him again and they insisted that he leave, but he felt strongly that it was his option to finish the week.

By this time, however, Jerry's parents had seen a lawyer and a family physician, and appeared at the seminary with a document that gave them the right of conservatorship over their son. Jerry quickly consulted the church leaders. After some deliberation over strategy, he opted to slip away from the compound and seek refuge in a remote Unification Church center, while members of the group began to obtain legal advice for preparing his defense. The adversity Jerry was facing contributed to the consolidation of his beliefs. He not only espoused the creed of the church, but also had to defend it.

Jerry may have begun his involvement with the Moonies under a misapprehension, but his affirmation of their beliefs was now clear, and his mental competency to stay on (or undertake any course of action he chose) appeared intact. He was introduced to a new set of beliefs by subterfuge at a time when his own distressed mental state made him vulnerable. The malaise he felt over his father's alcoholism and his own uncertain career plans had left him open to the offer of a universalist solution. He was gradually drawn into a belief system that provided a sense of certainty and a needed dose of hope and commitment. Proponents of unpopular belief systems have long revealed only what they felt wise during initial recruitment.

SEEKERS

Unlike Jerry, however, some converts have had long careers as seekers[19] of spiritual experience before joining one of the new religious movements. Becoming involved in an active quest for a comprehensive approach may represent an effort to resolve conflicts about life's meaning. Such preoccupations are of course common in adolescents, but for some they can become compelling and protracted, and may serve as a primary focus for intellectual commitments. The culture in which a youth grows up can also do a great deal to prime the person for such a mental set, and the counterculture perspective of the 1960s and early 1970s led many young people to seek a guiding philosophy. Yet, for many seekers, the specifics of ideology in the sects they joined were apparently less relevant in their particular choice than coincidences surrounding their initial encounters with the group. That is, if the time, people, and place were right, any movement might have caught their attention.

One person who ended a protracted quest by joining the Moonies is named Bill; his experience illustrates the career of a seeker. Like his parents, Bill thought of himself as agnostic from an early age, and maintained no formal religious identification. In his mid-teens, he became interested in his Jewish cultural background and traveled to Israel after his high school graduation. While spending a week in Europe, he ran into members of the Unification Church, but was not, as he later recalled, attracted to their lifestyle or religion.

The next year, as a college freshman, he took two courses in philosophy hoping to gain a better understanding of "essential issues," and spent much of his spare time with a neo-Hindu group, but eventually lost interest in it.

He went to a lecture at the campus headquarters of the Unification Church, looking for "some ideas about the way the world turns." Although the group offered interesting views, he chose other opportunities to find a meaningful identity. For some months he "became a hippie, to see if drugs were a route toward understanding," and then, as he put it, an "intellectual; I read a lot. I was big on the value of 'ideas' as the essence of life."

Bill began participating actively in the antiwar movement during his second year at college; he again went to Israel to spend the summer in a Hasidic Moshav. Here, too, he became disenchanted, feeling that he could not accept the Hasidic position that Jews have a special place as God's chosen people.

Bill returned to college that fall, but only as a part-time student, feeling uncertain of his future goals. He dropped by the campus headquarters of the Unification Church again, but remembers feeling no great camaraderie and no sense of connection with his own experience. Still, the Divine Principle interested him and he offered to help with tasks around the building, regarding this as a convenient way to make an acquaintance with "offbeat" aspects of the local scene. As we spoke, he surmised that he was feeling the need for some group he could relate to more permanently, having exhausted his role as a movement "buff."

Bill was soon invited to a four-hour lecture on the Divine Principle, which he attended with misgivings, thinking that its origins were not compatible with his own Jewish background. After the lecture, though, his response to the group's philosophy was one of "glee. I had found my purpose in life. I now had conviction and belief, something which had been lacking before." He had reached a resting place in his career as a seeker, and six years later, in recounting his experiences, he pointed out that subsequent exposure to the group's beliefs had strengthened his commitment.

IDENTIFYING

Other converts joined as a way of identifying with values they perceived in their own parents; for them the group often represented a meaningful cause from the outset. One young woman, Barbara, remarked that the most important reason for her joining was that its members had the same kind of dedication to social values as her own mother, whom she had admired greatly since childhood. Her mother had been deeply involved in the struggle for racial equality and had worked actively for peace from the early years of the Vietnam war.

As a college freshman Barbara became interested in the women's movement, and wrote a comprehensive paper on contemporary women musicians. On her professor's suggestion, she adapted the paper for an article in her college newspaper. She said, "I pursued this idea because I was committed to change, but I decided that we were only scratching the surface. Like my mother, I wanted to believe in a philosophy of action to build an ideal world, and as soon as I became acquainted with the Church, I sensed that their beliefs could bring it about."

OPPOSITION

In contrast to Barbara, a potential convert may assume an oppositional position. Many youths like to engage in conflict with an established authority, in this case represented by a new religious movement. What is at first most visible is the blustery autonomy and rebelliousness of adolescence. But in the end their underlying need for dependency, against which they do battle at this stage of life, emerges in their attraction to the group's totalistic demands. An independent stance may serve as the basis for conversion to the very position they oppose, as they become involved in battling over the sect's ideas. Similar observations have been made in studies on the social psychology of attitude change.[20]

One young man, Carl, was introduced to the church at a time when he felt relatively content with the circumstances of his life. His friend joined the Unification Church, and Carl tried to convince the friend to leave, relishing the opportunity to argue against the sect's position. The friend prevailed on Carl to attend a church workshop, claiming that he could not really communicate effectively unless exposed directly to the Divine Principle. Carl recalled the workshop as an "interesting" experience, but said it left him tense and irritated since he felt compelled to refute the views of its leader as they spoke together after the formal sessions.

The crucial point in Carl's conversion came three days later when he was challenged by two acquaintances to justify the interest he seemed to be showing in the church. An argument followed and, in insisting on his own neutrality, Carl's ambivalence shifted to more positive feelings. Later that evening, he decided on impulse to telephone his friend at the church center. He found himself saying that he would be coming over the next day to a session at the center to "get more familiar" with the church. That night, Carl felt an intense longing for the church, and the truth it now seemed to offer. "Now I wanted to believe in the Principle so that I could find comfort in it. The next day I decided to join."

This experience is similar to that of many alcoholics who join Alcoholics Anonymous, also a charismatic movement. Their association with the group is born out of a need to establish a safe base in opposition to their compulsive attraction to alcohol, but they are often skeptical about the quasireligious commitment inherent in AA. Nonetheless, the alcoholic's own oppositional position against dependency on the group and its creed can ultimately yield to a strong commitment. This is reflected in the comments of one alcoholic concerning the First Step of AA, the acknowledgment of helplessness before a Higher Power.

> I thought it was preposterous at first, submitting to a Higher Power. I knew better than that, and I even argued the point with some members. Then, after a while, I realized that they *were* right and that all along I

had *wanted* to acknowledge my belief, but had fought it off for too long. The strength of these principles became clear when I realized how hard I had to fight to avoid them.

Often the need to aggressively oppose the creed of a charismatic group is fired by a convert's psychological defense against dependency needs, which are heightened by the seductiveness of submitting to a set of absolute beliefs. As the convert becomes more intimate with the group, even in rebellious anger, the need for dependency may produce submission.

A Study of the Members

As I began planning for a study that would address the issue of shared beliefs in a charismatic sect, it became clear that church officials would not impose *a priori* restraints, so it then seemed feasible to touch on some sensitive topics such as drug use, physical coercion, and attitudes toward sex. I prepared a questionnaire on these as well as other psychological and demographic issues from the Divine Light study. The questionnaire was to be completed anonymously to avoid concern by members that their responses might somehow be monitored.

The group's leadership was also quite cooperative in helping with arrangements for administrating the questionnaire at a large meeting at the New York Church headquarters, where members would attend a routine program of evening entertainment. The meeting was typical, and because of the considerable mobility of church members throughout the United States, this sample included individuals from all regions of the country.[21]

Our research team was present to distribute the questionnaires and coordinate a cadre of members whom I had previously prepared to answer questions that might be raised. As we began, the National President introduced the exercise, asking that members be frank in responding so that an accurate picture of the church would be given. There were 307 members present that evening, and, of these, questionnaires from the 237 who were native-born Americans were analyzed; they had been members for an average of almost three years.

Responses showed that the backgrounds of Unification Church members were similar to those observed among the Divine Light Mission. Also reflected, however, was a dislocation that preceded their joining the sect, both in terms of disruption of their education and emotional problems, as well as antecedent interest in other sects. For example, members began to withdraw from the usual sequence of education before they encountered the group, since less than a third of those who were students right before conversion were actually enrolled full-time. In addition, although most (58%) had begun college, only a minority (25%) actually graduated. Although most (67%) regarded themselves as moderately or strongly committed to their family's religious orientation before they reached the age of fifteen, the overwhelming majority (90%)

reported a subsequent history of some commitment to one of the other new religious movements—reflecting at least some experience as religious seekers.

Psychological difficulties before joining also were not uncommon (as also shown in the Divine Light Mission study). Thus, a sizable portion (39%) felt that they had experienced serious emotional problems in the past, problems that led many to seek professional help (30%) and even hospitalization (6%). The nature of the members' current emotional status was ascertained by means of a standardized instrument developed by the National Center for Health Statistics, the psychological General Well-Being Schedule. This instrument allowed us to compare Unification Church members to a representative sample from the general population based on national survey data.[22] From their responses, it was apparent that even at the time of the study, members' sense of well-being was notably below that of a matched group from the general population.[23] This is all the more significant because members' Psychological Distress scores for the period *before* joining were considerably (48%) higher than those obtained for the time of the survey. This suggested that members had as a group been experiencing a notable level of psychological distress prior to joining, which no doubt left them vulnerable to a set of beliefs that promised to provide them a renewed sense of purpose. Furthermore, the data on members not completing their college education and reports on their contact with other sects suggested a behavioral concomitant of this emotional disruption.

To examine the relationship between members' acceptance of the Unification Church beliefs and their current emotional well-being, I had developed a scale for religious commitment (Table 3-1), in which subjects rated a series of items according to how they had felt at three different times: for the period immediately before joining, the one immediately after, and at the present time.

Not surprisingly, members' current commitment to their religious beliefs was very high. For example, the bulk of the members (74%) felt a "close connection with God . . . very much." Their proselytizing zeal was also reflected in their strong feeling that nonmembers should "adopt the same religious beliefs" as their own (80%). In addition, in relation to transcendental religious experiences, most (90%) reported that they had "intensely . . . seen a special new meaning in life . . . during daily prayer."[24] These feelings were reported much more strongly than for the period before joining.

How did this degree of commitment affect members' emotional status? In the first place, a large majority (91%) indicated that their level of psychological distress was lower for the period right after conversion than the one right before. The average decline was equivalent to a change from "moderately" to "slightly" anxious on the Distress Scale (from a score of 3 to 2). Equally important, the actual decline in symptoms was directly correlated with the strength of members' religious feelings, so that those who improved the most in their distress had shown a markedly greater increase in religiosity scores over the course of conversion.

Table 3-1. *Religious Belief Scale*

Each item is rated from 1 ("not at all") to 5 ("very much") relative to the period in question.

1. I feel a close connection with God.   ( )
2. My religious beliefs give me comfort.   ( )
3. I should avoid thinking about sex.   ( )
4. I should avoid getting "high" from alcohol.   ( )

   People who are not members of my religious group should:
5. adopt the same religious beliefs that I do.   ( )
6. avoid thinking about sex.   ( )
7. avoid getting "high" from alcohol.

8. Prayer or meditation give meaning to my life.   ( )
9. Prayer or meditation raise my spirits when I felt troubled.   ( )

Three variables in question could now be considered together, so that we could evaluate the impact of the members' religious belief and cohesiveness on their emotional well-being. This analysis showed that items from these two scales of group affiliation—belief and cohesiveness—were strong predictors of members' sense of emotional well-being (that is, together they predicted 36% of variance in General Well-Being scores). Two items of religious belief, "My religious beliefs give me comfort" and "I feel a close connection with God," were the highest-ranking predictors in this analysis.[25] A member's ongoing emotional state was strongly related to the degree of affiliation felt to the church. If the member was closer to the group in terms of beliefs and social ties, he or she would experience considerably more psychological general well-being than if more distant.

It was also interesting to ascertain the extent to which members' beliefs affected their actual behavior, since behavioral change is certainly a test of true commitment. Two areas of attitude and related behavior were considered: sexual relations and use of drugs and alcohol. Members indicated a striking increase in constraints over sexuality after joining. Only a few (11%) reported that they had felt very much that they "should avoid thinking about sex" immediately before they joined the church, but by the time of the questionnaire, the large majority (76%) felt this way, and a similar portion of the respondents believed that such avoidance was appropriate for nonmembers too. Members also put these views into action, since sexual contact of any sort was unheard of among the many members I interviewed, and proselytizing to bring in others to accept these norms was a principal activity. As I later observed in studying members engaged to be married, a prohibition on all sexual contact was adhered to over the course of more than three years of engagement and even afterward, for months of a prescribed "separation period" following the marriage.

The impact of people's beliefs on their behavior was further seen in the changes in their use of drugs and alcohol. As creatures of their contemporary culture, members had used intoxicants fairly extensively before joining, so that a fair portion of them (23%) actually reported having serious drug problems in the past. The large majority had smoked marijuana (79%) or drunk alcoholic beverages in the past (90%), and almost half (45%) had used hallucinogens. At present, the bulk of the members (88%) strongly accepted the preferred norm, to "avoid getting high from alcohol," and only a small minority (13%) had drunk any alcoholic beverage during the previous two months. Only one respondent (0.4%) had used alcohol daily during this period, in contrast to a fair number (17%) who had done so at some point before joining. In my subsequent study on the induction experience (discussed in a later chapter), I found that such religiously grounded attitudes were acquired quite rapidly: Workshop participants expressed levels of commitment similar to those of long-term members after no more than two days of exposure to the group.

What emerged from the interviews and survey was a picture of the individual convert's pliability in acquiring strong beliefs over a relatively short period. Once receptive to the charismatic group and then part of it, the convert's psychological status becomes engaged with these beliefs. A state of well-being is maintained insofar as one adheres to these beliefs, but distress emerges when one feels less committed to them and to fellow members. This close relationship between affiliation and emotional well-being reinforces compliance and continued ties to the group, without need for external coercion. This mechanism is not consciously perceived by the member, any more than most people routinely ponder why they go home to their families each night or why they repeatedly seek out their friends for social engagements. Norms for belief and associated behavior become internalized very rapidly and considerable distress would emerge if some undue circumstance led a member of a charismatic group to violate these commitments.

We are often surprised at the deviant behavior of cult members when it is dictated by beliefs at variance with our own. When a Moonie spends his or her day soliciting in the street, we find this incomprehensible, just as we think it bizarre when a Hare Krishna member appears in flowing robes with shaven head. Nonetheless, so long as a particular behavior pattern has been adopted in association with a system of cultic beliefs, and in association with a charismatic sect's close-knit social network, it is not experienced as unusual or strained by the members themselves, even though it may shock or repel the general public.

The Attribution of Meaning

To consider further how the convert acquires a set of beliefs different from prior attitudes, we may draw on attribution theory. Originally outlined by the social psychologist Fritz Heider,[26] this theory deals with how people ascribe meaning to events by drawing on their existing attitudes and environmental cues. It has been applied to the way people interpret their experience in spheres as diverse as psychotherapy, politics, and religion.[27]

One way people acquire their attitudes is literally by observing themselves. Daryl Bem[28] pointed to this aspect of self-perception when he wrote that individuals come to "know" their attitudes, emotions, and other internal states, partially by "inferring them from observations from their own overt behavior, and/or the circumstances in which this behavior occurs. . . . The individual is functionally in the same position as an outside observer, an observer who must necessarily rely upon those same cues to infer the individual's inner states."

People may, for example, attribute meaning to important experiences in life by recourse to their family's religious background, but usually they had adopted these attitudes without formal intention, in part because they *observed themselves* engaged in that faith as they grew up. One does not necessarily arrive at a conscious decision about one's religious orientation, but rather acknowledges "I am a Catholic" or "I am a Jew" because one has repeatedly carried out practices associated with that faith.

This type of attribution also applies to more transient experiences. A person can be thrust into uncertainty by a confusing series of events, and then draw on any readily available explanation suggested by the *social context* in which those events took place. The individual may then use that explanation in other situations where it seems relevant. Given an uncertain state of mood and perception, the individual responds with the most readily available credible explanation. We tend to deal with uncertainty by looking to past experience or cues in the situation, and may then come to an understanding without carefully evaluating all available data. Certain situations actually tend to increase the likelihood that an individual will be influenced by circumstantial cues rather than making careful observations and verifying them. Harold Kelly[29] proposed that this is most likely if someone has

1. Little social support.
2. Prior information that is poor and ambiguous.
3. Problems difficult beyond one's capabilities.
4. Views that have been disconfirmed because they were inappropriate or incorrect.
5. Other experiences engendering low self-confidence.

These ideas shed light on the way potential recruits begin to acquire new beliefs while attending the workshops of the Unification Church. For example, when the recruiter telephoned Jerry at college and asked him to attend the weekend workshop, Jerry met these criteria for dislocation. He had recently quit the job he had taken while on leave from college, was uncertain of his future career, and felt adrift. His father's difficulties with drinking were also weighing heavily on him, contributing to his malaise and low self-esteem. In the Unification Church workshop, he was subjected to an unexpectedly intense group experience, one that forced him to develop some perspective, if for no other reason than to make sense of the unanticipated affection show-ered on him. In addition, the contrast between the uncertainty he felt before and the certitude shown him by members of the One-World Crusade (as these Moonies called their group) primed him to attribute some broader meaning to the experience. At this point, the workshop leaders offered him the tran-scendent role of their Crusade as an explanation for this remarkable display of commitment.

Jerry was also influenced by observing his own behavior, as he found him-self mobilized into taking part in the workshop: a full schedule of group dis-cussions, singing, sports, and the sharing of intimate feelings. Participating in these group activities shaped his perception of himself as a member of the Crusade who shared the group's values. Thus, his own behavior in complying with the group's exercises and the messages imparted by the workshop's lead-ership both attributed meaning to his experience.

Once established, this attribution helped guide his subsequent behavior, and implicitly served as an explanatory model around which he defined his later experience. This becomes clear in what he told me about his feelings after the weekend workshop.

> It was strange, but the intensity of the two days left me much clearer about why I had been so uncertain, and where I might head for the future; it was as if a haze had been lifted. I began to understand things that had made no sense before, why most people rushed around for no reason, without any lasting sense of purpose. I had a sense that I could look for direction to my friends in the One-World Crusade.

In later joining the Unification Church, Jerry acquired a small community of comrades whom he knew personally, but in addition a much larger *pseudo-community* now existed for him—the full membership of the church. This group, most of whom he had never met, was becoming as much a reality as the members he actually knew. This use of a large interpersonal network, existing only in the individual's mind, allows the charismatic group member to feel close to many people who support the attributions he or she had just established. A deviant belief, an idiosyncratic mission, and fidelity to a cultic figure are all more tenable if there are thousands who hold the same position. A newly acquired philosophy is more likely to be maintained when its tenets are accepted by many others.[30]

The concept of the pseudo-community is also relevant to the understanding of certain types of psychopathology, particularly paranoia. For the paranoid, a pseudo-community is autistic—it is conjured up without any consensual validation from others. As originally described by John Cameron,[31] the pseudo-community consisted of persons whom the paranoid imagined to populate the world, usually potential assailants, who might be members of the FBI, the Mafia, or similar menacing and powerful groups.

For Carol, a pseudo-community had included the devils she and Bobby were battling. In the hospital, she was able to free herself of this deluded state by adopting a different attribution set—a Pentecostal religious perspective—and her alienation was relieved by joining a new pseudo-community, that of the Pentecostal believers awaiting salvation. Jerry, the seeker, on the other hand, provides an interesting contrast. His exposure to the Unification Church before his weekend workshop had been brief, and the group's beliefs bore little relationship to his prior attitudes. One might wonder what led him to acquire a commitment to the broader community of the Unification Church and its transcendent mission. This should be most revealing, reflecting on the remarkable capacity of church workshops to engage participants into the sect's system of beliefs.

Two studies highlight the role of group conformity in altering individuals' judgment. Solomon Asch[32] had an experimental subject join a group of six people seated around a circular table. The six were actually collaborating with the experimenters, and had been rehearsed on how to behave. All seven were shown a board with a vertical line drawn on it and then shown three other lines and asked to select the one identical in length to the first. The task was structured so that the correct choice was easily made. A series of trials was carried out in which the six collaborators, each responding *before* the subject, gave correct answers. In a final trial, however, all the collaborators made the same *incorrect* response. When his turn came, the subject could either conform with the unanimous majority and make an incorrect choice or choose correctly and be at variance with the group. In a series of these experiments, only a third of the subjects gave the right answer every time. Less than one in ten conformed and answered incorrectly on almost all occasions, while most responded incorrectly intermittently. Here we see a prototype for a nonmember's acquiescence to the group view.

The importance of unanimity among the collaborators was revealed in a subsequent study in which one gave the *correct* response during the last trial while the other five did not. Conformity to incorrect responses among the subjects declined considerably (from 32% of trials in the original study to 6%).

These experiments indicate why cults must maintain a high degree of conformity to the group's views in their recruitment efforts. The Unification Church typically includes a majority of active members in its induction workshops, rather than a lone member as leader in a group of nonmembers. The tenor of communications is thereby more easily managed by the committed majority. Similarly, in Alcoholics Anonymous, recruitment generally takes place at meetings in which the majority of persons present are active members who tell of their salvation through AA and their commitment to maintaining complete abstinence.

During the Unification Church workshops, Jerry conformed to the group's activities and observed himself acting like other adherents to the One-World Crusade, individuals he had come to like and respect. As he said, "I went along in all the activities because they were sincere people doing things for a good cause, even though sometimes it seemed silly." As time went on, though, his perception of his own attitudes was no doubt influenced by observing his own behavior. As Bem suggested, after a point the person who willingly acts out a set of attitudes will come to feel that those attitudes are his or her own.

As the workshop progressed, the group's values gained credence through his observations of his own behavior and the emotional well-being he was beginning to feel. Jerry recalled that "I realized the Principle had to be important. I could see what it was doing for me." Increasingly, he saw the group as a reference point for his perceptions of the world around him and as the basis of his decision making.

Consider the nineteenth-century Oneida Community in this regard. Members' acceptance of its utopian beliefs and their compliance with the ideals of their leader were reinforced at daily meetings of the entire community in the Mansion House, in which personal problems were raised and arbitrated by recourse to group values. Decisions regarding daily activities, from kitchen work to sexual practices, were explained and implemented by recourse to the views of John Noyes, the group's charismatic leader, thereby promoting attribution of all experiences to the Community's worldview.

Attribution to the group's perspectives may also be carried out in small group meetings, as in Synanon, a therapeutic community for drug abuse treatment that originated in Southern California in the late 1950s. The Synanon "games" are protracted group sessions in which participants meet several times a week. In these games, members aggressively address minor problems in their relationships and deviations from prescribed norms among members' attitudes until they achieve a consensus for compliance with the community's values.[33] This small group format is potent; it has allowed members to achieve abstinence from heroin addiction early in the group's history and later served as a basis for establishing a rigidly controlled, closed community with its own self-contained residential and occupational arrangements. Throughout its history, this community was tightly controlled by its charismatic leader, Charles Dederich, whose views were transmitted to members through a network of these games. Controlled communication in the small group also characterizes coercive persuasion, or brainwashing, where the individual is forced to adopt a group's views *against* his or her will. Robert Lifton has observed that brainwashing like that in Chinese Communist prison camps required full control over the context of communication[34] but in voluntary conversions contact must be maintained in a subtle (or deceptive) way, without forcing the individual to comply with the group's views.

Individuals in highly structured group situations can be led to make judgments in ways very different from their decisions while on their own. When properly primed by the social setting, they may accept unusual beliefs that the group they have affiliated with continually reinforces. As we will see, these beliefs can be further intensified when an individual's feelings and state of consciousness have been altered within that group setting.

4

ALTERED CONSCIOUSNESS

People are more vulnerable to social influence when they are made to think, sense, and feel differently than usual, when someone or something disrupts their emotional balance. Such changes in subjective experience (or alterations in consciousness) can undermine the psychological matrix in which our views are rooted, so that we lose track of customary internal signposts. They may also introduce a feeling of mystery, or a sense that forces beyond our control are operating. Thus, they can prime us to accept unaccustomed explanations for our experiences and adopt new attitudes implied in these explanations. In this respect altered consciousness can help shape members' attitudes in a charismatic group.

I was struck by the significant role of alterations in consciousness when studying the Divine Light Mission. From my first contact with this group, members mentioned the importance of the four "meditations" to their personal commitment. Each drew on a different sense, causing unexpected visions, tastes, and music. The sect itself was named for one of these sensory experiences, the "Divine Light," that members reported seeing during their personal meditation. At first these meditation practices did not seem compelling, perhaps because of my own inclination to dismiss as self-deceptive or pathologic those experiences that could not be verified by independent observation. Their importance became clear, however, as I spoke with one person, Raymond, whose views I tended to take more seriously, since he too was a psychiatrist. Sharing a profession made it easier to empathize with him. In addition, Raymond was a bright young man, well-versed in contemporary psychological thought, and willing to consider all sides of an issue. Nonetheless, in his recounting he seemed almost obsessed with the alterations in consciousness he ascribed to his religious experience.

While in medical school, Raymond wanted to be a general practitioner and decided to do his internship in family medicine. Then he took a position in a small-town clinic to have the personal contact with patients he had long anticipated. After two years in this crowded clinic, he became disenchanted with the limited opportunities for working closely with patients and began to wonder about other possibilities. An acquaintance invited Raymond to attend satsang, the religious sermon of the Divine Light Mission. He did and found in the group members a sense of conviction lacking in his own life. He had begun to feel bored and the group offered a focus of interest. He attended satsang again, and described the following experience from his third visit.

He was sitting comfortably in a group of a dozen people, mostly members, listening to a young woman speaking about the importance of the guru's mission. He was not attending too closely to her words, but was instead lulled into relaxation by the rhythm of her speech. Suddenly, he saw a bright light emanating from her body, forming a halo around her. He later recalled

> The light was intense. She glowed as if she were a religious figure in a movie, and it gave her the appearance of holiness. It was a real light, as real as the lightbulb in a lamp. So I sat there listening carefully to her words, and they were no different from the ones she had spoken minutes before. Now, I'm a fairly cynical guy, and I don't take the unexpected at face value, so I did a double take and looked away, expecting the light to disappear—but it was still there. No one had even told me to expect a light like this, and no one else seemed to see it.
>
> When she finished I got up to leave and, as I walked toward the door— she was still glowing—I realized that something had happened to me that I couldn't dismiss. The experience would somehow have to become a part of my understanding of the world around me. Over the next few weeks I found myself getting involved further with the group, and soon decided to ask to receive Knowledge [to join].

Raymond continued to work at his clinic for a few months, but then decided that he had to carry the group's message to others, so he took a position in an alcoholism treatment program where he hoped to help his patients by conveying to them the sect's message. After six months in that program, his patients were unresponsive to his message, and Raymond decided that a career in psychiatry would offer him a better opportunity to deal with the spiritual issues his conversion had raised. He took his training in psychiatry and continued to meditate, occasionally experiencing intense visual and bodily sensations and changes in his sense of time.

This episode of altered consciousness was not very different from many in the literature on religious conversion, but was nonetheless difficult to explain from a psychiatric perspective. Raymond's vision of the halo might be construed as a hallucinatory experience in conventional psychiatric terms, and thereby ascribed to causes of perceptual change such as a dissociative reaction, transient psychosis, or even mass hysteria. But his history, his behavior, and his demeanor as we spoke gave no hint of such a diagnosis. This "vision" also fit in nicely with his later experiences in meditation, and could not be dismissed as an isolated phenomenon.

I was left with a tale told by a perceptive and lucid observer who described a phenomenon that did not fit into my handbook of diagnoses. Nonetheless, the experience had clearly served as a basis for the attribution of a new meaning to his life. It set him off balance and he turned to the philosophy of the sect to explain the puzzling event. From that point, Raymond's relationship with the Divine Light Mission followed with seeming inevitability, and served as a basis for his understanding of his own role in life. This experience had many counterparts in my interviews with other members of the Divine Light Mission, as it became clear that altered consciousness in the form of inexplicable perceptions and transcendent emotional states was common in their conversion and subsequent religious experience.

These reports made a compelling argument for the role of altered consciousness as a force in the charismatic group, even though the phenomena reported were difficult to integrate into contemporary models of psychiatric function. Research on mental function is generally conducted at the level of observable behavior or neurophysiology, and does not usually address subjective aspects of experience. Nomenclature is based on what can be seen and measured by independent observers, whereas altered consciousness is usually only subjectively perceived.

Altered consciousness, however, can be a prime motive force among both well-adapted and disturbed individuals. Like group cohesiveness and shared beliefs, it acts as a vehicle for the identity transformation and engagement that draw people into a charismatic group.

As a starting point for understanding the role of altered consciousness in charismatic groups, we must turn back nearly a century to the work of William James. James reasoned that "the distribution of consciousness shows itself to be exactly such as we might expect in an organ added for the sake of steering a nervous system grown too complex to regulate itself."[1] This concept of consciousness as a meta-organ is useful, and serves as a credible basis for Arnold Ludwig's definition of an altered state of consciousness:

> any mental state(s), induced by various physiological, psychological, or pharmacological maneuvers or agents, which can be recognized subjectively by the individual himself (or by the objective observer of the individual) as representing a sufficient deviation [from] . . . alert, waking, consciousness.[2]

But given these definitions, what specific aspects of perception are actually altered in the altered state of consciousness? We can consider consciousness as if it were a multidimensional space, with each dimension representing some aspect of perception or sensation.[3] Different altered states may then be defined in relation to the dimensions altered. We will discuss a variety of dimensions relating to charismatic groups, such as time sense, personal identity, appetite drives, and visual perception. Each dimension contributes to the totality of a person's state of consciousness and allows for mapping out similarities and differences between altered states. When altered by a charismatic group experience, each can serve as a nidus for the attribution of new meaning to one's experience.

Consciousness and its alterations are grounded in physiology, so that states subjectively perceived as similar may also have similar physiologic characteristics. This is illustrated by the changes in neural function found in some states of mental relaxation and reflection. For example, electroencephalographic (EEG) studies of experienced practitioners of Transcendental Meditation reveal an increase in alpha wave activity[4] during meditation. This calming state can be compared to that experienced during marijuana intoxication when people are allowed to relax in the absence of social input. Here the EEG is characterized by alpha waves of greater amplitude.[5] An increase in alpha-wave activity coupled with similar mental relaxation can also be achieved through biofeedback training.[6]

The fact that altered states may be substituted for each other also suggests similarities. For example, many members of the new religious movements switched from drugs to meditation to achieve similar mental effects. The Divine Light members who previously had "serious drug problems" and frequently experienced altered consciousness from drug use were more likely to practice meditation routinely after joining the sect than those who had not used drugs extensively.[7] Crossing over between one vehicle for achieving altered consciousness to a second one suggests an inherent relationship between these subjective states; it also complements the observation that states may be induced by different means.

Meditation

The important role of altered states in the Divine Light Mission was set in relief by the responses from members describing their own transcendental experiences during meditation, which almost all of them (95%) practiced daily.[8] In answering the questionnaire summarized in Table 4-1, they used a scale designed to register increasing levels of hallucinatory-like phenomena, and thus more profound alterations in consciousness. In the auditory sphere, for example, members were asked whether they had "heard something special that no one else could hear," the first item on this scale. The large majority (92%) reported having such experiences during meditation. Of these, about half (49%) reported hearing it "only inside" them; a small number (14%) answered, "I could almost hear it in my ear"; but almost a third (29%) gave the most literal response for such hallucinatory experiences: "I heard it with my ears." This response is most striking since it would be compatible with a diagnosis of psychosis outside the context of religious experience.

Table 4-1 reflects a widespread alteration in subjective and sensory states during meditation, but the way in which meditation was practiced is also

Table 4-1. *Altered Consciousness During Meditation*

Each respondent indicated the extent to which he or she had the following experiences during meditation, using a scale of 0–3. The first figure after each item is the portion of members who reported any such experience at all (scale responses 1–3); the second figure is the portion who reported the experience most intensely (response 3).

1. I heard something special that no one else could hear. [92%, at all; 29%, I heard it with my ears]
2. I saw something special that no one else could see. [92%, at all; 30%, I could see it clearly with my eyes]
3. I had strong sexual feelings without physical sexual contact. [39%, at all; 14%, clearly more intense than orgasm]
4. I had a special and unfamiliar feeling in my body. [91%, at all; 49%, very intense]
5. Time passed faster or slower than usual in a very special way. [90%, at all; 34%, very intense]
6. I felt myself to be different from my usual self in a very special way. [94%, at all; 56%, very intense]
7. I saw special new meaning in my life. [96%, at all; 61%, very intense]
8. I felt better than ever before in a very special way. [96%, at all; 66%, very intense]

important. Members not only set aside a specific time to meditate, they also practiced it while involved in daily activities, as suggested by the guru. Almost all (99%) did this sometimes and a majority (54%) did it "usually."

The relevance of such experience to participation in a charismatic group may be clarified by considering how these members attribute meaning to their daily experiences. A compelling alteration in a person's subjective state, whether from drugs or to a novel social context, leaves the person open to ascribing new meaning to experiences. This certainly applies to the altered consciousness associated with meditation, which serves as a vehicle for destabilizing old attitudes and preparing the meditator to accept the group's beliefs. It acts to support the group's cohesiveness and stabilize and even enhance a member's acceptance of the group.

As in Raymond's case, meditation also serves as a basis for *joining* the charismatic group. This is illustrated by the responses of the Divine Light members, who were asked whether the experiences of altered consciousness listed in Table 4-1 had taken place at the time of their conversion. It turned out to be almost as high then as it was during their subsequent meditation, even though their exposure to the group had been modest up to then. A large majority reported that during the conversion period to some degree they "saw something special that no one else could see" (90%) and "heard something special that no one else could hear" (83%). Such experiences must have made them more responsive to the group's influence.

Over the long term of membership, meditation also played an important role in supporting a convert's continuing involvement. An analysis of the relationship between the time members spent in meditation and the decline in their level of neurotic distress revealed that greater meditation time was associated with diminished neurotic distress. This association suggests that the emotional response to meditation acts as a reinforcement for its continued practice.[9] That is, the more a member meditated, in general, the better the person was likely to feel. Members apparently used meditation to relieve distress, both at scheduled times and on an ad hoc basis. This tranquilizer, as it were, had its own reinforcing qualities and no doubt helped cement commitment to the sect. In this way, it had an addicting effect.

The role of meditation in altering individuals' perspectives on life is shown in an interesting manner by American practitioners of Transcendental Meditation (TM), followers of Maharishi Mahesh Yogi. This sect initially had a straightforward approach to achieving a meditative state, based on a formula in which the meditator concentrated on a personal code word, or mantra. The ability to facilitate relaxation with this technique made TM popular in the early 1970s and aroused interest in both lay and medical communities. Certified trainers would impart the technique to clients who paid for a course of instruction, taught with a minimum of cultic trappings although there were some, such as the secrecy surrounding trainees' mantras. By the mid-1970s, 350 TM training centers were scattered across the nation, with 10,000 persons taking up the practice each month, most of them well educated and successful. Professionals involved in the economic and cultural mainstream reported having transcendent experiences while meditating. One senior editor at a New York publishing house had mild hallucinations if she exceeded the prescribed forty minutes per day, "not frightening ones; just flowers and birds and fountains."[10] Acceptance among health professionals was widespread too, and TM was used to allay everyday tension, provide pain relief in dentistry, and for other clinical purposes.[11]

In time, TM evolved into something of a charismatic movement, with a belief system that transcended the domain of its practice. The scope of the movement broadened considerably with the establishment of Maharishi International University, named after the guru of TM, in Fairfield, Iowa. A variety of unreasonable beliefs came to be accepted as literally true by the more committed members, such as the ability of experienced meditators to levitate. Group meditation was thought to effect direct changes in international political and economic affairs, and even to reduce traffic accidents in remote cities. Indeed, at one point movement leaders mobilized a conclave of thousands of Maharishi's followers who expected by their conjoint efforts to shape the course of ongoing military conflicts in the Middle East and Southeast Asia.[12] In this movement, the altered state associated with meditation clearly contributed to members' acceptance of an unlikely set of beliefs.

Drug-Induced Altered Consciousness

Because of their potent effect on perception, thought, and feeling, psycho-active drugs such as marijuana, cocaine, heroin, and alcohol can shape social behavior and social structure. Quite aptly, the term social pharmacology[13] has been used to describe the interplay between the physiologic effects of drugs that alter the mental state and the impact these drugs can have on social interactions. Psychoactive drug use is almost always part of the fabric of rit-uals and accepted behavior within a society, and thereby usually contributes to the stability of the social structure. Alcohol, for instance, is so closely associated with norms of accepted social behavior in contemporary culture that it is difficult to change such customs, as we learned during Prohibition. Cross-cultural studies indicate that psychoactive drugs generally help inte-grate members of a society into patterns of social conformity. This observation has been made in diverse social settings and in different historical periods, from primitive to complex cultures. In preindustrial cultures where ritual use of psychoactive plants is found, little if any abuse occurs, and drug use almost always is a means to a socially approved end, such as contacting the super-natural.[14] Even in nineteenth-century United States, where opiates were used widely in tincture form, their role was accepted as part of the standard phar-macopoeia.[15]

Drugs and the Counterculture

Consciousness-altering drugs played a prominent role in spearheading the acceptance of counterculture values in the 1960s, abetted by their ability to alter the individuals' subjective state and thereby prime the person for accep-tance of a new world view. The psychedelic movement, fueled by marijuana and ignited by psychotomimetics such as LSD, psilocybin, and mescaline, came close to meeting the definition of a charismatic group. Participants ac-quired a good measure of social cohesiveness, a mix of shared ideologies and beliefs, and considerable changes in personal values.

Some of those experimenting with LSD attempted to generate new per-spectives rooted in the presumed value of self-realization inherent in altered consciousness; we will examine these attempts since they illustrate the incom-plete development of a potential charismatic movement rooted in the use of mind-altering drugs. Best known was Timothy Leary, who emerged from the relatively value-free perspective of a psychological research laboratory. Leary was exposed to LSD in the context of his early investigations into its psy-chotomimetic effects. The motto he later popularized—"Tune in, turn on, drop out"—became a catchphrase for the counterculture, but was primarily a negation of values. His subsequent flirtation with establishing a more tran-scendent quasireligious movement, the "League for Spiritual Democracy," whose acronym is LSD, did not carry sufficient meaning to engage young people. As an effective orator, Leary drew sizable crowds at first, but interest in the nascent movement evaporated, and drug use did not become the basis of a new religious movement.

Because little historical relationship exists between psychedelics and Christian mysticism, drug-induced altered consciousness was also not seen as the high road into Christian tradition. One attempt at studying how drugs can help attain transcendent experience within the framework of an established religion is fascinating. Walter Pahnke[16] was a researcher who undertook a variety of investigations into the consciousness-raising effects of psychotomimetic drugs. In one notable study, he gave the psychotomimetic psilocybin to ten Christian theology students, and an active placebo (one whose marginal effects might lead it to be mistaken for the drug itself) to an equal number of control subjects, also theology students. Both groups had been prepared for the possibility of a heightened spiritual response and were brought to a Good Friday service in a chapel right after.

Pahnke found that those who received the active drug rated themselves appreciably higher on descriptors of mystical experience, such as feelings of unity and transcendence of time and space, than did the controls. On the basis of a six-month follow-up, he reported that the experience also provided "life-enhancing and-enriching effects similar to some of those claimed by mystics" and had a profound impact on the lives of eight of the ten subjects given the active drug. He emphasized that the experience took place in the context of a religious service whose use of symbols was familiar and meaningful, and that the design of the study provided an appropriate framework for the students to derive meaning and integration from their experience.

Such an approach to promoting a Christian mystical experience was quite interesting, but, in the end, Christian mysticism is associated with asceticism and denial of bodily pleasures, whereas the use of psychedelics, at least within the counterculture generation, came to be allied with a hedonistic orientation and a rebellion against traditional values. Ultimately, the contradiction between these two perspectives made their combination unlikely.

Others sought to revive established religious values through drugs, but drew on Eastern religions rather than Western views. This was more apt because of the acknowledged place of altered consciousness in Eastern meditation. Although Eastern spirituality is not traditionally associated with psychedelic drugs, a lack of familiarity with these traditions allowed youths to relate the drug experiences to their newfound meditation practice. American-born drug experimenters exposed to Indian culture, such as Richard Alpert, who later took the name of Baba Raam Dass, articulated this position.

For many a natural transition occurred from drug-related altered consciousness to the altered states associated with meditations within an Eastern charismatic sect. Engagement within the cohesive setting of the Divine Light Mission helped many fend off their abuse of drugs, but the experience of these young people also reflects the interchangeability of drug use with the meditation practice of this Hindu-oriented group. Ellen's case was presented as an illustration of how a woman about to return to full-blown heroin addiction had been able to respond to such an experience. She was on the verge of relapse when she encountered the Divine Light Mission in Colorado, and was drawn into its supportive network. She initially accepted the social support offered at the ashram, but later found that the group's meditation practice was essential to stabilizing her abstinence. As she said,

> At first all I had to hold on to was the other premies, but I still kept thinking about heroin. After a week or two I was able to meditate, and after a while the meditations began to stand in for the drugs I was craving. At times the sensations I had while meditating felt like the high I used to get from drugs, and soon I could put myself into a drug-free space just by meditating—for a few minutes at first, and later for most of the day. Eventually I could summon it up when I had to.

Some Eastern sects were quite explicit about the direct transition to mystical meditation they offered drug users. For example, Alexander Deutsch[17] studied a small Eastern-oriented cult, and found that most members had made at least moderate use of LSD prior to their encounter with the group. Indeed, Baba, their leader, referred to the psychedelic experience as a "preview of coming attractions." Devotees saw their use of psychotomimetics as influential, even essential, to their embrace of this cult, and reported that those drug experiences with a mystical content were most important to their entry into the group.

The adoption of irrational beliefs in this group was also clearly supported by members' experiences with psychedelic drugs. As one follower of this guru reported, "Baba says that he knows that someone is coming if that person thinks of him on the way here. At one time that would have seemed ridiculous to me, but after all the unusual things I've experienced under LSD, I can believe it." This statement reflects the potency of altered consciousness in preparing the individual to accept unaccustomed beliefs.

The psychedelics spearheaded the introduction of a movement espoused with great zeal by many counterculture members, but it lacked the leadership or mission to crystallize into a true charismatic group. Since it was incompatible with traditional Christian mysticism, it could not coalesce with established Western belief systems. Experiences of altered consciousness, however, did leave a vacuum of commitment among the young that primed many of them to accept the new religious movements of the 1970s, particularly insofar as they offered meditative states as a substitute for drug experience. For many parents it served to generate a contrary movement in their explicit battle against drugs.[18]

Social Induction

Inducing an altered state of consciousness in group religious experience by suggestion from the social milieu is not a contemporary phenomenon. The mystical experience of trances, visions, and speaking in tongues has for the most part been undermined by the influence of rational empirical thinking. The success of the physical and biological sciences in yielding material progress has appeared to validate objective observation and experimentation as the only legitimate basis for inquiry, and with this a worldview based on spiritual values has been dislodged.

Although religiously grounded transcendent experience has waned in recent centuries, certain charismatic denominations within contemporary Christian practice espouse a tradition of altered consciousness and mystical experience, particularly during group prayer. These groups assert the validity of nonrational subjective experience guided by belief as a definitive basis for seeking out a "higher" reality. They introduce their adherents to altered consciousness in a social context where the culture of the group leads them to anticipate transcendent experience. This anticipation primes members for intense and moving experiences, like those from previous centuries.

On the contemporary American scene, this is found among Pentecostal Protestants and charismatic Catholics, as well as members of the Unification Church. We will consider each of these movements, and then examine socially induced altered consciousness of a different sort, in a contemporary *non*religious setting, the self-help-oriented est workshops.

The Unification Church

Altered consciousness may be experienced among devotees of religious sects who publicly tout its importance. Typical of these are the Eastern, meditative new religious movements. In other sects, they may occur often but are only infrequently discussed with outsiders. Although the Unification Church is not known for such experiences, these are both common among its membership and important to their continuing sense of religious commitment. Their role in conversion is illustrated by the story of Ed, a Moonie who had unusual perceptions at the time he decided to join. Ed was invited to a recruitment workshop by an older member who participated in the group experiences along with him, serving as a spiritual mentor. After a few days, the mentor became concerned that Ed's attitude did not reflect a proper understanding of the group's mission and advised that he devote his time to prayer for two full days; he also gave him suggestions on how to heighten his spiritual awareness. For example, he told Ed to eat no solids, but drink whatever juices or other fluids he chose.

Ed spent most of the next two days at home, visiting the workshop center each day for a short time. He soon began to experience an unfamiliar state of consciousness, which he described as follows.

> I felt a bit weak, but less cluttered inside, and in my body could sense that I was closer to liberation from my old concerns. The prayers soon developed a rhythm of their own, and now that I had removed myself from my friends, there was a loneliness I could almost feel. It was strangely pleasant.

At the church center he had been told about dreams in which spirits could appear, and indeed did have vivid and intense dreams on the first of the two nights. He also heard about how one may enter into a "condition of indemnity" in which a rapport is established with supernatural spirits.

On the second night, he finished his prayers and read from the Divine Principle while alone in his apartment. Suddenly he felt he was in the presence of Reverend Moon, and heard the minister speaking to him directly

> as real as we're talking now. I didn't turn around but I knew that Reverend Moon was there. His presence was as real as any person I've sat with. He told me that I was doing the right thing and should continue on my course, that I would find spiritual enlightenment.

Ed could not fall asleep, and paced back and forth until after sunrise, when he broke his fast. He had never had an experience like this, nor was he suffering from any psychiatric disorder so far as I could tell.

The demand characteristics of the group (expectations implicit in the social context) had primed this young man to experience perceptual distortions. He had been exposed to a seductive social setting in the church center and its workshop, and the church members whom he had come to trust had convincingly stated that they could experience alterations in perception and consciousness. Furthermore, his isolation, prayer, and fasting had altered his mental state so that his usual sense of his place in the world was destabilized, leaving him open to accept the group's perspective.

A social setting's demand characteristics can determine a person's behavior in unexpected ways. This can happen even if those setting up the group *don't* want to prejudice events, a problem sometimes arising in psychological research laboratories, where the demand characteristics of a scientific project implicitly lead participants to be "good subjects" and perceive their state in a subjective way that will give the experimenter results that will fit his or her hypothesis.[19] Ed wanted to be a good disciple, and tried somehow to feel in a manner that he implicitly knew would please the group and his mentor. Both the demand characteristics of the workshop setting and the altered subjective state Ed established through prayer and fasting led him to attribute his unaccustomed feelings to the church's "spirit world." The consequences of this attribution may have been startling, but they were nonetheless in keeping with the group's expectations.

Members of the Unification Church do indeed experience alterations in sensation and perception like those reported by Divine Light members. In our study of the Moonies, we applied the same questionnaire items as in the Divine Light study to reveal similarities between the two groups.

The Moonies' experience *outside* formal prayer was particularly relevant, as their lives were often touched by transcendent states during the routine of their daily activities. This is illustrated by changes in time sensation. A majority (72%) had experienced a distorted sense of the passage of time outside the prayer experience, and most of this group (50% of the total) felt it "clearly" or "very intensely."[20] Such experience is not without consequences for an individual's judgment and perception of everyday events.

A parallel can be drawn from an experimental study by Fred Melges and his associates on subjects who smoked delta-9-THC, the active component of marijuana.[21] They studied the change in time sense produced by the drug and examined its effect on attention and goal-directed thinking. Subjects became susceptible to alterations in their perception of themselves (feelings of depersonalization) and delusion-like ideas (such as feelings that they were being influenced by outside forces). The researchers likened the situation to one observed in some psychiatric patients and also in normal individuals who may report feelings of clairvoyance. Under these circumstances, subjects drew intuitive "connections" while often disregarding commonsense considerations.

Similar changes may occur in the subjective distortions of time sense promoted by the social context of Unification Church membership. For the majority of Moonies, transcendent experiences may help effect changes in their usual style of thinking. They may draw conclusions they would not otherwise arrive at if they applied the norms for inference accepted within the general society. In this altered state of mind, however, they are more likely to accept unusual attitudes and beliefs promoted within the group, and perhaps to be open to further hallucinatory experiences.

Repeated experiences in which the parameters defining consciousness are altered also serve as opportunities for renewal of commitment to the group's views—mini-conversions, as it were. For example, most members reported experiencing outside the context of prayer "a special and unfamiliar feeling in my body" (52%) and seeing "a special new meaning in my life" (90%). And some members had more intense alterations in the sensations that define consciousness: more than a third (39%) reported feeling themselves "to be in the physical presence of someone important to [them] even though most people couldn't have seen him" or seeing "something special that no one else could see" during their usual state; half of this group (18%) reported that they "could see it clearly with [their] eyes."

Consider how these experiences are integrated into the group's belief system. A sizable majority of members (74%) reported that they *strongly* felt a "close connection with God," and that they had "no doubt at all about the relevance of the Divine Principle in [their] personal life." These feelings were associated with a strong commitment to the sect, so that transcendent episodes were likely to be perceived as divine messages, interpreted within the framework of the group's expectations, associated with the "spirit world" and a member's "condition of indemnity."

Accounts of visions were, of course, much more common in medieval times. Could it be that the worldview brought about by the age of empirical science has stamped out the consensual acceptance of mystical experience? Might not such experiences be more accessible today if they were more widely perceived to be a valid part of our subjective existence?

Closer to the Mainstream: Pentecostals and Charismatics

The Protestant Pentecostal movement claims several million American members and its influence has spread to millions more overseas.[22] What makes the movement distinctive is its zealous religious experience characterized by rituals involving a significant degree of altered consciousness in many participants. Among these are speaking in tongues, or *glossolalia,* strange utterances thought to represent the voice of God; *possession behavior,* during which a person may dance and gyrate or roll on the floor; and the *testimonial,* a fervent and spontaneous statement of the person's faith, typically made after rising to speak in the course of a Pentecostal service. Interestingly, careful empirical study of the Pentecostals reveals that all three behaviors associated with altered states are also associated with the relief of emotional distress; the more frequently members of a Pentecostal congregation engage in these rituals, the less likely they are to report symptoms of distress on a standard psychological measure.[23] This offers a parallel to the relief of distress associated with meditation among Divine Light members.

Glossolalia is a form of pseudolanguage said to be available to all persons that can be acquired by inspiration or determined practice.[24] It derives from citations in the New Testament and Pentecostals consider it to be evidence of baptism in the Holy Spirit. The contemporary Pentecostal movement dates to 1901, when the Reverend Charles Parham left an established pulpit in Topeka, Kansas, and began to practice faith healing. Despite local opposition, he soon established a Bible college. Parham assigned some students the task of investigating the experience of "baptism of the Spirit," sometimes called the Pentecostal Blessing, and asked them to report back after the school's Christmas holidays. He later wrote that to his "astonishment, they all had the same story. . . . The indisputable proof on each occasion was that they spoke with other tongues."[25]

The identicalness of all the stories came to assume great importance for the growing Pentecostal movement, and similar experiences were soon reported elsewhere in the western states. Within a few decades Pentecostalism had spread across the country, and the phenomenon of speaking in tongues came to be seen as the culmination of the rediscovery of Christ as a personal savior. As Pentecostal religious services took shape, they acquired a free and loud participatory style, with sermons and songs frequently interrupted by cries of "Amen," calls in "tongues," and testimonies of faith and supplication. Some of these raucous outbursts and physical paroxysms helped label the Pentecostals as Holy Rollers.

The practice of glossolalia frequently (but not always) serves as a vehicle for achieving a trance-like state. In a process called "driving,"[26] the leader of a congregation, typically a gifted orator, impels the audience into a high state of excitement. Driving often takes place in stages; the first is singing of hymns with clear repetitive beats and clapping in time, often enhanced by musical accompaniment. A particular supplicant is next prayed for by members of the congregation and by the leader, usually very loudly and in beat. Soon this evocation passes into a final stage of glossolalia where singing and prayer merge into unknown tongues, usually shouted by the supplicant, who may now enter into a trance.

States of altered consciousness may act as the basis for stabilizing highly idiosyncratic group rituals. Within the Pentecostal movement, snake-handling cults of the southeastern United States exemplify this. In rural Tennessee, for example, members of the Holiness Church of God in Jesus' Name draw their religious practice from the literal interpretation of the following Bible verses.

> In my name shall they cast out devils; they shall speak with new tongues; they shall take up serpents; and if they drink any deadly thing it shall not hurt them; they shall lay hands on the sick and they shall recover (Mark 16:17–18).

While speaking in tongues, often to the accompaniment of screams and lashing, jerking movements, members of this congregation not only practice faith healing but also expose themselves to the risk of death by drinking poisons and handling poisonous snakes. One member described how he would wait for the right state of mind, or "anointing," during a church service so that he would be ready to handle the congregation's poisonous cottonmouth snake.

> When I get anointed, a numbness starts in my face and in my hands, and it feels like oil dripping out of my fingers. It's symbolic, too, as if your arm went plumb to sleep. But it's full of joy . . . a real good feeling. I feel like I'm walking in another world. It's hard to explain.

Another congregant described the experience in these terms:

> It's just like a small still voice. Calmness comes over me from the top of my head to the bottom of my feet. When I hear that voice I go ahead and move. But I want to be doubly sure that it is God . . . [Then, discussing a time he was bitten by the snake,] it stings just like a bee. Like two needles. I hurt for about 12 hours on this one. I suffered, but it didn't make me sick. Both arms swelled up. . . . I don't believe in going to a doctor when I get serpent bit. See if God lets the serpent bite you, I don't see that you have the right to do anything about it. God can heal you.[27]

In actuality, between 1910 and 1960 at least nineteen persons were reported to have died in the United States from snake bites incurred during such religious services, and the first of the two congregants just quoted estimated that ten persons in his church alone were fatally bitten over a period of ten years. Indeed, the Holiness Church to which these speakers belonged gained international attention because of court disputes over their right to such practice when two members died from drinking strychnine during a religious service.

More than half a century after their emergence in Kansas City, Pentecostal practices began to spread to the American Catholic Church. In 1966, two young faculty members at Duquesne University in Pittsburgh made a pact to pray for their spiritual renewal. They attended a Protestant prayer meeting and soon became inspired to speak in tongues. With other faculty members and students at the university they formed a prayer group involved in charismatic activities, and their mission spread to the campuses of Notre Dame and the University of Michigan.

In a typical Catholic charismatic meeting at that time,[28] neophytes would report their experience of religious revival, often revealing that this had followed their involvement in the drug subculture. States of altered consciousness were called "gifts of the Holy Spirit" and were expected to lead members to a spiritual rebirth. These experiences included glossolalia, involuntary motor activity, and trances, all generated by the dynamics of the prayer meeting.

This movement spread rapidly and, within the decade, as many as 350,000 Catholics across the United States worshiped in derivative prayer meetings.[29] As the similarities in the ritual practice of the Pentecostals and Catholic charismatics began to surpass the differences, they soon served as a basis for bringing together many members of the Catholic and Protestant traditions in interfaith services and joint religious publications, an ecumenism long considered difficult to achieve.

Experiences of altered consciousness, however, are not restricted to religious settings since they are also reported among the public at large. Andrew Greeley studied a representative sample of Americans, asking them if they had ever felt as though they "were very close to a powerful, spiritual force that seemed to lift you out of yourself," and found that more than a third (35%) answered positively. When this group was then asked what situations triggered these experiences, the most common responses were religious in nature, such as prayer, attendance at a church service, and being alone in a church.[30] Cross-cultural evidence also provides support for the widespread potential for such altered states. Erika Bourguinon[31] reviewed data on 488 societies drawn from the *Ethnographic Atlas*, a standard cross-cultural reference; most were preindustrial and tribal in structure. A full 90% were found to have institutionalized practices that included some form of altered consciousness, trance-like in nature, and, in the majority, trances were ascribed in one way or another to possession by some religious force. Indeed, the linkage between beliefs and trance states is thought to date to Upper Paleolithic times.[32]

In the Secular Mainstream: est

For another view of the role of altered consciousness in promoting membership in a charismatic group, we might ask how a contemporary population can be made susceptible to such influence when the right social setting is established. Consider an "experimental" problem in the psychology of the charismatic group: How might one engage a population of sophisticated, well-educated adults from metropolitan centers in a new, zealously espoused ideology, where the techniques employed can include the development of a cohesive group setting and the promotion of attitude change via altering consciousness? One answer comes from the example of est, an acronym for Erhard Seminars Training.

This secular movement was started in 1971 by Werner Erhard, a man with no formal experience in mental health, self-help, or religious revivalism, but a background in retail sales. Within only five years of its founding, est had reportedly put over 83,000 generally affluent and well-educated people through its training, aimed at "transforming your ability to experience living."

Erhard and his trainers combined aspects of a number of popular philoso-phies, from Eastern religion to psychoanalysis, in a program that would sup-posedly make participants appreciate the need to confront their own conflicts and social circumstances and dismiss long-standing illusions.

The training program consists of two weekend-long workshops with evening sessions on the intervening weekdays. Workshops with about two hundred enrollees are led by a trainer designated by Erhard and several experienced assistants. Over the course of nine days, enrollees are cajoled and emotionally battered, and encouraged to regress up to the point where they have finally "got it," a state akin to a conversion.

Certain alterations in consciousness and subjective state within this large group context are apparently used to promote this conversion-like experience. Workshop members are subjected to a variety of unsettling circumstances for long hours at a stretch that act to peel away those layers of psychological stability that normally bolster their usual state of consciousness. Several in-junctions are issued: no watches, no talking unless recognized by the trainer (which means rarely), no leaving one's seat, no smoking, no eating, no going to the bathroom except during breaks separated by many hours. Participants undergo long periods during which they must keep their eyes closed and listen to diatribes, abuse, and obscenity dispensed by the trainer. They are also generally kept in rooms where there is no daylight, at temperatures that may become uncomfortable (such as 40°). In addition, they are usually exposed to a number of individuals within the group who respond with intense emotion, crying copiously or screaming. A variety of physiologic and emotional para-meters are therefore disturbed, disrupting the enrollees' homeostasis. Partic-ipating in the program is not without psychiatric risk, and a number of cases of psychotic reaction have been reported among those enrolled.[33]

What it means to "get it" in est is hard to define. After an initial corre-spondence with Werner Erhard, I met at some length with the movement's director of research so that we might consider studying this transformation. Our discussions of getting it, however, yielded no operational definition (or any viable basis for a study, for that matter).[34] One account of the attitude of an est trainer may be helpful in defining this observation further. Just before graduation, the trainer always asks if people "got it." Some say yes and are applauded. Another group isn't sure. The trainer talks to them and they all say they got it. Finally, one or two people are sure that they haven't got it, and the trainer says, "Well, you got it, because there's nothing to get." The whole thing is treated as a joke, discomforting the new converts.[35] Nonethe-less, one study of a large sample of est alumni who had completed the training at least three months before revealed that the large majority felt the experi-ence had been positive (88%), and considered themselves better off for having taken the training (80%).[36]

Psychological sophistication does not seem to breed skepticism among those exposed to the program. In the study of est alumni, for example, there was no significant difference in the proportion of professional therapists or lay-people who gave positive reports. In another study, an experienced clinician evaluated a series of his psychiatric patients who took the est training and concluded that the majority derived some benefit from the program.[37]

One psychologist who had been through the training told me of his distress at the psychological assaults against some of the more labile workshop members, but his words also revealed the role of altered consciousness in overcoming these apprehensions.

> The physical discomfort and badgering left me horrified, and feeling very weird. Time had stopped running in any usual sense, and I was having unexpected feelings of all kinds. At one point, when the trainer called my friend an asshole for trying to console a woman who was crying, I got enraged; I wanted to see the trainer dead. I realized that I was beginning to lose any sense of where I was in the real world, and even who I usually was.
>
> And then suddenly it came clear! I was the prisoner of *my own* compulsion to help everyone and be kind to them. The trainer was right; I didn't *have* to be tied down by this attitude. I was free to choose what I might think and feel, independent of forty years of programming. Then the whole room seemed to slip away, and I no longer cared about eating, peeing, or how long the whole damn thing would run on. I felt liberated, released from a long prison term.

In one sense, this represented a transition to a full-blown "culture of narcissism" in which the individual owes allegiance only to the self. Participants in the est program often feel released from the commitments born out of fidelity to their fellow humans, allowing them to indulge themselves without guilt. In another sense, however, est underlines how much we each act on our own set of comfortable misconceptions. Whether or not the realization of this psychologist ultimately proves useful to him, it did indeed come after his feeling and thought had been altered from their usual state.

II

A MODEL OF
THE CHARISMATIC
GROUP

We have discussed the psychological forces that allow a cult to exert its potent influence on members, and now turn to developing a model that will explain how these groups actually function. To do this, we must link three levels of human organizations—biology, psychology, and social structure. Behavior is rooted in biology, even though it is moved by psychological forces affecting the individual as a whole; the individual group member is engaged in social organizations that themselves assume a life of their own.

5

BIOLOGY AND
BEHAVIOR

We have examined the remarkable power of psychological forces within the charismatic group to shape its members' attitudes and behavior. We will now consider the origin of these forces. Are they innate in human nature, or merely the product of culture and circumstance?

The inclination to participate in local social groups is observed in the most diverse cultures, emerging no doubt from the advantages a community confers in meeting daily needs and contending with adversity. This inclination is intensified, even caricatured, in the paramilitary groups that arise in nations racked by internecine conflicts, such as contemporary Northern Ireland and Lebanon. The intense commitment that participants in military groups can develop toward each other may entail extreme self-sacrifice, as in the human wave tactics involving young Iranian boys in the war with Iraq.

In the Unification Church, as in other contemporary sects, members put themselves at risk in a variety of ways out of fealty to the group. They may go through long periods of arduous work, subject themselves to public ridicule, and postpone childbearing for many years.

The inclination toward such self-sacrificing group behavior is observed in almost all cultures; it can obviously help meet the needs of a group to wage war, endure dislocation, or survive in times of economic privation. This pattern of behavior may even serve as the mechanism for survival of the group and its conjoint goals.

The human affinity for close-knit groups is a ubiquitous and apparently innate trait. If so, how would this trait have evolved? Is an instinct for group affiliation based on the evolutionary advantage that the group—including the charismatic group—confers on its overall membership, particularly at times of crisis and outside threat?

In *The Descent of Man*,[1] Charles Darwin revealed his interest in developing a method of psychology that would explain the appearance of similar social traits in very different species. He even incurred allegations of "extreme anthropomorphism"[2] in writing

> with what care male birds display their various charms, and this they do with utmost skill. . . . it appears that actions, first perhaps intentional, have become instinctive. If so we ought not to accuse birds of conscious vanities; yet when we see a peacock strutting about, with expanded and quivering tailfeathers, he seems the very emblem of pride and vanity.[3]

Konrad Lorenz[4] would have considered the vain strutting observed in both peacocks and *Homo sapiens* as behavioral *analogues*. Lorenz observed that such analogues arise as two different species independently develop similar biologically grounded means for adapting to their environment. To be analogous, the traits must be found in species that are separated in the chain of evolution by others that do *not* carry such a trait. For an example of a social analogue, Lorenz looked to the behavior of geese, a species he studied at great length. He acknowledged that terms like "falling in love, marrying, or being jealous" might seem awkward when speaking of birds, but pointed out that behaviors comparable to these human ones may be found with little difficulty among monogamous pairs of geese. In addition, they have very much the same role and survival value in both species.[5]

The possibility that ethologic insights may help explain some puzzling aspects of human behavior is therefore most attractive. For our purposes, we may invoke evolutionary paradigms to address the following central paradox of charismatic group behavior: Affiliation with such groups is observed in many settings, both in full-blown or muted form, and appears to represent a universal potential in human beings; nonetheless, such affiliation frequently runs contrary to the interests of the individual, sometimes contrary to the person's very survival. Why should people have retained such a potentially self-destructive trait over the course of evolution?

We do find that most social traits confer a clear-cut adaptive advantage for the individual carrying the trait, such as the strutting behavior of the peacock or the assertion of status in a regional band of primates. Some traits, though, are not clearly adaptive. For example, the inclination to assist others in need offers an adaptive advantage to *other* members of a social group, but does not necessarily enhance the fitness of the individual with that trait. Such an altruistic trait may often operate to the individual's detriment, when he or she sacrifices self-interest for other members of the social group. This trait is similar to the human inclination to join a charismatic group, which often demands great personal sacrifice. Explanations for the evolution of altruism may therefore shed light on behavior in the charismatic group.

The altruist who saves a drowning swimmer or the worker honeybee who stings an assailant and thereby loses its life have one thing in common with the person who becomes engaged in the charismatic group. From an evolutionary standpoint, each sacrifices individual interests and survival potential

for the group's benefit; they will diminish their fitness for subsequent repro-
duction by virtue of carrying the trait. How do such traits persist over the
course of evolution, if their carriers are *less* likely to survive? Let us consider
the following. A trait observed in a given individual may serve to improve the
reproductive advantage of *other* individuals who themselves may carry genes
for that same trait. The enhanced genetic fitness of those other carriers then
promotes transmission of the trait to the next generation, since they are now
more likely to survive and transmit it themselves. When such principles of
population genetics were elaborated and applied to a variety of puzzling ethologic observations such as the self-sacrificing behavior, a new outlook on
behavior emerged, one Edward O. Wilson termed sociobiology,[6] which has
become both provocative and controversial in recent years.[7]

The concept of inclusive fitness goes to the heart of sociobiology. As proposed by William D. Hamilton,[8] this form of genetic fitness reflects not only
the fitness of a given individual carrying a genetic trait, but also the fitness
of all others who might carry that trait, since their survival also ensures its
transmission. Inclusive fitness can therefore allow a trait to persist in a species, even if it does not aid the individual carrier to survive.

Consider, for example, the concept of *reciprocal altruism*. Robert Trivers[9]
pointed out that an altruist trait need not be based only on the advantage it
gives actual relatives who are assisted. It can reflect the reciprocal benefits in
a family or a larger population of remotely related individuals who act toward
each other in an altruistic fashion, thereby assuring some measure of reci-
procity when later in need. Furthermore, interesting models have been developed by Lumsden and Wilson[10] for conceptualizing how certain engrams
of cultural behavior may be transmitted. All this, we will see, offers an explanation for the survival of traits that do not necessarily endow a given individual
with greater genetic fitness.

The inclination to join cohesive groups per se may well have emerged over
the course of human evolution as one particular manifestation of inclusive
fitness. In the first place, individuals may not have experienced greater personal fitness because of this inclination. The groups they affiliated with, composed of many individuals with this same trait, *could* work together better in
the face of adversity and therefore survive better.

The Relief Effect

When one joins a charismatic group, one gives up the opportunity for independent decision making and complies with the group's norms, which may
conflict with one's own adaptive needs. The human inclination to join such
a group can therefore lead to diminished personal fitness.

Persistence of this inclination may be explained by inclusive fitness—the
enhanced potential for survival of all carriers of the trait in the group, as
distinguished from personal fitness alone, the potential for survival of the
individual. Thus, if a trait found in a given population promotes the survival

of the population overall, we say that the inclusive fitness of the population is enhanced—even though any given individual may be less likely to survive when manifesting this trait. We will now see this demonstrated with regard to the enhanced inclusive fitness conferred by affiliation in a cohesive group. Individuals carrying this trait may suffer from the self-sacrifice it engenders, but the cohesive group as a whole, consisting of carriers of this trait, is more likely to survive and thereby assure its transmission.

The enhanced fitness conferred by the group derives from how this social entity as a whole can act as a highly adaptable instrument of social organization, particularly in times of crisis. A zealous cohesive group can mount collaborative efforts that a more loosely cooperating group cannot. The persistence in the gene pool of a trait that leads individuals toward such zealous group behavior is thereby promoted at the same time that the group's needs as an entity are met.

In some circumstances this behavior may be the only way of guaranteeing that individual members undertake the considerable sacrifices necessary to ensure the group's genetic survival. But what psychological mechanism implements the inclination for maintaining affiliation with the charismatic group? What motivates people to join and stay, often disregarding their own personal interests? To understand this, we must posit a mechanism that ties the individual to the group, one rooted in human physiology. Furthermore, if this mechanism is grounded in the human evolutionary past, it should have homologs in the behavior of other primates.

At the heart of this process lies the relationship between a pattern of social behavior and a biologically grounded motivation, or instinctive drive, that I have termed the *relief effect*. It operates as follows. *When people become involved in a charismatic group, an inverse relationship exists between their feelings of emotional distress and the degree to which they are affiliated with that group.* Individuals' capacity for commitment to the group is mediated by the relief of neurotic distress, relief that they experience on affiliation and continued membership; the closer they feel toward the group, the less distress they feel. Conversely, if they disaffiliate from the group a bit, they are prodded to return by the increased distress they are likely to feel. Thus, zealous group members feel unhappy or dysphoric when removed from their group. A committed member of Alcoholics Anonymous, for example, typically reports feelings of unease or being out of sorts when he or she misses a number of meetings.

A member is therefore poised between reward for closeness and punishment for alienation. Each minor episode of reward and punishment, on moving closer to the group or further away, functions as an operant learning experience that conditions subsequent involvement. The process is indeed similar to a conditioning experiment in which an animal is rewarded each time it spontaneously carries out a particular behavior or punished for acting in a contrary way. After several such spontaneous acts and their associated consequences, the experimental animal will carry out that behavior consistently, even when further rewards are given only infrequently. For example, a mouse can be rewarded with cheese every time it taps a lever. Eventually, it will tap the lever frequently although bits of cheese are few and far between.

A charismatic group member resembles an experimental animal or human subject in an operant conditioning study. He or she can be made to adopt a behavior pattern if at first rewarded whenever the person acts in a particular way. If, whenever the member feels close to the group, his or her distress is relieved, the member will tend to stay close, and the feeling of closeness to the group becomes the source of operant reinforcement. Such habituation can occur without the individual's awareness. Similarly, the repeated dysphoria associated with feelings of alienation tends to make members avoid distance from the group; it is a negative reinforcer for staying close.

After a member undergoing induction has come close to the group a number of times and been rewarded each time, the member "learns" to comply with the group so as to feel close to it and experience the consequent well-being. The new group member, a product of a reinforcement process, will continue in a pattern of maintaining closeness even if rewards are provided only intermittently. The relief effect thereby serves as a reinforcer for continued group involvement.

Thus, by relieving neurotic distress individuals are engaged into the charismatic group and learn to comply with the behaviors it promotes. The relief effect is mediated by the affiliative attitudes of social cohesiveness and shared beliefs—that is, by both social and cognitive means. A series of propositions, supported by data on members of the Unification Church and Divine Light sects, may explain how this effect underlies affiliation within such groups.

Evidence in Contemporary Sects

I will now review a series of propositions based on findings on members of the Unification Church and the Divine Light Mission. These will be used to support the model first described on the origins of affiliative behavior.

When joining a charismatic group, an individual experiences relief in neurotic distress in direct relation to how closely affiliated he feels with the group. Initiation into a group involves remarkable personal commitment. For a member to become fully involved, there should be a dramatic psychological impetus to commitment, and engagement should yield considerable relief. Using the Unification Church and Divine Light findings, we may consider whether this is so.

The needs of potential recruits before joining contribute to understanding the nature of this relief, since those who were attracted most to the group had experienced the greatest distress, as evidenced in the reports of 104 participants in Unification Church initiation workshops. Scores on the general psychological well-being scale revealed that those experiencing the greatest stress were more likely to join.[11] Those who remained after the initial weekend but did *not* join were less troubled; those who left earliest were least distressed. Importantly, though, each group was well below the average in psychological well-being in relation to a comparable sample of young people drawn from the general population. Yet when a cohort of long-standing members was studied, their well-being scores were much closer to the level found in the general population, reflecting a considerable improvement in their psychological well-being over the course of induction and membership.[12]

This is also corroborated by reports given by members of the Divine Light Mission for the periods both before and after joining. Two years after joining they described their psychological distress as having been a good deal less (37%) right after joining than immediately preceding. For example, a considerable decline occurred in the degree to which members viewed emotional problems as interfering with their adjustment in life (35%), with a similar drop in feeling nervous and tense (41%). This decline was highly correlated with the members' feelings of cohesiveness toward the group. Those who felt closest to the group were more likely to experience a relief in neurotic distress. Altogether, the items reflecting group cohesiveness accounted for a large portion of this decline in neurotic distress and these observations are at the heart of the relief effect.[13]

Furthermore, it can be said that mobilization into a charismatic group is most likely in times of distress. From the standpoint of group adaptation, a bold course of action involving mutual commitment and self-sacrifice is in fact usually needed at such a time, so as to address pressing problems that face the group.

In the proper group setting, it is possible to elicit commitment to the charismatic group quite easily. Members or potential members are not necessarily open to involvement in a group for extended periods of time, and it must be possible for engagement to take place when the need arises. The experience of participants in the Unification Church induction workshops was striking in this regard. Of those participants who remained beyond the initial two days, all rapidly developed an intense feeling of affiliation to the sect, whether they eventually joined or not. Their answers reflected very high levels of cohesiveness toward members in their immediate induction group, and rapid acceptance of basic church tenets. Indeed, the attitudes of those who later left differed from those who joined only in that those who dropped out had stronger ties toward persons outside the group. That is, those who refrained from joining did not do so because of a lack of strong feelings for the group— they left because of commitments to family and friends.

This rapid development of affiliation during the induction experience demonstrates how easily a person can become psychologically engaged in the group setting, as long as he or she demonstrates some initial interest. Recall the rapid transition to commitment that Jerry, the depressed college student, experienced when he entered the Moonie induction program. Within several days he had thrown off his previous social bonds and chose to become a fugitive from a court order rather than cut his ties to the church.

Over the course of induction, individuals' attitudes and behaviors came to conform with those expected of group members. In addition to acquiring a cohesiveness toward the group and belief in its creed, recruits also adopt the group's standards of behavior. In the Unification Church, inductees' attitudes and behavior regarding the use of alcoholic beverages illustrate this point; the Church discourages intoxication with alcohol, but does not prohibit its use. The large majority of long-standing members (86%) reported using alcoholic beverages right before contact with the sect, but only a third still used them at all two years later. More important, daily use disappeared entirely.

This pattern was a reflection of newly acquired attitudes. Members' agreement with the statement "I should avoid getting high from alcohol" increased appreciably with members' length of membership. Whereas a minority (42%) said that they strongly agreed with this statement before joining, more than twice that number (89%) felt this way right after joining, and the same proportion concurred after a period of membership. Among Divine Light members, hallucinogen and heroin use almost vanished over the course of membership (hallucinogen use went from 35% to 3%, and heroin use from 14% to 0%).

The relationship between the relief of neurotic distress and affiliation with the charismatic group continues over the course of membership. This relationship is essential to the group's perpetuation since it assures that members will maintain their commitment. The proposition is supported by our data on the psychological status of long-standing members of the Unification Church. Two aspects of their affiliative feelings toward the group were examined: social cohesiveness and shared beliefs. Scores on a scale reflecting group cohesiveness accounted for an appreciable portion of members' psychological well-being at the time they were studied, indicating a very strong relationship between the strength of these social ties and level of well-being. Furthermore, a scale of shared religious beliefs added even more to the statistical correlation between members' well-being and group affiliation. The two items on religious belief that best predicted a member's psychological well-being were "My religious beliefs give me comfort" and "I feel a close connection with God." The relief effect apparently continues to operate over the course of long-term membership in the charismatic group, thereby serving as a motivation for continued commitment.

Conformity to a group's behavioral norms is implicitly perceived by members as necessary for maintaining their well-being. This motivation for conforming was seen in the long-standing Unification Church members who had been matched for marital engagement by the Reverend Moon.[14] These members had been born into typical American families but were nonetheless going along with the betrothal—something that few, if any, youths of their background could be expected to accept. They were, in fact, pleased to have their spouses selected for them with no input of their own. Here was a remarkable example of conformity to the behavioral norms of a charismatic group. The vast majority (95%) of these engaged members were still active in the group four years later, almost all now married to their designated mates. Clues as to why these members so readily complied were found in the way they implicitly perceived their emotional vulnerability to disruptive life events.

It has been established[15] that people are more likely to suffer psychological problems when they have recently experienced life events requiring appreciable social readjustment such as a change in residence, the illness of close relatives, or being fired from a job. With this in mind, these Moonies' recent histories of disruptive life events were assessed with a standard scale. As with other populations, a higher incidence of such events was associated with lower levels of psychological well-being. More important, members were buffered from this emotional vulnerability by the degree of their commitment to the church. Those who felt closest to the church were least likely to undergo emotional distress after experiencing disruptions in their lives, and those who were less close were more vulnerable.[16] Specifically, life events predicted 15% of the variance in well-being; this percentage would rise to 31% when affiliation items were incorporated.

A member's responsiveness to the group's expectation is therefore likely to be supported by the person's implicit perception that he or she is protected from life's emotionally disruptive experiences by commitment to the sect; the member comes to see the group as a shield from threatening experiences. This relationship is succinctly expressed in the high percentage of members (88%) who strongly agreed that "My religious beliefs give me comfort."

This mechanism of conformity was again observed in the same group of engaged members followed up three years after their engagement. By now, the large majority (91%) had been married for one year and many (24%) of the wives were already pregnant. For most of these members, the previous year was full of numerous disruptive life events, such as moving out of church residences, setting up new households, assuming responsibility for their own finances, and for many, being uprooted to serve on mobile fund-raising teams. Nonetheless, their scores on the belief and cohesiveness scales had not changed significantly, and these were still strong predictors of their level of psychological well-being. Members' vulnerability to disruptive life events was still muted by the degree of their commitment to the group. This leads to the following corollary proposition.

The group acts like a psychological pincer, promoting distress while at the same time providing relief. This is evidenced in an ironic sequence of events. The group promotes behavioral norms that may expose a member to potential distress. Then, as we just saw, the member comes to feel that the relief of this distress depends on fidelity to the group. This in turn makes the member more responsive to the demands of the group and its leadership.

A cycle of this kind is evident in Alcoholics Anonymous, which uses group dependency as a means of escape from alcohol addiction. Recruits are made to feel that they must give up their use of alcohol when, over the course of induction, they accept the group's creed of abstinence. Giving up alcohol, however, raises fear in recruits over their inability to do so without considerable craving and anguish. The group heightens this fear by making recruits face what they have attempted to hide, that they cannot effectively control their drinking. It then offers an answer to this conflict: as AA becomes more important to the new members, they are told that regular attendance and acceptance of AA's rules are necessary for maintaining abstinence. Since they have come to see their psychological well-being as dependent on abstinence, they are trapped into depending on this large group and agree to go along with its demands. In this way many AA members attend meetings on a regular, even daily basis for months or years and succeed in staying sober. But they become highly dependent on the group.

The magnitude of the relief effect is not enhanced by a history of psychological disability. If emotional distress is relieved by affiliation, wouldn't a background of psychological illness make for a more committed member? In a psychological sense, this might make sense, but from an evolutionary standpoint it does not, for if the relief effect were a correlate of disability, sounder members would tend to disaffiliate, and such groups would retain only their most troubled members, while losing their most able. That obviously would not improve the group's chances of survival.

Our own findings showed that a serious emotional disability is not related to the strength of members' ties to the group. Among members of both the Unification Church and the Divine Light Mission, those who reported that they had experienced "serious emotional problems" at some time prior to joining (39% in both samples) were compared to those who had not. No significant correlation existed between this background trait and the degree of relief experienced on induction or the degree of cohesiveness felt toward the group.[17] Thus, among those who joined, responsivity to the group did not depend on a background of serious emotional problems and therefore did not come at the expense of diminished personal fitness.

The relief effect is correlated with a sense of exclusivity. In the Divine Light Mission, the single item on the cohesion scale most highly correlated with the relief of neurotic distress was "I am suspicious of nonmembers,"[18] reflecting a gulf between attitudes toward insiders and outsiders, a mistrust of outsiders that serves as a basis for excluding them. The factor is among the differences between the Unification Church, a self-contained charismatic group, and the Federation of Parents for Drug-Free Youth, composed of zealous community-based parent groups who share a commitment to combat teenage drug abuse. The Federation of Parents is a more conventional self-help program, well integrated into the community. Although Federation members exhibit considerable cohesiveness and shared beliefs, the movement does not function as a socially circumscribed, self-supporting large group, meeting its own economic, social, and cultural needs. Moonies and Federation members did not differ significantly in cohesiveness scores toward their own respective compatriots. With regard to outsiders, however, the Moonies had much lower scores.[19] This difference in feelings toward outsiders indicates that the benefits of Unification Church members' considerable sacrifice will not be casually available to outsiders and reflects the self-protective nature of the true charismatic group.

These propositions help to explain how members of a charismatic group experience a decline in neurotic distress relative to the intensity of their involvement in the group. Since all these propositions are based on measurable psychological characteristics of large-group members, they provide empirical support for the operation of this relief effect.

We will now look for further support for the relief effect hypothesis to very different sources: our knowledge of our evolutionary past and contemporary studies on the behavior of primates. These anthropologic and ethologic data complement studies on contemporary groups to support the ideas about social bonding just presented.

Ethologic Observations

If the relief effect, presumed to underlie charismatic group behavior, is a valid sociobiologic model, supporting ethologic evidence should exist, for example, in homologous behaviors among other primates.

Australopithecus, a direct ancestor of *Homo sapiens,* inhabited forested areas of East Africa from about five million to one million years ago. Over many generations they developed stable patterns of large-group social organization to sustain adequate nutrition by hunting large game.[20] Indeed, *Australopithecus* is thought to have formed groups of thirty to one hundred members, as do hunter-gatherer tribes today. In addition, it was necessary to develop behavior patterns allowing them to share in the allocation of spoils of the hunt, and ensuring that outsiders would not gain access to the spoils without having contributed to that communal activity.[21]

Like contemporary hunting tribes, prehistoric bands are thought to have dispersed at intervals, depending on their immediate needs and ecologic circumstance. They consistently reaggregated, however, thereby establishing stable regional groupings.[22] These behaviors also bespeak the value of a psychological mechanism that would ensure cohesiveness among the individual members of large groups.

Complex social traits such as speech, empathy, and interactional skills make for more effective group behavior. In lower species, complex traits may evolve relatively quickly.[23] Nonetheless, the extent to which social traits have evolved since the emergence of Australopithecus is striking. Hominid cranial capacities, for example, doubled between australopithecine times and the appearance about a million years ago of *Homo erectus*, a more recent precursor of *Homo sapiens*.[24] Such massive increases, in cortical matter primarily, have underlain significant changes in the behavioral repertoires of our hominid ancestors.

The social cohesiveness in early hominids is also represented in homologs among nonhuman primates. As with hunter-gatherers, social band size of forty to eighty individuals is common in the community organization of several monkey and ape species. It is seen in the discrete groups formed by chimpanzees in the wild, who migrate, collaborate, and maintain proximity to each other in groups of this size.[25]

There is also experimental evidence for homologs of the relief effect in lower primates. A body of empirical research involving rhesus monkeys supports the relationship between group affiliation and good mood. In classic observations, Harry Harlow[26] demonstrated the emotional vulnerability of lower primates to loss and separation, using the model of mother-infant separation.

Of more direct relevance to behavior in large groups, Stephen Suomi[27] followed Harlow's work with a series of studies inducing depression-like behavior among young monkeys by separating them from their peers. Removal of a young monkey from the cage where he lived with other young monkeys with whom he had been raised eventually resulted in diminished activity, a doleful expression, and a crouched posture. Thus, severing the bonds that these monkeys had to peers in their social network seemed to produce behavior similar to that associated with depression and anxiety in humans. Interestingly, Suomi then studied two ways in which he could overcome the experimentally induced depression in these monkeys—either by reestablishing social ties to peers or by administering antidepressant medications. In one study, the isolated monkeys were introduced into groups of nondepressed peers and thereby achieved relief from their depression. In a second study, imiprimine, a common antidepressant drug, relieved the depression without return to a peer group. Both social and physiologic intervention were thereby able to mimic a relief effect.

Changes in affect may serve in additional ways to ensure cohesiveness and thereby stabilize large social groups—not only by means of the relief effect. Russell Gardener,[28] for example, has drawn attention to the alpha and omega roles (dominant and submissive positions) observed in bands of lower primates. The alpha member of a monkey troupe, the highest in its hierarchy, aggressively initiates action and continually asserts control over other members, much like a manic or hypomanic human. The omega, on the bottom of the heap, moves slowly, acts with hesitation, and is not able to prevail when confronted by assertive members, much as depressed human beings behave. Among monkeys, these contrasting roles are determined in large part by heritable factors and are also shaped by individual experience. The potential for expressing these behaviors serves to stabilize the social structure of primate troupes by determining the ongoing rank of its members and hence helping define its working organization.

This is of interest to us as an additional example of the role of affect in regulating social structure. Its function of maintaining a dominance structure in a large social group is different but complementary to that of the relief effect. Affective status, in terms of depression or contentment, probably helps regulate social functions secondary to group affiliation, such as dominance roles, mating behavior, and work satisfaction.

Shared beliefs also have a place in the paradigm of the relief effect, and the biologic underpinnings of this conception can be introduced by considering how the religious symbolism implicit in these beliefs may be mediated in neurobehavioral terms. One useful model for relating symbolic function to brain physiology deals with the imagery reported in dreams.[29] Just as the symbolism of dreams is generated in the biology of brain function, so is the symbolic nature of religious belief.

Recent research has demonstrated that the occurrence of dreams depends on periodic activation of the forebrain by lower brain centers during sleep. Because of this, the existence of a dream "generator" rooted in reticular, oculomotor, and vestibular neurons is posited, one that provides a programmed neural basis for the drive to dream. The random but nonetheless characteristic nature of these generated signals serves to provide "frames" for dream imagery, and clusters of runs of generator signals constitute time marks for dream subplots and scene changes. In a sense, these neural signals serve as the bursts of current that will produce the dream images. Ultimately, the forebrain, automatically activated by such generated signals, synthesizes the dream by combining the stimuli initiated in the brain stem circuits with "re-membered" information stored in the cortex.

On the basis of current understanding of the physiological roots of emotionality, it is reasonable to posit a psychobiologic mechanism from which man's *beliefs* may gain expression, as follows. Man's vulnerability to dysphoria is mediated in large part by lower centers of the brain that developed earlier in the course of evolution, by the limbic system of the midbrain in particular. Among limbic centers, the hippocampus, cingulate gyrus, and septal region are thought to be most concerned with emotional states related to interpersonal relations. These limbic centers may serve as a generator for driving higher cortical centers to ensure the presence of affiliative ties. This takes place by virtue of two presumed functions: the ability of limbic centers to produce an affective state vulnerable to changes in these ties, and the capacity of the neocortex to create the imagery associated with previous social relationships and learned symbols related to such social interaction. Thus, the affective components of one's need for social affiliation may be generated in lower centers but experienced on a conscious level in relation to symbols and content introduced from memories stored in the neocortex. The generated need may be requited by expression in action, such as by establishing ties with one's peers.

Rules for generating the ideas, symbols, and communication patterns that compel behavior are in good part grounded in our evolutionary past, just as the ties of social cohesiveness are. Consider the *innate releasing mechanism,* a device found in lower species, which has its counterparts in observed human behavior. This neurosensory pattern triggers behavioral sequences in lower species when certain stimulus configurations are automatically recognized by virtue of an engram that is genetically predetermined. When the animal is exposed to that stimulus configuration, it will instinctively undertake a complex sequence of behavior. The recognizable behavioral trigger is called a *sign stimulus;* it clearly bespeaks a rather specific inborn neurosensory mechanism, one that can yield the release of a specific inborn behavioral repertoire.

Anthropologic findings also shed light on the role of shared beliefs in cohesive groups. In one classical formulation, Radcliffe-Brown[30] emphasized the importance of religious ritual in assuring linkage among members of primitive societies and suggested a mechanism similar to the hypothesized relief effect. He draws on ethnographic observations, pointing out that anxiety emerges among individual members of tribal societies who fail to uphold the religious rituals of the tribe and suggests, with some irony, that "magic and religion give men fears and anxieties from which they would otherwise be free." But he also makes it clear that these rituals assure the upholding of communal standards of behavior. In this way, an inverse relationship between dysphoria and affiliation is suggested, quite similar to the one described in the relief effect. The social norms associated with the group's symbols and rituals help to guide its members' behavior and ultimately enhance the entire group's adaptive capacities. In this chapter, we initially saw how the concept of inclusive fitness might be applied to affiliation in the charismatic group, particularly evident in certain cult-like settings, and then considered its role in relation to two aspects of group affiliation, group cohesiveness and shared belief. In both cases, physiologic, anthropologic, and ethologic observations were found to support an evolutionary basis of this affiliative behavior.

6

THE CULT AS A
SOCIAL SYSTEM

At the interface between the charismatic religious sect and society at large, strange things happen. Many people have noted the glazed look of members of such sects as the Unification Church when they venture outside the fold and mix with nonmembers. It has been suggested that such behavior is symptomatic of psychopathology, specifically a dissociative state. Others who studied the sects, however, have not made such observations. In this chapter, we will see how the discrepancy represents different aspects of behavior at the boundary of a social system.

Another common observation is the animosity cults elicit from outsiders. In a pluralistic society such as the United States, one may wonder why such hostility exists. Again, we will see how this reaction represents a characteristic process that occurs at a sect's boundaries and will explain some troublesome interactions between members and nonmembers.

All social systems have certain functions that act to protect their integrity and implement their goals. The two previous examples are products of the group's boundary control function, its means of securing its perimeter in a potentially disruptive environment. To view sects more clearly in the broad social context, and to understand their interactions with society better, we will draw on systems theory.[1] We will try to see the cult group as a functionally integrated whole. Four functions characteristic of systems are transformation, monitoring, feedback, and boundary control, and we will consider each.

Transformation

Systems have been likened to factories: they take input from the outside, which can be raw material, energy, or information, and process it into output, a product. This function, called transformation, allows the system to carry out operations essential to its own continuity or to the needs of a larger suprasystem to which it belongs. In a given system, the most important transformation—the one that typically defines its identity—is its *primary task*; most components of the system are geared toward either carrying out this primary task or preventing its disruption. The primary task of most cults is to prepare for the messianic end they envision.

An unstable system, such as a cult in its earlier stages, is particularly susceptible to dissolution. Members may disaffiliate at any time since the ties that bind them together have yet to be woven into the stable network of a social structure. In this regard, the concept of transformation can be used as a model for the persistent attempts of certain charismatic groups to stabilize themselves by acquiring new members. This may be why members can become so deeply involved in conversion activities; they themselves are motivated only by an inchoate need to become engaged in the charismatic group, but they begin conforming to the group's needs as a system. Members would not on their own be inclined to go out and recruit for the group, but as parts of its system they come to act in accordance with its goals.

At some point in their evolution, most charismatic groups focus on making converts as a primary task. The process may ensure a larger and stronger group and, when successful, can also help confer legitimacy to the group's own ideology, thereby consolidating the commitment of its long-standing members.

Another important aspect of that transformation function is how it disrupts the psychological stability of potential recruits, the "input" to this process. Since an intensive mobilization of a charismatic group's psychological and material resources may be directed at the conversion of new members, they can create deep turmoil in the individual convert. On the one hand, the group is intensely seductive in its attempt to attract new members; on the other, it demands a disruption of antecedent social ties and a metamorphosis in the convert's worldview. Thus, when the full resources of the group are focused on a recruit, the potential for tearing the fabric of that individual's psychological stability is considerable. The result may be psychiatric symptoms in people with no history of mental disorder or psychological instability. The genesis of these symptoms may lie more in the conflict between the convert's needs and the group's demands than in an underlying psychological impairment of the convert.

The overriding importance to the group of these transformation activities helps explain a number of puzzling phenomena associated with religious conversion experiences, in particular, the manner in which the eruption of behaviors among potential converts may appear to meet standard criteria for psychopathology. Several pathologic categories outlined in the *Diagnostic and Statistical Manual* of the American Psychiatric Association[2] set in relief the congruence between syndromes associated with conversion and those designated as psychiatric illness. Among the illnesses to be considered from this diagnostic manual are dissociative disorders, pathologic adjustment reactions, major depressive disorders, brief reactive psychoses, and paranoid disorders of a psychotic nature. Each can be generated by the charismatic group as its forces are mobilized to implement the transformation function. An experience recounted by an ex-member of the Unification Church illustrates the potential within a charismatic group for creating a searing force as its transformation function operates against an inductee's resistance. In this case, the group's ability to engage and transform was great enough to disrupt an otherwise stable psychological condition, cause much guilt, and result in a severe psychiatric reaction.

Annette was working in a restaurant in a university town when she and her husband of two years separated. At first, the separation had been very difficult, but she invited her younger sister to move in with her and was beginning to readjust. She was dating occasionally, and had become involved in camping and mountaineering, interests that predated her marriage.

After Annette had been separated for three months, her sister became interested in the Unification Church at a sidewalk recruitment display. A few weeks later, the sister decided to leave Annette's house and move into one of the Church's communal residences. This caused Annette anguish, and she rushed to her sister to dissuade her from joining. The sister first refused to speak with her, but then agreed to discuss the matter if Annette would attend some of the church's classes and discussions to gain a better understanding of the movement's philosophy. Annette did attend, and then vehemently pressed her sister to recognize the importance of reestablishing her independent life. In the classes, Annette was at first argumentative, then sullen.

Soon she realized she was under considerable stress, and found herself becoming emotionally unstable. She often cried, but at other times felt euphoric. The world around her began to seem unreal and she herself felt unreal, sometimes imagining that her body was "separated from her mind," operating independently and automatically. This feeling would persist for hours and even a full day, leading her to fear for her own sanity. She took two weeks off from work and told a male friend whom she had dated for several weeks to stop seeing her because she could no longer "handle a relationship."

Annette now became compulsive about discussing with her sister the problems she had precipitated in joining the sect, but at the same time she also began to feel attracted to the group's ideology and well-ordered view of life. At this point her need to save her sister was coming into direct conflict with the capacity of the group to transform potential recruits. She described her ensuing experience.

> For two weeks I didn't know if I was a part of the world around me, whether my mind and body were connected; it was as if I were watching myself from the back row of a movie theater. I became so upset I couldn't sleep. One part of me was fighting for my sister, but the other began to wonder whether I might not be able to feel some relief by joining the Church. Soon I began to wonder whether the Church might not actually hold the truth for me. Then one day, I was with some brothers and sisters at the church house, and I was overwhelmed by an indescribable feeling. In a way it was an intense and physical feeling, of being torn between

wanting to be part of the church and wanting to be separate. Then after a few minutes I could anticipate a feeling of warmth, of knowing that I would be doing the right thing in accepting the Divine Principle. Suddenly I knew I would join the church, and said that to the brothers and sisters right there.

A clinician might be inclined to draw on the psychiatric nomenclature to describe the experiences that preceded Annette's conversion. What she reported would meet the diagnostic criteria for a dissociative disorder—"a sudden, temporary alteration in the normally integrative functions of consciousness, identity, or motor behavior."[3] In particular, it represents depersonalization, which involves an alteration in the perception or experience of the self, so that one's usual sense of reality is temporarily disrupted. This can occur when a person cannot resolve an unmanageable and intense conflict, and, as with Annette, cannot integrate the conflicting forces of her own unconscious expectations with those thrust on her by circumstance.

Though Annette's destabilization might seem pathologic, from a systems viewpoint it may be understood as the means of producing compliance in a potential convert through the strong forces of transformation orchestrated by a charismatic group. These forces emerge naturally from members as they act in concert, once the group's direction has been set. And it is this conjoint action that makes the process so forceful. Each member encountered by the inductee contributes to the unquestioning affirmation of the verity of the group's position, thereby enhancing its ability to transform the recruit.

Annette's case demonstrates the potential of the transformation function in engendering neurotic symptoms, but this process can also have sufficient intensity to shatter the sanity of a potential convert, particularly in situations where it is carried out under intense social pressure, with little attention to selecting and protecting fragile individuals. Thus, the transformation function is prominent in the recruitment activities of est, a quasitherapeutic charismatic group that systematically structured its "training" procedures. est maintained that it trained people to free themselves from the seemingly paradoxical and confounding social demands of everyday life. It has been of considerable interest to the mental health community,[4] and the possibility of casualties occurring among those who participate has been studied. Glass, Kirsch, and associates[5] reported on a series of est trainees who experienced symptoms of major psychiatric disorders including paranoid delusions, hallucinations, and severe depression. Because of their unstinting commitment to the transformation process, est trainers apparently ignored psychiatric symptoms precipitated in their workshops.

One mother of three began to develop ideas of influence and to elaborate grandiose projects after the first of two est weekend workshops. She returned to the final workshop and was allowed to continue despite her patent derangement. There she behaved bizarrely, rolling on the floor and laughing uncontrollably. The psychiatric problems for which she later required professional treatment went unattended. Another woman became apathetic, depressed, and isolated after the training sequence. She broke off with friends, began gorging, and gained thirty pounds. In an attempt to ameliorate her severely depressed state, she decided to participate in a postgraduate est course, but rather than being buffered from further pressure in this experience, she was labeled by the trainer as a misfit because she could not "get it." The experience left her feeling even worse because of her inability to connect with the group's message, and she too sought professional help.

One might wonder how these problems could be allowed to unfold since est trainers have developed psychological sophistication and use many techniques drawn directly from the mental health field. How can a group that touted its capacity for improving emotional well-being ignore the emergence of major mental disturbances among those who came to join it?

Considering how the est movement functions as a system will help answer this question. A variety of devices are employed in this group to intensify the forces operating on potential converts. The "training" is carried out in protracted sessions where disagreement with the trainer is actively discouraged, often by harsh verbal abuse. Little respite is afforded from the intensity of the group experience, and the training setting includes as many as two hundred potential converts herded together in a large hall, with their behavior tightly controlled. The dynamism of the experience further heightens the potential for energetic group influence and emotional contagion, and altered consciousness is promoted by a variety of contextual cues and behavioral controls.

Conversion is in fact the primary task of est, conducted at the expense of almost all others. Casualties incurred may have to be ignored, and the problematic issues they raise, repressed; this is in line with the shared belief of devoted est followers, who see "getting it"—achieving personal freedom through the est formula—as a more important goal than attention to the specific conflicts or encumbrances of their day-to-day relationships.

Suppression of concerns that might detract from the primary task of an intensely committed social system is actually quite common. In time of battle, for example, an army may be mobilized to achieve its immediate military objectives, and its primary task is therefore the transformation of all personnel and material into a fighting force. The psychology of the troops is bent to this mission to the exclusion of all else since victory in battle is paramount. Concern for the needs of the wounded may be secondary, since this could detract from the thrust into battle. In a similar way, mobilization for the transformation process in the charismatic sect cannot be deflected by the difficulties experienced by individual converts because the usual constraints on exerting social pressure are suppressed.

Monitoring

To operate effectively, a system must transform input from the environment into a form that meets its needs, but must also observe and regulate the

The Charismatic Large Group as an Open System

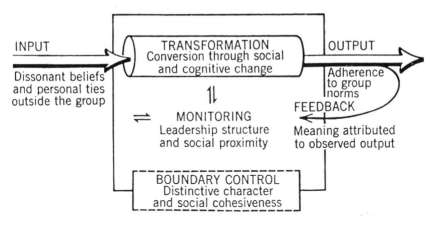

actions of its component parts, thereby assuring that their respective activities are properly carried out and coordinated. This constitutes its monitoring function. Such monitoring is essential to any system to assure the effective implementation of its primary task, whether that system is a living organism, a social organization, or a factory. The system must have an apparatus for monitoring its components. In the living organism, its nervous system serves this function, and in social organizations and factories it is some form of management structure.

An Illustration

A characteristic sequence of monitoring activities in a charismatic sect may begin with a specific plan undertaken by the leadership, which is implemented by proposing a suitable rationale to the members, which then is wholeheartedly adopted. A later shift in circumstances, however, may require a change in the group's agenda, and this in turn may necessitate a change in what is now a strongly held commitment of the members. Because such shifts are common, the system must have the means for observing and acting on the needed changes in attitude and behavior. The monitoring function will operate without undue need for communication or conflict resolution in an effective system. The system's components, the cult members, will respond automatically to the suggestions of the leadership, and the leadership will know how to observe and govern to stabilize the system.

An illustration of this sequence will help clarify the dramatic shifts of direction that often occur in charismatic groups. In 1982, over two thousand couples were married by Reverend Moon in a mass ceremony in New York. Shortly after these new couples had begun to settle down, Moon mounted a major recruitment drive. Mobile recruitment teams were activated across the country, and large numbers of recently married members were expected to leave the connubial status they had just established after more than three years of sexual abstinence. Despite this wrenching dislocation, the newly married members responded with enthusiasm, and many hundreds disrupted their living arrangements and moved to begin their work. Something of a religious crusade was at hand.

The undertaking soon proved unsuccessful, however, since the social climate of the country was becoming conservative in the 1980s, and young people had little interest in a movement that would require them to reject their familial values and disrupt their future plans. From the outset, very few youths approached in urban centers or college campuses considered joining, and no doubt it became clear in reports back to the leadership that potential converts were not to be had. Within a few weeks, the teams of recruiters who had been galvanized for action were deactivated, and had to drop their zealous goal. The situation was potentially tense, as much enthusiasm for the project had been generated.

Because of the effectiveness of monitoring within the sect, this major reversal in perspective was accepted without questioning. The shift away from the recruitment initiative was rationalized as being necessary to set up community-based family residences for individual couples, called "home churches." This change in policy was disseminated by the leadership and was accepted without question as to why the original initiative changed. Members applied themselves to the home church initiative with the same zeal as in the recruitment drive, and at no time did I hear any expressions of reservation about the viability of the initial undertaking or that there may have been a misjudgment by the church leadership about the potential for recruits. Whether consciously controlled or not, compliance with the group's announced perspective was complete.

To understand the means by which this charismatic group rapidly and effectively monitored the thinking and behavioral norms of its members, we must consider the psychological defense mechanisms employed by the group *as a whole*, which are not unlike those operating in individuals. These defenses are employed for the unconscious management of conflicting motives so that the group can function smoothly in the face of conflict. Although similar defenses may be observed in other social systems, the charismatic group responds in particular ways that distinguish it from less tightly knit groups, since the forces of group cohesiveness and shared beliefs in the charismatic group facilitate its operation as a functional whole.

These psychological defenses protect the group culture from unacceptable ideas, often "realities" produced by outdated initiatives or outside influences. Such realities may be ignored outright, by means of denial; forgotten through repression; or distorted through rationalization. In the shift from an active recruitment posture just described, the Unification Church leadership was able to rationalize its actions by maintaining that the same ends were to be accomplished by the home church movement, where members would recruit in their new neighborhoods. The apparent failure of the mobile recruitment teams was denied, as it could have exposed the leadership to question and caused demoralization. Members whom I spoke with gave no indication that the movement's momentum was in question because of the collapse of this recruitment initiative, or that an abrupt shift in attitude had occurred. In this regard, their views had been effectively manipulated to maintain the group's internal stability. *Identification* with the leadership's commitment to the home church movement completed the process.

Identification

In a social system, monitoring is most easily implemented when a voluntary collaboration exists between those in control and those being managed, since outright coercion necessitates undue expenditure of resources and detracts from cooperative efforts to carry out the system's primary task. It is best, in fact, if those monitored accept the leadership without conscious deliberation and, since the defense mechanism of identification operates in an unconscious fashion, those who adopt the attitudes of their leaders do so without deliberating over the wisdom of their actions.

Perhaps the most unusual type of identification takes place when the members' own safety and well-being are jeopardized by their leadership. An example of this is the Stockholm Syndrome, where individuals are cast together as hostages and their lives are threatened. Such captives may develop a positive bond toward the hostage-takers, not only complying with their expectations, but even defending them against people trying to secure the hostages' safety and release. A comparison between this situation and the monitoring process in the charismatic group is intriguing. In both settings the identification seems paradoxical to the outside observer, since those in the dependent position are actively participating with those in control in activities perceived by the outsider as directly conflicting with their own interests; yet they may maintain tenacious fidelity to the people who appear to be threatening their well-being.

Both the cult and hostage situation share the psychological pincer-like effect described previously: The agent inflicting distress on the dependent person is also perceived as the party who can provide relief. Thus, pressure is exerted on those experiencing distress to accommodate to the party who comes to be seen as the only one able to offer relief. The Stockholm Syndrome was first observed during an armed standoff lasting six days between a lone bank robber and the police in a bank in the Swedish capital city. After capturing the facility with an automatic weapon in an attempted holdup, the heavily armed gunman held four bank employees hostage for six days.[6] Reporters' contacts with the captives while they were still under threat of death revealed the startling fact that they had come to fear the police more than their captor, and even after being released the hostages could only puzzle as to why their sense of fealty toward their assailant persisted. For weeks after the incident, they were unable to dispel the feeling that he had been protecting them from the authorities, and could express little animosity toward him.[7]

It has been suggested that this phenomenon is an exaggerated expression of *identification with the aggressor,* a psychological defense mechanism originally described by Anna Freud.[8] Like all psychological defenses, this one represents an adaptive strategy whose purpose is to aid the individual in coping with unresolved mental conflict. In the Stockholm Syndrome, the hostage must avoid the threat of bodily danger but at the same time engage the support, or at least the benign neglect, of the very person who poses that threat. This can generate a conflict that is not easily resolved between the need to be cared for and an overriding hostility toward the person who can provide this care. The hostage, therefore, cannot readily act in a way that would engage the assailant unless the anger he or she naturally feels is not acknowledged and expressed. Once this repression is achieved, the victim may look to the captor for support and success. Victims implicitly hope that by means of fidelity and compliance, they may elicit the aggressor's protection. Like other psychological defenses, this one seems irrational at first glance, yet it may represent the best available means by which the person can respond to an emotionally untenable situation.

Identification with the aggressor is relevant here because it helps us better understand the monitoring process in charismatic groups. Members of these groups are often effectively under assault by their leaders. That is, in the consensual view of their surrounding society, they are pressed to participate in unpleasant activities, and are sometimes subjected to abuse. Members nonetheless have their own psychological need for maintaining affiliation with the leader and the group, since they are captives by virtue of the pincer effect, which makes their emotional well-being depend on involvement in the group that inflicts distress. In a sense, they have no choice but to unconsciously make peace with the potentially threatening agenda of the leadership and comply with its expectations to achieve emotional relief.

We saw this process in operation among the followers of Baba, who clung to their leader during the course of his protracted psychotic illness.[9] Baba became physically abusive and behaved in a highly erratic manner toward his devotees, inflicting them with adverse living circumstances and even sexual assault. Nonetheless, members remained faithful, using a series of rationalizations that, to the observer, were untenable. They claimed his madness was "divine," and said that he was "teaching them a lesson" with each bizarre demand.

Members who had become highly involved with the group, subject to its emotional pincer, found it necessary to identify with the leader-aggressor and sustain their dependency. The conflict between dependency needs and potential anger toward Baba was not unlike that observed in the Stockholm Syndrome.

SUPPRESSION OF AUTONOMY

Our discussion raises the question of how autonomy is suppressed in a charismatic group. Such suppression is vividly seen in the mobile street sales teams of the Unification Church. In these teams, members who had little acquaintance with each other rapidly adapted to living and working in very close quarters under considerable privation. They sometimes slept all together in cramped quarters and shared limited provisions of food. Often they would draw underwear from a common clothing pool, reflecting an unusual enforced intimacy established for economy. The religious injunctions for each team included "brotherly and sisterly" cooperation, typically rooted in citations from the Divine Principle, which offered the group's ideology as the basis for suppression of any deviant behavior.

Ex-members whom I interviewed said they had rarely experienced serious misgivings while on the mobile teams and certainly had not felt it appropriate to express reservations. Such hesitancy was born out of the guilt that disrupting the team's mission would have caused more than of fear of disapproval. Unlike army recruits, who might suffer similar privations, these sect members did not maintain a psychological distance from the leadership and did not complain or question the wisdom of the circumstances thrust on them, nor did they have consensual support from the broader society.

For a social system to regulate its functioning effectively, it must have the capacity to suppress members' deviation from its implicit or explicit goals. In charismatic groups, the penalty for those who deviate from norms is psychological distress; overt coercion usually is not necessary to induce compliance. How is this penalty exacted? We have seen that there is a decrease in psychological well-being among those who felt *less* closely associated with the group. Furthermore, members who were considering leaving the sect had attitudes most clearly at variance with those of the group, and their scores fell into the clinically depressed range.[10] Indeed, 36% of those who dropped out of the Unification Church reported the emergence of "serious emotional problems" in the period following their departure.[11]

These observations suggest that members may experience distress whenever they are inclined to think negatively about their affiliation. By recourse to learning theory, we may infer that attempts at achieving independence from the group's monitoring function would tend to be extinguished. One person suffering the penalty of distress was Allen, a young man who fell into conflict with the norms of a small neo-Christian cult. When I interviewed Allen he was sixteen years old and had just been hospitalized because of withdrawal from his peers at school, mounting disruptiveness in an aunt's home where he lived, and a two-week history of hallucinating Satan's voice. Allen had been a member of The Word of God cult for three years, but had left three months before his hospitalization. He had originally been introduced to the cult along with two siblings by his mother, who had been suffering from drug problems before she joined. The boy adapted fairly well to the group, but when he was caught smoking marijuana some members said he was tainted by the Devil. After this, he became a scapegoat of sorts, and his participation in the group's religious services was limited. By his own account and that of his aunt, he had previously experienced no psychiatric difficulties.

One of the group's leaders continued to harass Allen over his presumed satanic association, and it became clear that several cult members believed he was actually in communication with the Devil. As these views got back to him, the boy became increasingly frightened about the influence the leader would have on other members. He decided to escape the group and went to live in his aunt's house, but became anxious and depressed, ruminating over his possible diabolical taint, and after a few weeks began to hear the voice of the Devil on occasion accusing him of sinning in leaving the cult. He was soon admitted to the hospital, where he showed no other evidence of psychosis or thought disorder, but was preoccupied with the fear of the group's allegations of his relationship with the Devil.

In the hospital Allen was initially treated supportively, told he was free from supernatural taint, and led to understand the misfortune that had befallen him in being labeled as he was. His mother corroborated that his social adjustment had been adequate until the cult leader had seized on the episode of marijuana smoking as reason to question Allen's place in the group. During a one-month hospitalization, without medication, his symptoms abated and he was discharged.

Allen had fallen victim to the interpretation of the cult's ideology by one of its leaders, and was then made a scapegoat by members following this leader. In refusing to accept this role, he violated the group's monitoring functions and set up a conflict within himself. His departure from the group intensified this conflict and he began to manifest symptoms that meet the diagnostic criteria for a brief reactive psychosis.

Psychophysiologic reactions in such situations can be even more dramatic than the psychological consequences. The classical exposition of this phenomenon was made by the physiologist Walter B. Cannon in describing voodoo death. In the ritual of "boning," an Australian aboriginal may be rejected from the tribe, and when this happens the victim's

> cheeks blanch and his eyes become glassy and the expression of his face becomes horribly distorted. . . . He attempts to shriek but usually the sound chokes in his throat, and all that one might see is the froth at his mouth. His body begins to tremble and the muscles twist involuntarily. He sways backwards and falls to the ground, and after a short time appears to be in a swoon. . . . After awhile he becomes composed and crawls to his wurley [hut]. From this time onwards he sickens and frets, refusing to eat and keeping aloof from the daily affairs of the tribe. Unless help is administered in the shape of a countercharm administered by the hands of the Nangarri, or medicine man, his death is only a matter of comparatively short time.[12]

Cannon's contribution was to suggest a physiologic mechanism underlying such events and support it with both clinical observations and animal experiments. In the voodoo death syndrome, he saw that the tribe has been the individual's protector so that ostracism precipitates an intense fear from which the separated member cannot flee, because of a deep and long-standing emotional bond. This crisis produces an excitation of the sympathetic nervous system and adrenergic release, followed in time by cardiovascular collapse.

More recent studies have supported Cannon's views in demonstrating that the reaction to major environmental stress can precipitate ventricular fibrillation and death.[13]

Allen's case and the voodoo death syndrome both clearly reflect the remarkable potency of forces that may be mobilized *within* the group to monitor and regulate those who might be considered in violation of its norms. These complement the other facets of the monitoring function examined, namely benign identification and identification with the aggressor.

Feedback

Feedback is one way for a system to obtain information on how well it is carrying out its primary task. A portion of output is fed back into the system and this provides information for planning future operations. If a cult is trying to recruit, information on the relative response of potential members can be fed back to the cult leaders and guide them in improving the group's recruitment techniques.

Feedback may be either positive or negative. Positive feedback gives the system information that will increase the deviation of its output from the steady state, thereby yielding an enhanced or elaborated output. Negative feedback tends to diminish variations in the transformation function. When negative feedback ceases to be available, transformation activities may go unmoderated, the steady state can vanish, and the system's boundaries can be disrupted.[14] Consequently, the system must have unrestrained access to negative feedback to exercise a proper degree of self-regulation and not dissipate its energies.

This latter function is important in charismatic sects because they are prone to suppress negative feedback when it runs contrary to the group's internal stability. It is a special risk because of the highly effective monitoring function that allows the cult system to control the information made available to its members. Means of avoiding undue negative feedback are essential to charismatic groups because their ideology and practices often elicit hostility from the general society. If allowed to enter the system unobstructed, such negative feedback leads to suppression of the group's transcendent vision and a decline in members' morale.

Certain charismatic groups try hard to isolate their members from all negative feedback, but this can be dangerous as the group may lose information valuable to its own self-regulation. These groups usually are no longer actively recruiting and have little need for protracted contact with outsiders. We will see the potential for dire consequences of this phenomenon in Jonestown (Chapter 7). Other groups, however, rely on the successful recruitment of new members to provide them with positive feedback. Such successes are used to reinforce the merit of the group's own ideology and promote new initiatives that validate the group's chosen course. New converts give legitimacy to a group in the face of a hostile world and encourage members to carry the group's mission forward. Such feedback can be a useful tool for social regulation.

Successful conversion activities were widely publicized in the Unification Church. Overseas recruitment was also important, and here too reports of large numbers of converts were circulated. All this served to undermine the impact of the negative feedback from society at large. Accounts of the magnitude of converts were often exaggerated, betraying the leaders' motives. For example, members were consistently told of a very large enrollment in Japan, a sign of the movement's worldwide acceptance; one figure given to the press was 260,000.[15] When I visited the movement's headquarters in Japan, however, I was startled to find the figure of five million Japanese members in an English-language church publication. Such grandiose reports from Japan were apparently aimed at Americans and other English-speaking members. I spoke with American members in Japan in detail about the actual level of participation in the country and why the misleading brochures were produced. Soon it became clear that there were no more than a few thousand members in Tokyo and a similar number throughout the rest of the country. One member who was relatively at ease in discussing the issue was apologetic because he could not support figures used in the Church literature and explained that they represented a dubious count of signatories to a petition for world peace issued by the sect some years before.

In the United States, inflated figures were also regularly given to church members as evidence of its international impact. They were in effect counterfeit positive feedback.

Negative feedback assures that a system does not expend undue energy or embark on fruitless ventures. Because it can suppress initiatives needed to maintain commitment and group momentum, however, such feedback may engender conflict in a charismatic sect with an expansionist agenda, leading to its own suppression.

This occurred when Reverend Moon was first becoming known to the American public in 1976. He arranged for a large rally to be held in Yankee Stadium in New York City, to summon up the faithful, attract potential members, and draw attention to the movement. The leadership assumed that this would elicit a positive response from the general public. Before the gathering, hundreds of church members, including large numbers of Oriental followers of Moon, most of whom had recently been brought in from overseas, were sent into the streets of New York City to clean up refuse. In wearing white work suits that were a startling contrast to the way other pedestrians were dressed, these Moonies gave the movement an odd and unappealing image and strengthened the widely held view that members were turned into automatons. Despite a modest turnout, church leaders pronounced the venture a success.

Here too, as with the incorrect membership figures, a realistic assessment of the situation would have carried with it an undue amount of negative feedback, and might have forced the membership to confront the sect's limitations. The public's bleak view of the group's Oriental affiliations and alleged

dehumanizing qualities would then have implicitly discouraged the very initiatives the leaders were using to support the group's primary task at that
time, namely zealous expansion to a worldwide organization. So they suppressed the negative feedback.

Other examples of this can be found in a variety of commercial ventures
on which the Unification Church embarked. These included sizable commercial fishing enterprises in New England and on the Gulf Coast, and the publication of newspapers—*Newsworld* and *Noticias del Mundo* in New York and
the *Washington Times* in the nation's capital. These operations consistently
showed a deficit, and from any rational business standpoint should have been
closed early on.[16] But they promulgated the church's ideology and provided
continued positive feedback. The fishing enterprises were an expression of a
mystical commitment to maritime matters expressed by Reverend Moon, and
the newspapers apparently reflected the church's desire for a platform to
broadcast their view of public affairs, giving them credibility on national and
world events. Such ventures were seen as evidence of the viability of the
movement's ideology; to admit they had failed would have produced negative
feedback that could have been destabilizing.

Boundary Control

As we have seen, an open system must carry out its transformation functions
while maintaining internal stability by monitoring its own components and
responding to feedback. These functions, however, can be disrupted by intru-
sions from outside. For this reason boundary control is a vital function of any
system.

Boundary control protects social systems against dangerous outsiders. It
includes not only the screening of people but also of information, since information is a potent determinant of behavior. If a charismatic group is to
maintain a system of shared beliefs markedly at variance with that of the
surrounding culture, members must sometimes be rigidly isolated from consensual information from the general society that would unsettle this belief
system. During the initial phases of conversion to charismatic sects, novices
may be regarded as vulnerable and actively discouraged from establishing contact with their families. After their integration into the group, when their
beliefs have been consolidated, new members may be encouraged to reestablish ties with their families so as to promote a benign public image and
perhaps make other conversions.

Two important facets of activity form the boundary of charismatic sects,
each mirroring the other. The first is a set of behaviors and attitudes of members, often deviant, that is directed at outsiders. It reflects how the system
focuses its social forces to protect its boundaries. The second is a reciprocal
set of behaviors and attitudes of the surrounding society, often an aggressive
response of outsiders to the group's members.

The System Raises Its Defenses

Any group that coalesces around a cause or function must soon establish a boundary to differentiate those who are participating from those who are not. One situation I witnessed illuminated the potency of such boundary control phenomena. It occurred at a Tavistock training institute for experiential learning in group behavior (see Chapter 2). These institutes are designed to stimulate the circumstances under which certain group forces emerge and thereby illustrate the nature of group interactions. Participants, generally mental health professionals, sometimes other interested parties, use this experiential exercise to acquire a firsthand acquaintance with the processes underlying group behavior.

In one exercise, members of the institute were asked to select rooms within the training center where they would establish small discussion groups and then, in these groups, define a common position in relation to a certain social issue. Assignments to groups were arbitrary, but members of each group were able to choose their common perspective within a relatively short time.

As a participant, I was struck by a particular sequence of events involving Paul, a mature psychiatrist well respected in the Washington, D.C., community. He implemented the boundary control function for his group with undue zeal and aggressiveness, to the point that his behavior in retrospect seemed bizarre to him. Paul's group had shortly before begun to define its goals, and the members' mutuality was as yet uncertain, since they had only recently gotten together. A slight, elderly woman entered the room to observe this group as an emissary of her own, an undertaking that had been suggested in the instructions for the exercise. Paul, who had been assigned the role of screening outsiders, insisted that she not impinge on the group's territory and became quite curt. After an exchange in which the woman expressed little more than curiosity, he rushed over to her and tried to force her out the door, angrily throwing her to the floor and wrenching her leg in the process. He expressed no remorse, but instead admonished her for not knowing better than to intrude on a group deliberating among themselves.

The small group in which Paul was participating was involved in little more than a vaguely defined discussion of its "identity" and was created only for a daylong exercise. Nonetheless, it was beginning to delineate its borders. Paul felt it necessary to protect this perimeter, thereby assuring that the group's sense of purpose would be consolidated, without interference from outside. Paul had apparently become too closely identified with the system function he had been assigned, that of defending the system's boundary.

This episode illustrated in a small but chilling way the ardor that can flare up in those who defend a group, even a meaningless one, to which they belong. A month later I asked Paul what his thinking had been in accosting that defenseless woman. After saying with some embarrassment that he had located the woman the next day and apologized properly, he answered that

The exercise was artificial, but somehow we were swept up in it. At the time, I knew that our small group was vulnerable and I was committed to see our unity preserved. She wasn't just an intruder on our space. She seemed like the beginning of the unraveling of our work. I wasn't really pushing her out. As far as I can recall, I was keeping out over a hundred other people in the institute exercise who would inevitably follow after her, leading to our group's dissolution.

The boundary behavior of cult members that has made the deepest impression on outsiders involves the glazed, withdrawn look and trance-like state that some find most unsettling. Although this may appear pathologic, it can help group membership by reducing the possibility of direct exchanges with outsiders—it has an insulating effect. Thus, the trance-like appearance protects the sect's boundary. It would be more likely to develop in settings that threaten the group's integrity, so that an observer who is perceived as an antagonist is more likely to see the behavior than one who is not. This may help explain the puzzling discrepancies among observers' reports on contemporary cults since they may approach the sects' "safe boundaries" in different ways. Some researchers, such as John Clark and Margaret Singer,[17] have had a great deal of contact with people leaving sects and have addressed at length the ill effects of membership. Their writings question the place of these groups in a society that protects the right to free and independent thought. They underscore the emotional constriction and stereotyped behavior sometimes associated with cult membership, implying that it is equivalent to psychopathology. Other observers, such as Thomas Ungerleider and David Wellisch,[18] as well as my associates and I, established a positive working relationship with active cult members and tended to look at the more constructive aspects of membership. This second group has not found the same stereotyped behavior and emotional constriction. Sect members may thus respond to outsiders according to whether or not they appear to threaten the group's safe boundaries.

Fearfulness of outsiders, or xenophobia, a common characteristic of cults, is an important manifestation of boundary control. It holds groups together but it can reach the dimensions of outright paranoia. It represents a boundary control function carried to the extreme and is seen among those sect members pressed by family or strangers to give up their ties to the group. It is also evident in the way outsiders are often treated with a different standard of openness or honesty. (A "heavenly deception" is one perpetrated by a member of the Unification Church on a nonmember to further the Church's goals.)

At times, outright paranoia at the system's boundary may assume sufficient intensity to meet diagnostic criteria for a commonly held delusional system. Such a state is termed a shared paranoid disorder, wherein a delusional state is shared among two or more people so that the pathologic perspective of one person in the group is supported by that of the others. In a charismatic group, it can be characterized by persistent delusional thinking and occurs in the absence of other psychotic symptoms, since it springs from close association with others with a similar delusion rather than from innate psychiatric disability.

The Community Reacts

Defensiveness and paranoia associated with the boundary function of a charismatic sect elicit a complementary reaction from the surrounding community. This is seen in the animosity between family members of converts and the sects; in the breakdown in communication between sects and some religious groups; and in the hostility toward sects voiced by some former members.

Attempts at communication between parents and their children who have joined contemporary sects are often rife with misunderstanding and hostility. The convert often becomes an agent of the group's boundary control function and regards the relatives who make contact as attempting to disengage the person from the movement, whereas the parents, operating at the boundary of a highly cohesive group, frequently become preoccupied with the effort to dislodge the new member. Communications are often frozen at this level.

Two couples who came to me for consultation illustrate how these battles across the group's boundary take place. The first were parents of a young woman who had shortly before dropped out of college and gone to work as a waitress in a rural area. There she befriended an older woman who was a member of the Jehovah's Witnesses and who actively encouraged her to join the sect. When her parents heard of their daughter's growing interest, they drove to the town where she was living and approached her angrily, demanding to know why she was sacrificing her future for this "odd" group. In the absence of an acceptable reply, they consulted a psychiatrist who had treated their daughter for a transient problem while she was in high school. He suggested they adopt a more benign and accommodating attitude, but neither parent was able to respond in this fashion for fear of losing their daughter. Soon the girl made it clear to them that it was only through a more congenial attitude toward the group and its beliefs that they could gain the right to discuss the matter fully with her.

The parents felt their only choice if they were to "keep" their daughter was to either forcefully resist the girl's move or themselves accept the sect's views. They were torn between two compelling systems functions of the group: transformation, which demands compliance with the group's ideology, and boundary control, which rejects aliens and their views. Under these circumstances, it was almost impossible for them to establish viable communication with the girl.

Some parents continue their aggressive efforts to draw their children away from a charismatic sect long after they have become fully affiliated. Many sects want members to establish courteous relations with their families once the membership role has been consolidated, without compromising the members' own fidelity, and this gives parents an opening. But in their attempts to change their children's thinking, the parents may assault the group's boundaries and produce a breakdown in communication.

This was the case in a second unfortunate family that for eight years had been engaged in a tug-of-war with their son, who had joined the Hare Krishna movement. At first they sent their own local religious leaders as emissaries to encourage him to leave, but this only exacerbated his defensiveness. Subsequent encounters, which had become less frequent, were characterized by disputes revolving around the rituals of the sect in relation to diet, dress, and lifestyle.

Consultation with his family arose over their uncertainty as to whether to invite their convert son to the wedding of his older brother. At first, the parents were able to maintain a flexible posture in the exchange and their son agreed to attend. As further plans were made, however, they again began to express the hope that he would be sympathetic to the family's needs, a request perceived by the young man as suggesting their desire that he loosen his ties toward the sect. He then issued demands about the cultic food and dress he would bring to the ceremony and finally broke off communication, refusing to appear at the wedding. Conflicting demands on both sides of the boundary had not been surmounted.

The sect's boundary may also generate a reverse phenomenon in the form of an "anti-cult." This is seen most prominently among the members forced to leave these groups by deprogrammers. We may define deprogramming as the forcible indoctrination of a negative attitude toward the sect in an attempt to dislodge members from it. In our study of individuals who had left the Unification Church,[19] a striking contrast existed between members who had departed voluntarily and those who were deprogrammed. The first group had mixed feelings about their experience but expressed a relatively benign view of both their own involvement and the ongoing participation of their remaining compatriots. Most (62%) still felt strongly that they "cared for the ten members they knew best," and the large majority (89%) believed that they "got some positive things" out of membership. On the other hand, those who were deprogrammed had a much more negative attitude toward the sect and had apparently become more involved in a cohesive group of mutually committed persons attempting to deprogram other members.

These deprogrammed youths often became articulate and active critics of sects such as the Moonies and Hare Krishna, in contrast to the majority of ex-members who had left on their own initiative. In our own study, eight out of ten deprogrammed ex-members had participated in attempts to coerce other members to leave, whereas none of those who left voluntarily had done so. Their animosity toward the new religious movements in general paralleled the intensity of feeling found in the sects they opposed.

Members of a cult may be driven to behave as they do by forces that act within the social system to assure its stability and implement its primary task. On the other hand, the openness of each member to such influence can only be understood by recourse to one's biologically grounded responsiveness to group influence. We have considered the scope of both biological and systems perspectives. We can next look at more extensive examples of these perspectives in some representative charismatic groups.

III

CASE HISTORIES OF
CHARISMATIC
GROUPS

We used to think of "cults" as obscure offshoots of mainstream religions with their own devotional practices. But over the course of a generation the term has acquired grim connotations of the potential for mass suicide, assault, or fiery death. So far in this book, we have considered how cults engage the minds of their recruits, how they generate their unique psychological and social forces, and how they acquire structure as social systems. We will now consider how several cultic groups came to grave outcomes that have troubled a generation.

Charismatic groups generally attract public attention when their zeal is at its height. Some settle into a more routine adaptation, become bureaucratized, and assume the form of a more traditional religious organization, as did the Mormons over the course of a century. Another, more contemporary example of this transition is seen in the Unification Church, whose evolution we will examine at length. We will see how this group moved toward stability despite its controversial beginnings.

Other groups have come to shocking ends, showing how the encounter between a cult and the general society can result in suicide or conflagration, militant confrontation, or even mass murder. Events in the 1970s and 1980s at the Peoples Temple in Jonestown and MOVE in Philadelphia acquainted the public with the possibility of cultic disaster. After a time, the headlines were forgotten and the events receded into the past. Then came the Branch Davidians, Aum Shinrikyo, and Heaven's Gate. We will examine these latter groups and the circumstances that contributed the most to their sad outcomes.

7

TROUBLE AT
THE SYSTEM'S BOUNDARY

This chapter examines two examples of the disastrous outcomes that can take place in charismatic groups, and we will use the systems model to put the reported events into perspective. The first example is the Peoples Temple in Guyana, a cult that originated in a mainstream Protestant denomination but ended in the self-inflicted deaths of over nine hundred members. Although the events surrounding this episode are well documented, they still leave uncertainty as to how a group of relatively stable people might have evolved to the point that they so flagrantly abrogated the innate human drive for self-preservation.

A second example illustrates how aggressive actions taken by a cult-like group at its boundary can lead the society at large to embark on an uncontrolled assault designed to protect itself from a perceived threat from the group. In this case, members of the group called MOVE had been sequestered in a residential neighborhood in Philadelphia for several years and presented a highly provocative stance in attempting to foist their idiosyncratic views on their neighbors.

Jonestown

Events in an isolated village in South America gave the world a sudden shock in November 1978. In a mass suicide unprecedented for its magnitude in contemporary history, over nine hundred people died, mostly by poisoning. The casualties included almost the entire membership of the Peoples Temple, a cult composed of American-born religious converts residing in an agricul-

113

tural commune deep in the jungle of Guyana, about 150 miles from the country's populated coast.

Background of the Group

The Peoples Temple was led by Jim Jones, a charismatic preacher whose religious activities had begun to take shape while he was an undergraduate at Indiana University. With a background in pastoral training in the Methodist Church, Jones eventually settled in San Francisco. There he pursued his interest in developing community service projects, such as a child-care center and a kitchen to feed the poor, and also worked in the political campaigns of a number of local and national figures in the 1960s.

By 1974, Jones had already begun to establish the Jonestown commune in Guyana, where he wanted to create a secluded haven for his followers. The Guyanese government had been eager to support this reputable group, which had a largely black membership, because Jones and his followers were willing to set up in a township in the country's remote interior where local blacks had refused to migrate, and because they were sympathetic to Jones's socialist philosophy. The commune also benefited from its religious status, which enabled it to import goods without paying customs to the Guyanese authorities.[1]

The situation began to unravel with the arrival of Leo Ryan, a U.S. Congressman from San Francisco. Ryan had come to investigate the reports of mistreatment of converts in this isolated setting and was accompanied by several journalists and relatives of Temple members who hoped to persuade their kin to leave. After meeting with Jones and visiting the colony for a day, Ryan's group was joined by four cult members who had opted to defect. The entourage was accosted as they were about to board their plane at the nearby landing strip and most, including Ryan, were shot dead. Within hours of the murder, Jones ordered a mass suicide of all his followers.

What happened then is known from a small number of eyewitnesses who succeeded in fleeing into the jungle and from audiotapes made of speeches during the carnage. A physician serving as medical officer for Jonestown prepared a large quantity of fruit punch laced with cyanide, and Jones ordered his people to drink this mixture, threatening that they would soon be under attack by the Central Intelligence Agency and that they had to prepare for a revolutionary death. Babies and children were first made to swallow the drink by the older members, and were then followed by the adults themselves. In the end, 914 persons died, including more than 216 children.[2]

The amount of force exerted to complete the mass suicide varied among the members. For most, no coercion was necessary; only a small minority acted under overt threats from Jones's henchmen, who were brandishing firearms. A survivor noted that when one member challenged Jones's demand that all present in the assemblage participate, "The crowd shouted her down."[3] If threats were used, they were typically warnings as to the fate any survivors would meet at the hands of the outside world. By all accounts, suicide was therefore a voluntary act for the large majority of the adults.

A Perspective

These bare facts are shocking. They tell of an entire social entity gone awry in a seemingly incomprehensible way. Although the group was driven by a deranged and paranoid leader, the course of events was played out through a complex social system.

While Jones and his group were still operating in San Francisco, the *transformation* function of this social system was directed at enlarging the sect's membership and bringing the broader community around to a favorable view of the group. Thus, it was estimated that during Jones's years in San Francisco between 50,000 and 100,000 people came to hear him speak, even though the actual membership of the Temple never exceeded 3,000.[4] This emphasis on transformation based on a zeal for conveying the group's message is quite common in the earlier phases of charismatic sects and is associated with the presumption that the leader's ideology is unassailable and infectious, a view untempered as yet by a lengthy history of rejection by potential converts or dissipation of the members' initial enthusiasm. When the Temple's committed members moved to Guyana, however, recruitment ceased to play a role in the movement's activities. Its energies now came to focus primarily on the close *monitoring* of its members. There were implicit demands for an intensification of commitment to Jones's idiosyncratic views, and increasingly bizarre beliefs came to be expected of these long-standing converts. Jones, for example, now claimed to be the reincarnation of Jesus, as well as Ikhnaton, Buddha, Lenin, and Father Divine.[5]

This monitoring function is illustrated in letters to "Dad," the confessionals of Jonestown residents to their leader.[6] They are quite revealing, in that they show the striking intensity of the group forces of shared belief and social cohesiveness. Expressions of commitment were laced with an intensified ideologic orientation, illustrating the system's growing control over the worldview of its members. As one member wrote about his rejection of his prior views: "I am an elitist and an anarchist because I think back in the States when I wanted to do my own thing and did not want any situations for discipline. I didn't have the U.S. capitalism in me and I'm trying to get rid of it. Here I don't have any intention of becoming a traitor or going back to the U.S."

The letter of another member reflected the intensely cohesive force that was focused on Jones himself, and it foreshadowed the final act of commitment.

> I will endure until I am dead. . . . I shall not let this movement down. I shall not beg for mercy either in that last moment. I shall proudly die for proud reason. You can count on *me* even if all desert you. I shall be by your side whether it be tangible or in spirit. If, suddenly, a U.S. vessel

or plane will come to get us all to take us back with promises of all the luxury and benefits if we would sell you out, I would not go on board because I am attracted to your goodness as magnets attract one another. . . . Nothing will ever break your pull.

The theme of apocalyptic doom was part of the group's belief system from early on, originally reflecting Jones's fear of nuclear annihilation. In California, his preaching began to embody visions of CIA persecution and Nazi-like extermination of blacks,[7] but in Jonestown this theme of anticipated destruction soon became intertwined with the group's monitoring function. Because of their intense commitment, Jones's followers could be drawn deeply into this vortex of apocalyptic visions untempered by their independent judgment. Members were regularly scolded and punished by Jones; some were whipped or beaten before the entire community for "crimes" such as not conforming to prohibitions on smoking.[8] Others were punished perversely; in a typical incident, a woman accused of violating the rule of celibacy was forced to submit to intercourse with a man she disliked while the entire colony watched.[9]

On such occasions, an indistinct line existed between voluntary submission and coercion. On the one hand, members suffered a deluded identification with the leader-aggressor; on the other, they were realistically afraid of resisting his demands and too emotionally dependent to leave. This lack of clear distinction was evident in the words of one escapee.

> The beatings were all over. . . . People would be humiliated in front of the crowd . . . and Jones would just sit there and just smile. You could never say anything about wanting to come back to the States, you couldn't say anything negative . . . a lot of people thought he had their minds controlled, he would tell them if they'd say anything negative that they in turn would get sick or something would happen to them.[10]

Acceptance of the leader's perspective is essential in assuring affiliation with a sect, and it meets the members' dependency needs. But if that perspective is irrational, conformity can be hazardous.

Needing to preserve their bond to the group in Jonestown, members were unable to reject Jones as an aggressor. As in the Stockholm Syndrome, they clung to him for security, coming more and more to accept his punishments. Jones precipitated members' problems, but as the mediator of group affiliation, he was also regarded by them as the only viable source of relief from their feelings of distress.

The "White Nights" Jones staged in Guyana laid the groundwork for the final mass suicide. These exercises began with states of emergency declared by Jones when the commune's population was awakened by blaring sirens to go through a rehearsal for death. An excerpt from the affidavit of one Temple survivor describes the experience. She wrote that in these situations Jones's deputies would

> arm themselves with rifles, move from cabin to cabin and make certain that all members were responding. A mass meeting would ensue. Fre-

quently during these crises, we would be told that the jungle was swarm-
ing with mercenaries and that death could be expected at any minute.
. . . We were given a small glass of red liquid to drink. We were told that
the liquid contained poison and that we would die within 45 minutes.
We all did as we were told. When the time came when we should have
dropped dead, Reverend Jones explained that the poison was not real and
that we had just been through a loyalty test.[11]

The fact that this bizarre ritual could be carried out at all reflects the
strength of the members' commitment to Jones's demonic leadership. The
absolute nature of his control must have countered Jones's fear of defections.

In Jonestown monitoring was not mediated by an intermediary level of personnel who could exercise independent judgment and temper Jones's exercise
of power. The leader's psychology had become the template for the group's
monitoring, and this made the members agents of his inclinations. With Jones
(as with Baba) unbridled control over a cult generated grandiosity and even
delusion as the leader came to believe in his own omnipotence. And, conversely, antecedent psychopathology in a leader may itself encourage him to
seize absolute control to allay his deluded concerns. In either case, and both
probably apply here, the monitoring process becomes embroiled in the leader's
primitive mental defenses.

Such congruence between a single charismatic leader and the monitoring
function is not true of all cults. The value of a "middle management" in
moderating the role of a charismatic leader is evident in sects with a more
influential administration operating between the leader and the membership
body. In the Unification Church, for example, the impact of Reverend Moon's
policy making was considerably tempered by a group of his close advisers,
including the president of the church's American branch. Moon's initiatives
generally passed through this group for implementation by a deliberative process that shaped the way those initiatives were articulated.

Feedback from the outside world can also be helpful in moderating a
leader's deviant views. In the Peoples Temple, however, there was very little.
Jones's seclusiveness clearly played a major role in constraining the group's
access to feedback. The physical isolation, conceived by Jones as a means of
protecting the group from assault, denied members access to the reactions of
outsiders who might have raised questions about their bizarre beliefs and
behavior. Outside views would have provided negative feedback for the system, and helped counter the leader's psychopathology. As noted in Chapter
6, access to negative feedback is essential to the continuing viability of an
open system since it enables the system to assess its own effectiveness and
change so as to eliminate maladaptive behavior. Thus, if the Peoples Temple
had made active attempts at recruitment in Guyana, thereby engaging in an
open interchange with the Guyanese society, potential recruits would have
raised pointed questions with cult members about Jones's physical abuse of
them.

Jones's growing paranoia and defensiveness were glaringly apparent in his
drive to close all sources of feedback. He made a strenuous effort to avoid

exposing the colony to the news media. In 1977, he successfully suppressed the attempt of a reporter from the *San Francisco Examiner* to prepare a series of articles on the sect. This involved a campaign of phone calls and letter writing balanced by the offer of a $4,000 contribution for a journalism scholarship to placate the paper's editors.[12] A month before the massacre, communication between Jonestown and the outside world was severed. Members were told that Los Angeles had been abandoned because of a severe drought and that the Ku Klux Klan was marching openly through the streets of San Francisco.[13]

The arrival of Congressman Ryan and his entourage portended the imminent disruption of the group's *control over its boundary,* and thereby precipitated the final events at Jonestown. For a leader and charismatic group of paranoid orientation, such vulnerability may be intolerable. Ryan's visit jeopardized the system's integrity. The fact that four cult members chose to leave with him posed a challenge to the group's monitoring of the membership. Moreover, an intrusion by the U.S. federal government meant that suppression of negative feedback could no longer be absolute. On both counts, it was reasonable for Jones to fear that the cult could no longer operate in total identification with his will. For Jones, already highly sensitized and paranoid, this was a severe threat. In deciding to assault the Congressman, he realized that "they will try to destroy us."[14] Once it became apparent that his cult's boundary could no longer be secured, Jones chose to preserve its identity in spirit if not in living membership. At the last moment, this was underlined when he implied to the group that their deaths did not represent a failure, but rather a triumph of the group's ideology:

> So . . . you be kind to children and be kind to seniors, and take the potion like they used to in ancient Greece, and step over quietly; because we are not committing suicide—it's a revolutionary act.[15]

This commune was therefore to die in body. In terms of its spiritual mission, however, Jones was preserving its integrity and, in a perverse way, history may well serve to accomplish this end.

MOVE

Conflicts on the boundary of the charismatic group may unleash remarkably destructive behavior. We have seen how the Peoples Temple preserved its identity by surrendering the lives of its members when an incursion of its boundary was perceived to threaten its dissolution. In contrast, events may be precipitated by the general public itself in responding to a threatening charismatic group lodged in its midst. This happened with a cult called MOVE in 1985, in Philadelphia. The group had been responsible for a series of provocations at its boundary and the response by city authorities was overwhelming.

Background of the Group

MOVE was a small cult committed in an idiosyncratic way to a return to things natural and rejection of the accoutrements of industrialization. It occupied a modest row house on Osage Street in West Philadelphia. Members had a confrontation with authorities seven years before that left a police officer dead and nine members of the group in prison. They had now barricaded their current residence and were using it as a base to promote their ideas, often by railing angrily at neighbors through a loudspeaker.

A final breakdown in communications with authorities occurred when the sect's "defense minister," Conrad Africa, refused to negotiate with a city official regarding the group's disruptions unless the nine imprisoned MOVE members were released. Given this impasse, the group's hostility, and the possibility that members had arms in the house, the mayor and police chief decided that an assault was necessary to dislodge the cult. The police then evacuated five hundred residents of the immediate area and began trying to flush the group out of the building. This task turned out to be much more difficult than anticipated, however, since members had turned their house into a virtual fortress, having boarded over the doors and windows and constructed a steel-reinforced bunker atop the building. What happened next was remarkable for the lack of restraint by local authorities.

The first step was to hose several hundred thousand gallons of water through high pressure jets at the bunker on top of the building. This proved ineffective and cult members responded by shooting at the police. Instead of waiting the situation out, the police then unleashed a storm of gunfire, almost exhausting their supply of more than 7,000 rounds of ammunition in an hour and a half.[16] At this point, several officers wearing helmets and body armor and carrying automatic weapons tried to penetrate the house through its cellar wall, but were fended off by members of the cult who opened fire.

It was then decided to "neutralize" the armored bunker atop the building by using an incendiary blasting agent actually designed for underground mining operations.[17] After making several passes over the street, a helicopter brought in for the task hovered sixty feet above the building and dropped its makeshift bomb. A fire erupted within minutes, but the fire department, present in force with its high-power hoses, did not respond for a full forty minutes as the flames spread. Firefighters were apparently planning to let the fire burn through the building so that its occupants would be forced out or killed. This violation of firefighting standards was a tragic error, as flames soon engulfed the aging structure and spread rapidly to nearby homes. Sixty-one homes were destroyed in the blaze, leaving two hundred and fifty residents of the neighborhood homeless. Eleven MOVE members who had been in the house at the time, including four children, were killed before they could escape the fire; only two were known to survive.

In the aftermath, it was not clear why such a cataclysm had to happen. A four-day search through the rubble uncovered one rifle, two shotguns, and three pistols. None of the automatic or semiautomatic weapons, the underground tunnels, or hidden caches of explosives rumored to have been there were found.[18]

How could this assault have been launched at the children and adults in the building at a time when they were innocent before the law? How could a major American municipality, in an attempt to respond to the needs of a residential neighborhood, drop explosives on that locality and bring about its destruction? An attempt to answer these questions requires some background on the cult itself.

MOVE emerged in the early 1970s under the leadership of Vincent Leaphart, a charismatic black third-grade dropout who made his living as a handyman. Leaphart preached an ill-defined blend of primitivism and anarchy. His group was confined to Philadelphia, with a membership that never exceeded one hundred. The impact of the group's intense cohesiveness and its commitment to its ideology, however ill-defined, soon became evident. Both served to fuel the group's *monitoring* function, which removed members from the influence of common social norms of behavior. To demonstrate their unity and common identity, the members all adopted the surname Africa. Their belief system also came to serve as the basis for a variety of idiosyncratic activities. At first they staged a series of little-noticed protests against a wide range of social institutions, from the public education system to the ill-treatment of animals in pet shops. To act on these views, the members did strange things, such as constructing a makeshift shelter for stray animals, thereby obstructing public facilities adjacent to their house; allowing their children to roam naked, eat out of garbage cans, and steal from neighbors; and throwing large quantities of refuse into their front yard.

During the years preceding the final confrontation with Philadelphia authorities, the group stopped recruiting actively, and the small coterie of members remained stable in number, drawing in more around a paranoid center. As with the Peoples Temple in Guyana, its energies were channeled into monitoring its own members. Also like the Jonestown cult, the group increasingly cut back on the feedback it would accept from the surrounding community, shielding its members from opposing views. Jones enhanced this isolation by moving to a faraway jungle; MOVE secured its boundaries by boarding up windows and doors, refusing to listen to the complaints of its neighbors, and mounting a public address system on the front of its building. Through the loudspeaker they issued angry tirades and obscenities related to the group's ideology, while allowing no response from the community. The decline in conversion efforts coupled with the restriction of community input increasingly isolated the group and prevented negative feedback that would have undercut its activities.

In its final stage, the group contributed to its own tragic fate by aggressive management of its *boundary control* function. The group was the victim of its tenacious insistence on preserving its membership and its provocative fending off of outside authority. In refusing to accept the state's prerogatives to jail its members, the group had extended its own boundary into the proper domain of civil authorities. Vulnerability at their boundary made the cult members fearful and tense, obstructive in responding to the attempt of city authorities to negotiate. MOVE members could not exercise any flexibility for they, like Jonestown cult members, had good reason to fear that an intrusion on their boundaries would bring dissolution of their bizarre social system.

It is quite common for aggression to be directed at the boundary of the charismatic group by the surrounding community, but in the case of MOVE this resulted in unbridled assault. Tensions had risen for some time, and a theme of animosity had developed between MOVE and the police, precipitated in large part by the killing of one of the police seven years before. This animosity was reflective of the society's need to protect its own boundary from deviant subgroups. Furthermore, local community groups had been protesting the presence of MOVE in their neighborhood for many months before the assault since the cult members were unwilling to respond to issues of legitimate community concern. The degree to which MOVE had set itself apart as a threatening alien group was evident in reports that the mayor's office had been developing plans for an assault on the house for eighteen months before the actual event, while police were secretly testing explosives for eventual use.[19]

Views expressed after the assault also reflected the animosity a charismatic sect can arouse when it engages in aggression across its boundary. When the Philadelphia fire commissioner was asked why his department had not responded to the raging flames at the house for a full forty minutes, even though ample equipment was in place, he replied cynically, "We're firefighters, not infantrymen."[20] Not only did city officials respond angrily, but public opinion was also rallied against the cult on the day after the assault.[21]

MOVE and the Peoples Temple show how a hostile confrontation can ensue at the boundary between a charismatic group and the surrounding community. Protective functions on both sides of the group's boundary may become intensified, leading to mutual provocation and paranoia. If neither party takes steps to defuse the situation, grave consequences can result. This vulnerability to escalating destructiveness across the boundary of charismatic groups should not go unnoticed in dealing with terrorists and nations that have turned to religious fundamentalism with a vengeance. Here, too, failed attempts to neutralize the threat they pose may only fuel their anger and their tenacious pursuit of idiosyncratic goals.

8

A RELIGIOUS SECT:
THE UNIFICATION CHURCH

The Unification Church was established in the United States early in the course of its evolution as a religious sect, at a time when intense conversion experiences and fervent commitment were reflected in the way new members were engaged. Because of this, studies of the church during this period of expansion and active recruitment offer insight into the nature of the zealous feelings that can emerge in the early stages of such sects. The church provides examples of the idiosyncrasies of a religious sect, yet it also illustrates the underlying principles governing behavior in those charismatic groups that reach some form of accommodation with the society around them.

A History of the Sect

The Reverend Sun Myung Moon, self-styled head of his own neo-Christian religion, arrived in the United States from Korea in 1972, a year after the guru Maharaj Ji had come from India. Whereas Maharaj Ji eventually relaxed his hold over his followers, Moon was tenaciously committed to maintaining close and lasting ties between his devotees and the church he founded. Because of this stance, as well as his aggressive political and financial activities, Moon became perhaps the most notorious and heavily investigated religious leader of this period.

Moon's background is partly obscured by a lack of objective sources. He was born in North Korea in 1920 and maintained that "from childhood I was clairvoyant. I could see through people, see their spirits."[1] He told his followers that as a youth, while he was praying on a mountainside one Easter morning, Jesus appeared in a vision and called on him to carry out His unfinished task, and that he later met and conversed with Moses and Buddha. Moon further avowed that during these years he discovered the "process and meaning of history, the inner meanings of the parables and symbols of the Bible and the purpose of all religions." But it is also known that Moon, as a young man, was arrested on three occasions, with reports differing about the nature of the charges. His followers insist he was being persecuted by the Communist regime for his religious commitments, while early acquaintances, as well as some of his detractors, maintain that the arrests were made for acts of promiscuity and bigamy.[2]

By the age of thirty-four, Moon, now a self-ordained minister, had moved from North to South Korea and had taken out a charter for his newly formed religious sect, the Holy Spirit Association for the Unification of World Christianity. As this group grew, Moon made the acquaintance of the authoritarian leader of South Korea, General Park Chung Hee, and although the regime imprisoned hundreds of critics during this period, including many independent clergymen, Moon's fervid anti-Communism and support for the government's policies resulted in a good working relationship with Park. Moon's business activities also began to grow, and he became board chairman of South Korean concerns as diverse as a pharmaceutical company specializing in ginseng tea and a corporation that manufactured shotguns.

This successful minister and industrialist soon considered the possibility of overseas expansion of his sect and moved first to establish a branch in Japan, where he had initial success in recruitment, particularly among political conservatives. In 1959, Moon sent missionaries to the United States. Under Young Oon Kim, an English-speaking former university professor, semiautonomous state satellites were established, and a young Princeton graduate, W. Farley Jones, named national president. The following decade, however, brought relatively little success in America. The five hundred members scattered across the country were poorly responsive to a central national leadership and the American branch of the church often operated at a deficit.

Moon himself came to the United States in late 1971 to take charge of his American church. Unlike Japan, where his movement faced considerable political and religious opposition, and Korea, where it was at the mercy of an autocratic central government, the United States offered a relative measure of security because of the First Amendment. Neil Salonen, an articulate and active man, became president of the Unification Church in the United States at age twenty-eight and was successful in establishing a firm leadership and expanding the sect's membership.

Rather generously, Salonen reported more than 25,000 American members in 1974 and more than a million members each in Korea and Japan.[3] My discussions with church officials and a review of church records with the staff at the national headquarters in America and Japan around this time could verify no more than about 7,500 American members and not many more in Japan. The American members were similar in background to those of the Divine Light Mission. Most were unmarried (91%), white (89%) young adults in their mid-twenties. Protestants (56%) and Catholics (36%) predominated, although members of Jewish extraction constituted only 8% of the group, one-third their representation in the Divine Light Mission. This disparity in figures between the two sects probably reflected the absence of a history of conflict between Judaism and Hinduism.

Changes in members' lifestyle were evident in their embrace of new sexual and marital standards. Sexual contacts among converts were prohibited, and marital choices were generally arranged at the discretion of Reverend Moon, most dramatically in two mass ceremonies.[4]

Recruits to the Unification Church were offered a fairly elaborate theology, in contrast to the ill-defined views of the Divine Light Mission and many other new religious movements. Because these beliefs differed on crucial points from Christian theology, they alienated the group from mainstream denominations to the point that reconciliation with American Christianity was impossible. The sect's religious beliefs were spelled out in the *Divine Principle,* its principal religious document, which presented an interpretation of the New and Old Testaments based on Moon's revelations.

Although members of the Unification Church do not publicly claim Moon to be the new Messiah prefigured in his doctrine, this is clearly suggested by both Moon himself and other leaders of his church. Interestingly, it was alluded to in a federal court when Moon was called to testify in a lawsuit following the attempted deprogramming of one church member. In response to questioning, he acknowledged that his followers "believe" in him, and then avowed that "I have the possibility of becoming the real messiah."[5]

In addition to promoting his distinctive religious beliefs, Moon's anti-Communism was adopted as part of the sect's reinterpretation of Christian doctrine. Moon himself entered directly into the political arena. During the Watergate investigations, he organized a media campaign to support the beleaguered President, investing $72,000 in the effort.[6] His position, as announced in his newspaper advertisements, was that "at this moment in history, God had chosen Richard Nixon to be President of the United States."[7] As the Watergate crisis was mounting, Moon brought 1,500 followers to demonstrate in Lafayette Square across from the White House. Nixon's daughter Tricia Cox and her husband mingled with the group to express their appreciation, and Moon was invited to meet with the President the next day. It was later revealed that the church had committed other resources to political activities, creating a quasiautonomous group called the Freedom Leadership Foundation to promote public relations and conservative political causes. Such political activities, however, compromised the movement's protection under the First Amendment.

Moon's overseas political ties also caused concern. It was suggested that his church had links to the Korean government through certain members, such as Moon's translator, Colonel Pak, a fourteen-year veteran of the Korean army who served as a Korean military attaché in Washington during his early days in the church. In response to rumors of a relationship between the church and the Korean CIA, a congressional investigation was undertaken by Donald Fraser, chairman of the House Sub-Committee on Internal Organizations. Although no judicial action resulted, the investigation clearly put Moon in a bad light.

Public relations became increasingly important to the church since a good public image might facilitate recruitment and minimize persecution by community groups beginning to mount campaigns against its activities. To improve its image, the church conducted a number of large-scale public events. A widely publicized rally was held in Madison Square Garden in 1974 and another two years later in Yankee Stadium to celebrate the American Bicentennial. Both drew less than anticipated attendance.[8] For another demonstration at the foot of the Washington Monument, the church spent nearly $1.5 million on the event itself and its advance publicity, but this too fell short of projected numbers. An annual conference on the Unity of the Sciences was begun in 1972, and attracted at least 25 Nobel Prize winners in the following twelve years.[9] In this venture, the sect was successful in obtaining positive press coverage while expending relatively little capital, since speakers and attendees were attracted by the leading scholars who had agreed to participate.

The sect's finances garnered considerable public attention, and whatever it gained from its public relations activities it no doubt lost through publicity over its fund-raising. Mobile fund-raising teams traveled throughout the country and raised money in public places from the sale of small specialty items such as flowers or ginseng tea. It was reported that each of hundreds of members brought in from one to five hundred dollars on an average day, usually not revealing their affiliation.[10] The church also made sizable real estate acquisitions that were heavily mortgaged and served as long-term investments. Properties such as Moon's own residence on the Hudson River, a twenty-five-acre estate purchased for $556,000, and the New Yorker Hotel in mid-Manhattan, bought for $5.6 million and used to house followers, were widely perceived as lavish acquisitions made with funds earned by impressed labor.[11]

Ultimately, public concern had to leave its mark on the movement. The Jonestown tragedy in 1978 raised questions whether Moon's group might itself pose a similar danger. Moon was the most visible of the remaining sect leaders, and further congressional inquiry into his group was undertaken. A report by the House Sub-Committee on International Organizations stated that it "had found evidence that Reverend Moon's international organization had systematically violated the United States tax, immigration, banking, currency, and foreign-agent registration laws, as well as state and local laws on charity fraud."

In 1981, Moon was indicted for filing false tax refunds. The charges stated that he had failed to report more than $150,000 of his income in a three-year period. Before indictment, Moon had apparently deposited $1.6 million in New York bank accounts in his own name and failed to report almost all the interest.[12] During the trial, Unification Church officials, with support from several mainstream religious leaders, maintained that Moon had fallen victim to religious persecution and was being charged on grounds that might have applied to other religious figures. But Moon was convicted and after an unsuccessful appeal spent eleven months in a minimum-security federal prison.[13] Even after his release in 1985, the church placed newspaper advertisements insisting that in his handling of his tax liabilities Moon was no more culpable than many other leading public figures.[14] Throughout his period of confinement, I saw no decline in commitment among long-term group members. Toward the end of this period, some church members began publishing a periodical, *The Roundtable,* that aimed for more independence of thought within the movement. This clearly reflected a weakening in the church's monolithic system of social controls, but at the same time allowed for the expression of dissent by members who were interested in reform yet committed to their church.[15]

Induction

In the Unification Church recruitment occurred in two different ways. One was open, the other was by deception. The choice in a given area usually depended on the experience of those who had assumed control over the local program. In the San Francisco Bay area, for example, a major source of recruits for the sect, the process was generally surreptitious. Potential members were approached under the guise of introducing them to an innocuous socially oriented group and only when the potential recruits became fully involved in the group were they made aware of its association with the church. On the other hand, induction workshops that I studied in the Northeast and in southern California were generally labeled clearly as activities of the church and the young people who became involved were well aware of their developing association with this sect.[16]

Two Entry Routes

During the late 1960s and early 1970s the church operated actively in the Berkeley area, since the campus was a magnet for estranged youths seeking an alternative set of values during a period of considerable social turmoil. The church concealed itself under a wide variety of names and causes capitalizing on this situation. Youths might be presented with the opportunity to join a "Creative Community Workshop" in which they were introduced to an ideology more palatable than that of the Moonies. Ecology, world peace, improved race relations were all put to use in recruitment drives.

The outside world naturally took a dim view of such deceptive practice. One father contacted me for a consultation after his son became a Moonie in this way. After completing his second year at an eastern college the young man went with a classmate to California intending to work in Yosemite Valley for the summer. On arriving by bus in Berkeley, they were met by two young women who invited them to participate in a "New Educational Development System" conducted at a house not far from the university campus. A short

while later, the son called his father to say that he and hi[...]
take a three-day workshop in Berkeley for which each w[...]
boy was not clear in describing the purpose of the worksh[...]
would be discussed there, and added to his father's s[...]
avoided specifying its exact location. In a second call two[...]
said that he did not plan to return to college, but woul[...]
on the group with which he decided to spend his year. His parents w[...] [...]
concerned but were unable to gain further access to either of the two youths.

The next contact with the family occurred after six weeks, when the young man revealed that he had just become aware that the group he was joining was in fact the Unification Church. With prodding from his parents, he acknowledged that he might have been reluctant to get involved had he known this. But its philosophy now made unassailable sense to him and he was pleased that he had been introduced to it under circumstances where his suspicions had not been aroused. When his parents asked to meet him to discuss the matter further, he declined by saying that he had to devote his time to gaining a fuller understanding of the church's religious doctrines and did not want to be disturbed while pursuing that goal. He told them that he would be leaving for a camp in the nearby Napa Valley and asked that they respect his wish and not contact him.

Some members I interviewed mentioned similar experiences. They described a situation where close attention and concern had been focused on them, a process the group's detractors called "love-bombing."[17] This elicited commitments from many young people, but revelations about the approach figured prominently in criticism of the sect. The remarkable ease with which some recruits adopted a vaguely defined philosophy in these workshops attests to how readily individuals can be made to attribute meaning to any credible, or even incredible, line of reasoning in times of uncertainty if the context is highly supportive.

Induction by subterfuge was often used to attract young people casting around for new ideas. In these cases, the appeal of a fad might be the starting point for subsequent indoctrination. Bennett, for example, was doing well as a third-year college student when he attended a two-day workshop on extrasensory perception. His previous interest in the issue had been casual, based only on the whimsical notion that "there might be some way in which people can sense each other's feelings, even without talking." Bennett did acknowledge to me several years later that he had felt a certain lack of meaning in his life at the time, and furthermore said that he could not "raise the interest" to choose a major or plan for a career.

As it turned out, the workshop was actually sponsored by the Unification Church, and the woman who spoke there related the possibilities for extracorporeal communication to opportunities for a deeper sense of religious commitment, although she gave no clue as to the nature of that commitment. As Bennett listened, he began to get a sense of the speaker's wisdom and was attracted to the "ultimate truths" the group seemed to offer. As the meeting closed, it was apparent that a number of the people there knew the speaker ell, and as Bennett asked further questions, they took a strong interest in his own willingness to discuss more thoroughly the topics raised and expressed support and affection he had not felt for some time.

This modest example of "love-bombing" was not without effect, as he readily accepted an invitation to come back for dinner the next evening. But not until three or four weeks later, after his involvement in the group had become secure, did the members tell him that they were affiliated with the Unification Church. At this point, he had already accepted the group unconditionally and saw the details of dogma they now revealed as no more than a sensible way to help him gain a better understanding of their philosophy.

These covert recruitment techniques had both advantages and disadvantages for the Unification Church. Since the sect had been widely criticized in the press as practicing "mind control" on its members, leaders were reluctant to announce the group's identity to potential recruits for fear of putting them off. In this way, the need to operate surreptitiously perpetuated itself, and certainly outraged the families of young people who joined in this way.

Officials in the church public relations office in New York, and leaders in California and Boston whose workshops were carried out in a more forthright manner, expressed considerable uneasiness to me about the impact of this approach on the public. Although they sometimes voiced concern to their superiors, they had to acknowledge reluctantly that the techniques had proven effective in recruitment. Discussions with church members from different parts of the country indicated that during the peak recruitment years of the early 1970s about half of the new members were brought into the sect by deceptive procedures like those just described. The rest came in through encounters where the group and its workshop site were clearly identified.

The open format had its own problems. Most youths approached straightforwardly refused to listen to recruiters. Furthermore, parents were generally informed of the induction earlier on and might intercede before their children became fully engaged. At the time of the Jonestown debacle, I was observing this induction procedure in anticipation of a more elaborate study. Parents of five youths attending one workshop drove a long distance to the retreat where it was held and demanded that their children return home with them. One couple brought a police officer. Although none of the participants were minors, the church leaders felt obliged to accede to the parents' demands.

The potential converts in the open workshops were young people approached in the street or on a college campus and invited to visit the church headquarters for an informal discussion or a lecture. Those who did go were next offered the opportunity to participate in a two-day program in a nearby rural setting. Their motivation was usually modest, since their familiarity with the sect was generally based on no more than a few encounters. Their understanding of the church's creed was also quite modest since it was not presented in detail until the residential workshop, but they were aware of the identity of the sect and willing to be exposed to its philosophy.

Those who participated in the two-day workshop were usually driven in a group to a secluded site on a Friday evening. A van or two would arrive at the workshop center each weekend carrying potential recruits along with the members responsible for their "witnessing," or recruitment. Other recruiters were already present along with the workshop staff. In the controlled study that I conducted, the urban headquarters were located in west Los Angeles, and the workshop center was in the San Bernardino Mountains, some seventy-five miles away. The setting was informal, but comfortable accommodations and a full complement of meals were provided.

The program for the weekend ran from eight in the morning to eleven at night. The main component was a series of ninety-minute lectures, each concentrating on major points from the Divine Principle, followed by a half hour of small group discussion that explored the meaning of these religious principles relative to the individual participants' lives. Although a certain measure of emotional involvement was expected, intense, cathartic experiences were not encouraged. The discussions tended to be intellectually oriented, as church members felt that their religious doctrine had considerable intellectual content and could serve as a major source of attraction on this count alone.

Communication was regulated in subtle but nonetheless effective ways by workshop leaders. For example, recreational activities such as singing, sports, and skits were interspersed with the lectures and discussions, but these seemingly casual functions were well structured and provided a context in which information-sharing and communication about the church took place. Conversations and ideas that did not bear on the themes under discussion were discouraged in a congenial but firm manner.

The balance between active members and nonmember recruits during the small group discussions also assured control by the leaders over the context of communication. Most exchanges took place in groups of four recruits, the four members who had invited them to join the workshop, and the designated group leader. Thus, the majority were committed to supporting the church's philosophy through either overt or covert management of communication. Under these circumstances, it was possible to suppress deviant points of view, often before they were expressed. Potential converts were therefore engaged throughout the two days in an organized agenda determined by the leadership, and designed to discourage ideas contrary to the group's perspective.

The following exchange illustrates how communications were managed in one group, although the transcription itself cannot convey the many nonverbal cues, such as a glance or frown, by which important communications were often made. The setting is a small group discussion at the workshop involving a leader, four potential recruits, and the four members who had shepherded these recruits through the initial stages of their involvement with the sect. The group had been examining a fundamental element of church doctrine that God had intended Adam and Eve to marry and bear perfect children and thereby perpetuate the "Kingdom of God on Earth." According to the Divine Principle, Eve was literally seduced by Satan and, thus tainted, brought Adam to sin as well, which made Satan a spiritual parent for all humanity. This sequence is what the church views as the original sin that led God to cast the first family out of Eden. The doctrine is difficult for a contemporary youth to accept because of its very literal interpretation of the Adam and Eve story. Furthermore, the church's retelling alters its outlines in the Bible, so that it is incompatible with the traditional Christian view. The discussion that took place after this theology lesson reflected these difficulties and showed how the church dealt with them.

One of the workshop guests, a fairly headstrong young man named Steve, expressed doubts about the literal nature of the material presented, and appeared uncomfortable, saying, "I don't understand. How can you say that the Devil actually existed and literally seduced someone?"

One church member turned to him and said, "I had trouble understanding that too. It took me quite a while to catch on, but if we don't understand the literal meaning of the Principle, well then it's just another book." By saying this, the member supported Steve in having to deal with uncertainty, but at the same time conveyed the view that his doubts were actually unfounded.

Because this member had informally played the role of an "assistant leader," over the course of the discussion, Ellen, another workshop guest, now turned to him as if he were an authority who might help her to clarify her thinking and asked, "But is it literally true?"

A second member then turned to Ellen and said, "Yes, this all becomes clearer when you understand how evil and misunderstanding are felt everywhere in the world. It's little surprise how many people have died in senseless wars over the course of history, even though people have tried to prevent them." At this point, another member added, "We lose out when we treat the Bible as a relative thing, as something that can be made into just a story." By underlining the views of the first member, these two members have therefore relieved him of the burden of arguing alone for church doctrine. The voices of three church members together have greater credibility than one, and they seem to take on the quality of a consensus. Since none of these three was the formal leader of the group, they also carried the credibility of peers rather than imposing authority as a leader. Ellen was reluctant to contradict their statements and simply said, "Oh, I see" in response.

It was probably not coincidental that the focus of the exchange had shifted to Ellen, since the church members could sense that Steve was more forceful in presenting his doubts and thus more likely to take issue with them if pressed to acquiesce to their position. The leader now looked around the group as if the issue had been resolved and turned to Ellen saying, "So you can see how it's hard to accept this bit of history at first. But later on we will see how it's a base we can build on."

In fact, Steve's doubts were later addressed by the group, but in a way more suitable to him, and that avoided confrontation. He was showered with support and affection, making it less likely that he would want to press his reservations further. The church members in his group complimented him profusely for his insight into the Divine Principle and his ability to pick up on the hardest issues to understand. In this way, a more argumentative guest such as Steve could be won over to compliance without thrashing out points of doctrine on their merits.

By Sunday night of the first weekend in these workshops, the talk turned to the choice open to those who participated. Did they wish to stay on for another workshop that would run through to the end of the next weekend or would they return home? Members were free to choose; those who left were reminded that they could come back at some other time, and many of those who left were in fact contacted again. Usually, only a minority of participants agreed to continue, but this is hardly surprising since the church had presented an unusual set of views along with the suggestion of further involvement.

In the weeklong workshop lectures and discussions were longer, with a three-hour session each morning. This was followed by an afternoon of sports, hiking, and maintenance work at the induction center. In the early evenings there were further discourses and, after dinner, further sharing among the workshop guests and members.

Guests also kept "reflection notebooks" so that they could write down their feelings about the week, sharing their thoughts with other recruits before bedtime. During these late-evening discussions, emphasis was placed by group leaders on the importance of dreams, and guests often found that they could recall their dreams much better than usual, not unlike psychoanalytic patients who are also in a setting where such recall is encouraged. The very vagueness of the dream material lent itself to interpretation by the workshop group, usually directed to support a participant's deepening commitment.

One member recalled having the following dream after four days in a workshop.

> I had fallen and hurt myself while rushing to get to my college class.
> There was a strange man nearby who said he would help me, but I felt
> I couldn't trust him because he reminded me of a neighbor I had been
> afraid of as a child. I decided to run on, hoping to find help, but was
> frightened because my arms and legs were bruised. I came to a large
> building and was given directions. I had made it to safety.

The members of the group interpreted the threatening man to be the dreamer's past sins, and the large building symbolic of the safety of the workshop center. They were no doubt trying to persuade this young recruit that the center and hence the church were a safe haven from the distress in his life. They did not speculate that the dream might have been interpreted otherwise, to represent the dreamer's fear of a disrupted life if he succumbed to the views of Reverend Moon (the stranger) and his need to escape the workshops and return to the large house in which he lived.

In any case, several members reported dreams that were seen as leading to an acceptance of the views proposed by the church. It was not uncommon for a member to say that such a dream had helped crystallize a decision to become more deeply involved.

After the second weekend of the extended workshop another decision point was reached. The remaining guests now had the option of participating in a final workshop, which meant spending two more weeks with the group. Recruits who stayed on were brought into activities that resembled those of regular members. One week was devoted to full-time recruiting and the other to fund-raising; both were usually spent in the urban center the recruits had come from.

The daily schedule during these two weeks was quite rigorous. Recruits slept in modest communal settings in the city, rising at six in the morning and spending most of the day promoting the church. Early in the morning, at midday, and late in the evening, time was set aside for prayer and lectures, as well as notebook entries.

One striking aspect of this two-week segment is the adversity faced by the recruits as they spent long hours toiling for the church. Street-corner recruiting was regularly punctuated by the derision and hostility of pedestrians and the potential recruits they approached. Fund-raising required long hours of streetside peddling. Typically, these fledgling recruits experienced very limited success or return for the effort they invested.

Because so many people whom they now encountered ridiculed the views they had just come to espouse, these recruits were forced to argue in the face of considerable opposition. Yet this seemed to enhance their emerging commitment to the sect. As we have seen, there is experimental support for the contention that argument against opposition can bind a person more closely to his or her viewpoint, even when the person had taken the position only because asked by someone else to do so.[18] In any case, participants generally agreed that the two weeks of labor for the church contributed materially toward strengthening their ties to the group.

At the end of the workshop series, the remaining participants were given the option to choose whether they would formally join the Unification Church. Those who did—only a small fraction of the initial number—were made full members, and their names given to the U.S. national headquarters in New York. They were soon assigned to a church center or mobile team at whatever location they were needed, generally at a site hundreds of miles from where they had encountered the church.

A Study of Induction Workshops

Whatever the relative political consequences of the two recruitment settings, the open workshop sequence offered a structured format whose operation and effectiveness might be studied. The church used a standard format that was systematically reproduced in a number of metropolitan areas across the country. The site for our study was the Southern California Workshop Center, because the number of "guests" there would enable me to obtain a sizable sample in a relatively short period. A new workshop sequence began each week, and all guests who entered the center over a two-month period would be evaluated. Eight workshop sequences were studied in all, including 104 guests.[19]

In framing the study I hoped to ascertain the differences between those workshop participants who joined and those who did not, and to use the

Table 8-1. *How Far into the Workshop Sequence Did the 104 Participants Continue?*

Subgroup	Stayed for	Percent of Participants	General Well-being Score
Early dropouts	1–2 days only	71%	74.7
Stayed beyond the first weekend	More than 2 days	29	67.2
Stayed beyond the first week	More than 9 days	17	—
Actually joined	More than 21 days	9	61.9
Control group	Community residents, nonmembers	—	83.4

relative roles of group cohesiveness, shared beliefs, and psychological well-being to distinguish between them. Questionnaires about these and other factors were administered on five separate occasions so that members' views could be monitored over the course of the workshop sequence. They were filled out anonymously, but each participant marked all five questionnaires with an individual code so that they could be grouped together at the end of the study.

The responses revealed no difference between the background of these recruits and the members studied previously. The workshop guests were predominantly single (94%) and white (77%), with an average age of twenty-two. Perhaps the most interesting findings about the workshop experience were the number who actually agreed to continue in the sequence at each juncture, and how many actually joined (Table 8-1). These findings are quite similar to those reported by Eileen Barker, a sociologist who studied a large sample of people who participated in similarly structured workshops in London the following year.[20]

After the first weekend, almost a third of the participants agreed to continue. Of this group, a majority stayed through the first arduous week.

As noted, participants had the option of joining the church after the full three weeks of workshop sequence. There could be little doubt that this was a major step, reflecting a commitment to enter into the uncompromising communal living situation the group offered. Nonetheless, half of those who had embarked on the final two weeks decided to join.

I was able to ascertain the status of all nine individuals who joined four months after their entry into the sect. By that time, three had already left the group. One had returned to his family overseas; another was reported to have been abducted by relatives while visiting his aunt's home on the way to another church center, and the third was said by those who knew him to have been "not serious" in his original commitment. The remaining six were still active in the church.

Altogether, after four months this sect had retained as members a total of 6% of the sample of potential recruits who had agreed to participate in the initial two-day workshop. Although this was a modest portion of those attending, it represented a considerable potential for recruitment when the times were ripe for initial engagement in the streets. Furthermore, a larger number had been more strongly influenced than they had anticipated when they volunteered for the two-day workshop and might reconsider joining at a later date.

The next step was to characterize the workshop participants who went on to join the sect. Two issues turned out to be most important in this regard: their relative emotional distress and the alienation they felt before entering. Table 8-1 shows that the psychological well-being scores of those recruits who dropped out early were considerably below those of the general population, and that the recruits who stayed longer in the induction period scored even lower. The scores of those who decided to join were lower still—actually in the clinically distressed range—confirming that the sect tended to attract people who were experiencing distress. This is all the more notable since the workshop leaders themselves screened out recruits who seemed unlikely to be able to withstand the rigors of membership for emotional reasons. Three workshop participants were asked to leave for this reason. Clearly, the Unification Church did not want to be a haven for people who would draw their own psychological stability from it without contributing much in return.

In addition to psychological distress, affiliativeness to the sect was an important discriminator between those who joined and those who did not. Recruits' feelings of social cohesiveness were measured by means of the scale described on pages 30–31. Shared beliefs were assessed with a series of items related to church creed such as "Some of the problems I see around me began with an immature use of love by the first human ancestors," and "My understanding of Jesus' mission to restore God's ideal of Creation will lead to a more meaningful life for me." Both the cohesiveness and the creed scales were completed on each of five separate occasions in the first nine days of the workshop series.

Some telling results emerged when the responses were categorized in three groups: the *early dropouts*—the 29% of the participants who left by the end of the first weekend; the *late dropouts*—the 20% who stayed after the weekend and chose not to join; and finally the 9% who *joined* at the end of three weeks. The early dropouts scored lowest on both cohesiveness toward the workshop participants and on the creed items. But no significant difference was found between the joiners and late dropouts in their scores on these items. Not only did they seem equivalent in their enthusiasm for the sect, but they developed this attachment equally early in the workshop sequence, as reflected by their scores on the repeated questionnaires.[21]

How were the late dropouts distinguished from those who finally did join? The dropouts scored significantly lower on the scale for cohesiveness toward persons *outside* the sect.[22] Lacking strong ties, they would not as readily be drawn back into the community. Those likely to join the Unification Church were unhappy young adults with limited feelings of affiliation toward friends or family who were sufficiently responsive to the group to become strongly engaged early on in the workshop sequence.

Another way of evaluating the induction experience is to see how members assessed it in retrospect. Relevant information had been solicited during our initial study of long-standing church members. Most of these active members recalled their conversion period in a positive way. As noted previously, when asked to assess their feelings on a scale of psychological distress, the overwhelming majority (91%) indicated a decline from the period before joining to the one after joining,[23] and more often than not they "felt an appreciation of the reality of God very much" (76%). Some, however, did allude to the psychological disruption of the experience, and indicated that they had encountered much more than usual conflict or unhappiness (18%) or disruption in eating (22%) and sleeping (21%). Only a few felt that they were "under someone else's influence" during the experience (12%)—a surprisingly small number, and quite telling in light of the considerable degree of group pressure actually applied during the recruitment process.

Transcendental experiences were not uncommon during conversion and many respondents reported that they had experienced the following "pretty clearly": "a special unfamiliar feeling in my body" (45%), "time passing slower or faster than usual in a very special way" (39%), and "the presence of someone important to me, even though most people couldn't have seen him" (35%). These items, however, capture only a part of the alterations in consciousness experienced during the protracted and intense group encounters included in the various conversion formats. Thus, it was not uncommon for workshop members to report the return in waking hours of dream images they had written about in their reflection notebooks. Sometimes they would perceive the presence of persons important to their religious thinking, such as Reverend Moon himself, while they participated in workshop activities.

A statement from one young woman reveals her intense feeling during the induction experience. She described the point at which her decision to join crystallized.

> I had just begun witnessing, and made the mistake of approaching a disagreeable, matronly woman who glared at me after I told her why I was speaking with her. She said, "Get away from me you little fool." I was crushed by the thought that she could dismiss everything that I wanted to express without even listening, and with a feeling of hatred at that. But my mind flashed back right then to what the workshop leader had told us just before: that we had to expect people's anger, and that this was the beginning of a path that we'd follow in God's steps. I hadn't really understood that at that time, but suddenly I knew that it was literally true, and I felt warmed by an intense feeling of faith throughout my body. Suddenly I knew I was literally in the company of Jesus and Reverend Moon themselves, carrying God's mission forward. I didn't dare

to turn around to look. It was a remarkable feeling of not being alone; they could have spoken to me if they chose to. I knew at the time that my commitment would hold fast, whatever might follow.

Family and Marital Structure

The mass engagement and marriage ceremonies of the Unification Church created some of the most memorable images of the new religious movements. In 1979 over the course of two days, 1,410 members were matched to their future spouses in a ritual engagement held in the church's World Mission Headquarters in New York. Mates had been selected by the Reverend Moon in a seemingly random fashion and appeared to have little doubt that they had indeed been provided an ideal choice of spouse. They were apparently pleased to wait patiently and endured a protracted period of engagement. Three years later, in a widely publicized ceremony, over 4,000 members were wed en masse in New York's Madison Square Garden. These events left the public incredulous over how this social rite could be so profoundly altered yet remain acceptable to young people who had grown up in the American mainstream.

I examined this process in some depth because it dramatically illustrated the way a charismatic group is knit together as a social system that regulates its members. Through it Reverend Moon was placing his own stamp on the lives of his American members and shaping their participation in the church for years to come. He could do this, however, because the marriage rituals in the Unification Church were deeply embedded in the group's ideology and its command structure. They epitomized the lockstep coordination of members within a charismatic group, who, as a rule, adopt the attitudes prescribed for them without question.

The Engagement Experience

The announcement by Reverend Moon of his plans to carry out a mass engagement was greeted with enthusiasm by church members. By this time, many of Moon's American converts had been devout followers for a decade or more and had been of an age suitable for marriage for some time. In particular, many women felt they would soon be rather old to begin a family. There was also a precedent in the movement for this unusual ritual, as mass marriages had been held by the church in Korea and in Europe.

Because of the large dimensions of the project, members applied for engagement to a church Blessing Committee; the Blessing referred to Moon's sacred wedding rituals. The requisite forms asked for very little: name, age, term of relationship. In addition, applicants were also asked whether they had been divorced before joining the sect and whether they had committed any sexual indiscretions during their term of membership. The Blessing Committee was composed of senior female members of the church, including Neil Salonen's wife. Although appropriateness for marriage was reviewed by the Committee, final decisions about some postponements were left to Salonen.

After the Committee made its decisions on eligibility, the members approved for engagement eagerly awaited notice of the matching ceremony, knowing that Reverend Moon would designate their future spouses at that time. The proclamation that Reverend Moon had decided to begin a two-day matching ceremony was made only a day or two before the event. Eligible members from around the country were told to appear at the church's World Mission Center, located in the New Yorker Hotel, a church-owned facility in midtown Manhattan. Its large ballroom could accommodate the entire eligible group at one time, if crowded together.

Moon began "matching" his assembled flock by designating several small subgroups among the applicants. He first called the black members and asked them whether they wanted to be married to persons of their own race; few of them did, since a commitment to racial integration was strongly emphasized by the movement. Moon then proceeded to match members who had volunteered to marry blacks and did the same with Orientals.

Two additional groups of members, students at the church's religious seminary and high administrative figures, were next asked if they wanted to have mates chosen within their respective subgroups or from the full body of those assembled. Finally, Moon made selections for those who were previously divorced and others over thirty-five years of age. The remainder of the crowd, the large majority of those assembled, was paired off without any designation of subgroups, in seemingly random fashion, with the assumption that the matches reflected a divine choice. Although Moon was accompanied by a member or two of the Blessing Committee in his rounds of the hall, he made all matches himself. Only a very small number of those present were paired off with someone they had known from a relationship predating the ceremony.

Those matched were allowed to speak with each other for fifteen minutes to see whether there was any reason why they might decide against becoming engaged, but needless to say, some potential spouses had problems that were not evident in the brief encounter. To remedy this, subsequent matching ceremonies were arranged so that persons with specific anomalies could be labeled as such. On later occasions, for example, members actually wore tags to this effect: "unable to bear children," "taking medications for mental illness," or "problems with homosexuality."

The following accounts of members' experiences with the engagement are quite typical, each reflecting different aspects of the psychological impact of the ritual. Nicole had joined the Unification Church twelve years before the matching ceremony at the same time as her boyfriend. The couple parted ways, since unmarried members were to abstain from all sexual relationships. When the engagement plans were announced, she had been witnessing in Boston. Along with other eligible members on her team, she made arrangements to fly to New York immediately. Within a few hours, she found herself in the hotel grand ballroom sitting toward the back of a large throng, wondering when she would be matched. Suddenly she heard Reverend Moon ask for those who had been divorced to stand up as a group, and she did so since she had been married for a short time several years before joining.

Only now did Nicole fully realize that her turn to be matched was approaching. She had consciously avoided thinking about who her fiancé might be since she felt that it would be a violation of the character of the occasion to second-guess her leader. Soon she was taken by surprise as she heard her name called. She walked calmly up to the front of the ballroom to stand next to Reverend Moon. There were so many faces in front of her that she could not distinguish them. She felt a bit dazed, and hoped only to follow Moon's wishes. As he had done many times that day, Moon turned to the audience, pointed to a man across the large room, and said, "You."

Nicole later described her initial response to her fiancé-to-be.

> I looked at him and it was like looking at my own brother, someone in my own family. Our relationship was immediately special. I sensed that he could really love. . . . It was like love at first sight. I had tested myself so much that I could accept anyone in my relations with church members. I would always find the points that I liked when I developed relationships with people in the church. . . . I'm pleased to accept what the church had offered me, and see only a happy future. I could never have doubted the choice that Reverend Moon made.

Immediately after they were matched, Nicole and her fiancé-to-be stepped aside to talk for about ten minutes and felt no reservations about each other.

The next day a ceremony was held to consecrate all the engagements. Members' callings had to be pursued, though, and since intimacy or cohabitation were not permitted during the engagement period all fiancés returned to their respective work sites, however great the separation between them might be. Thus, Nicole drove to Boston and her future husband flew to the West Coast.

Although Nicole was profoundly content, even beatific, while she described her matching to me, she still seemed to convey the specifics of her experience with reasonable accuracy. Some other members embroidered the experience, adding miraculous events to the recollections of the two days. Wally, for example, was a sensible young man who supervised repairs at the World Mission Center. I had met him on several occasions while making preparations for the Unification Church studies. He reported neither transcendental experiences nor psychiatric difficulties before joining the Unification Church, but his description of the matching included supernatural events.

Wally told me about a dream he had three days before the announcement of the matching ceremony in which he saw Reverend Moon introducing him to a young woman whose identity and even general appearance he was unable to ascertain. But he awakened the next morning "fully aware" that the ceremony was imminent. He said that the dream presaged Reverend Moon's making the best choice for him. There was no doubt for him that a divine hand led him to this premonition.

Wally recalled his experience in the ballroom while Reverend Moon was selecting a fiancé for one young woman who was standing in front of the assembled throng. Wally did not recognize her at first, but soon remembered that they had worked together briefly on a mobile fund-raising team, and that he had found her an earnest and likable person. He laughed to himself quietly, surprised at knowing her, but then perceived that the recognition was a divine signal that he would be chosen for her. Slowly, Reverend Moon looked around the auditorium and settled on Wally as the woman's mate.

Wally concluded that two divine interventions had taken place in relation to his engagement. He did not see either event as coincidental or a retrospective distortion. Such reports of presumed supernatural experiences, no doubt precipitated by the sharp sense of anticipation among members, were quite common. They illustrate the plasticity of perception and recall in the highly charged situations created by charismatic groups.

Nicole and Wally experienced the engagement somewhat differently. Nicole seemed content to be a passive recipient of a divinely inspired act, and was filled with joy by her new status. Whatever the church offered, she could accommodate. Wally, on the other hand, believed that he had predicted both the ceremony's occurrence and the identity of his spouse and hence saw himself playing a more active role in the selection process. Apparently, he took comfort from having a hand in the course of events. Both engaged members, however, shared the belief that their leader would select a satisfactory partner and did no more than adapt psychologically in their own ways to the church's expectations.

This kind of unfailing faith in Reverend Moon's choice was expressed most clearly in what members came to call the "Kodak matches," a format probably initiated because of a modest excess of male members in the United States. For these pairings, Reverend Moon matched an American man with a woman who was born in Japan or Korea and still resided there. As an aid to selection he would rely on photographs of the young women and men, since none of the participants were present. This arrangement was announced before the actual matching ceremony, and the American volunteers who were allowed to participate regarded themselves as a fortunate cadre chosen to articulate the church's goals. After Moon made the matches, the fiancées from overseas usually did not appear in the United States for months.

Six months after his Kodak match had been completed, one young man tried to explain why an engagement under these circumstances was such a good opportunity.

> I had been involved in three relationships before joining and was glad to be rid of that looseness. Not one of them had any real meaning to it beyond worldly interests. Now it was like being a pioneer and starting out anew in a new world. So I knew that this relationship would be a pure and lifelong commitment. . . .
>
> Since I joined I'd always felt that the Korean women had a very special quality about them. Most of all, they had been church members since early in their lives and could bring to a marriage the real seriousness of

religious commitment. This was the right person to start out a spiritual family modeled after Reverend Moon's.

He then took a photograph of a church-sponsored Korean dance troupe from his pocket, and proudly pointed to one of the twenty women, saying that she was his bride-to-be.

He had met her two months after the engagement when the troupe toured the United States; the couple now exchanged letters every week or two. The engagement perplexed his parents at first, but they were well disposed toward his membership since his life had improved after his conversion, when he stopped moving from city to city and using drugs heavily.

The way Reverend Moon was able to make this highly personal choice for his members cries out for explanation. In one sense, it can be seen as an expression of the church's religious creed. In another, as an articulation of the group's needs as a social system. In fact, doctrine and social function coincided in this case.

According to its theology, the Unification Church is the vanguard of a universal brotherhood that will form once its word has spread throughout the world. The church will herald the Second Coming. For this reason, the recruitment of new members, or "spiritual children," is essential to the growth of the United Family and hence to Moon's divine mission. After a new member becomes committed, he or she eventually attains the role of a perfect child in Moon's United Family. In time this "child" may qualify to join in the "sacrament" of establishing a family in the church. His own family is then modeled after Reverend Moon's perfect family, and thus brings salvation closer. This religious concept also contributes to the complete acceptance of Moon's authority over the United Family, justifying authoritarian regulation of members' lives by him and his agents.

On theologic grounds, nuclear families must be consecrated to embody Moon's messianic vision, which is much more important than any personal gratification a family may offer a couple. With regard to monitoring the membership, each couple must mesh well with the system of central figures. A couple's autonomy must not compromise the exercise of social control in any way. As sociologist Arthur Parsons has pointed out, members do not protest this unlimited power held by Moon; instead, they find repugnant any restrictions on his personal authority precisely because such limitation would pose an unwanted ambiguity.[24] In the end, the marriage is part of a tightly woven web that they must be sure to protect.

The engagements therefore draw on the forces of the charismatic group in shaping members' behavior. An intense social cohesiveness was evident in the members' pleasure in responding to Reverend Moon's call for the matching ceremony, and the virtual interchangeability of members as potential spouses demonstrated a remarkable merging of identities within the group. Their beliefs allowed them to make the leap of faith for relinquishing traditional aspects of mate selection, and to believe that their leader's choice was divinely inspired.

A Study of Engaged Members

To clarify how this sect carried out mass coupling, I wanted to undertake a study that would examine the details of the engagement ritual and its underlying psychology.[25] Permission to carry out this study was given by Dr. Mose Durst, then the sect's newly designated American President.

I began with extensive interviews of engaged members and planned to administer a structured questionnaire one year after the engagement. Four test sites would be used: two centers in New York City, one in Boston, and one in upstate New York (which included the church's religious seminary). Because church members frequently moved between cities, these centers drew on a population representative of engaged members across the country.

A number of scales from previous studies were included in the questionnaire and others were introduced. The questionnaires were completed at the end of one of the meetings required of the betrothed members, held for the purpose of discussing the engagement and planning for their future marital lives. In all, 321 of the 1,410 members matched in 1979 were studied a year after engagement.

Almost three-quarters (72%) of these participants were born in America, while 10% were Europeans and 9% Japanese, a breakdown representative of the population of the Unification Church in America at that time. Their mean age was twenty-nine and they had been members for an average of nine years. Almost all had at least some college experience (81%) and quite a few (15%) completed graduate or professional training. In summary, they were largely American-born, middle-class, educated young adults with a long-standing commitment to the church.

Respondents and their fiancés had had very little contact during the year after the engagement ceremony—a sign of the sect's effectiveness in abrogating conventional norms of engagement behavior. Only a small minority (16%) lived within a mile of their future mates, and many (42%) were separated by more than five hundred miles. Over a third (38%) had not seen their partners during the previous two months. Sexual contact between fiancés was strictly forbidden, an injunction scrupulously observed according to all reports.

Most salient in the disruption of conventional engagement practices however, was how members experienced the elimination of their independent choice in mate selection, since Reverend Moon had determined all matches on his own. Almost a third of the men (30%) had been paired in the Kodak matches to Japanese and Koreans, and a large majority (87%) of the respondents indicated that they had felt no preference at all for a particular individual before the matching ceremony. This fit in well with the attitudes expected by the leadership, and reflected the ability of the church to suppress the natural curiosity and personal desires of the members.

A modest remaining number reported they had felt some preference for a specific mate before they were matched. Of those who did, a minority (4% of the total) said they *had* been matched to the person they hoped for. Most of these had probably petitioned the Blessing Committee to allow Reverend Moon to match them with a particular member, but it is also possible that some decided after the fact that the fiancés chosen for them were indeed the ones they always wanted. The remainder (9% of the total) also reported that they had actually felt a preference for a particular fiancé but had not been paired with the one they preferred.

The general well-being scores of the members who had Kodak matches (30% of the men) and of those who did not get their preferred choice were not different from the scores of other respondents.[26]

A small number (3%) indicated that they were contemplating ending their engagement. These members about to break a major commitment made through the church had lower well-being scores than the balance of the group, falling within the range of clinically significant distress.[27] Clearly, they were not unaffected by the psychological consequence of disrupting the engagement, though their ties to their fiancés must have been minimal.

Current sociologic thinking about mate selection emphasizes traits that individuals consider desirable in a spouse. Marital choices are believed to be determined by a market economy of sorts, a tacit decision-making process in which the marketable assets of potential husbands and wives are entered into a calculus of relative desirability.[28]

In line with this, I included seven traits commonly felt to be important in a prospective partner, such as "sufficiently intelligent for you," and "looks attractive to people." Seven additional spouse traits related to the values of the church were also included, such as "can convey the church's spiritual values to your children" and "is profoundly committed to the Divine Principle." Each of the fourteen spouse traits was scored by the respondent in terms of how the person saw its relative importance in a potential spouse. Remarkably, *all* the Unification Church items were ranked higher than the "secular" traits. The members had moved far away from the value system of the general public in their thinking about marriage. Their responses suggest that they would be fairly content with Moon's selection, and they raise the question of what mechanism might underlie such pervasive conformity.

To answer this question, I tested two hypotheses by means of scales included in the questionnaire. The first one drew on observations made in the general population, namely, that a person's psychological well-being is adversely affected by disruptive life events such as moving or losing a job. I hypothesized that the engaged church members were similarly vulnerable to disruptive life events, including those relative to their life in the church.

Second, I hypothesized that the emotional distress caused by such events in the life of the sect member would be muted by the relief effect operating in charismatic sects. That is, the distress caused by these events would be countered by emotional support derived from a member's commitment to the sect: the more closely the person felt affiliated, the more he or she could place disruptive experiences in the perspective of the sect's beliefs and thereby avoid a sense of hopelessness and despair.

One scale developed by Thomas Holmes and Richard Rahe[29] has been widely used to assess the incidence of forty common disruptive events in a person's life; it was a convenient measure for my study. Typical items are "experienced a major personal injury or illness" and "began or ceased formal schooling." I tailored the scale to the experiences of church members by adding thirteen additional events such as "a major change in your method of witnessing," and "attended a church workshop."[30]

Altogether, members experienced about the same number of disruptive life events as a normative population, but the *relationship* between these events and the group experience was most revealing. My first analysis revealed that these disruptive life events predicted a small portion (15%) of the variability in members' well-being scores; thus, church members reacted like other population groups in their vulnerability to the psychological effects of disruptive life experiences. A second analysis, on the other hand, included items reflecting members' feelings of affiliativeness toward the church (cohesiveness and shared beliefs) as predictors of emotional well-being in an attempt to assess the degree to which attachment to the church affected members' general well-being. The life events and affiliation items together predicted an appreciable portion (31%) of the variability in members' well-being scores.[31] This supported the notion that sect affiliation acts as a buffer against the effects of disruptive life events: disruptive life events detracted from members' well-being while affiliative feelings enhanced it. Members not only experienced psychological well-being in direct proportion to the intensity of their affiliative feelings for the church, but they also enjoyed a corresponding relief from the depressive effects of those disruptive events.

From studies on operant conditioning we learn that such emotional rewards (or reinforcement) lead animals and people to persist in the behavior that brought about the reward. The emotional support they receive in unsettling circumstances reinforces members in their commitment to the sect and obedience to its authority.

Members' compliance with the engagement ritual parallels their malleability in all other areas of conduct. They accept what they are told because they have been conditioned to stay closely affiliated with the church. A long history of operant reenforcement of compliance prepares the members for accepting or rationalizing whatever is asked of them by the leadership. In this case they discarded their conventional views of marriage and rationalized their acceptance of Reverend Moon's choice.

Other models of group conformity are relevant in understanding the impact of the church on long-established behavior patterns such as marital engagement rites. One compelling example is found in studies on obedience to authority. Stanley Milgram[32] has shown that in certain settings people can easily be induced by an authority figure to perform acts that conflict with their usual values, even to the point of harming innocent people. Milgram solicited volunteers for what were actually sham experiments, carried out in a seemingly legitimate psychology laboratory. Typically, the volunteer was instructed by the "researcher" to help condition a second subject played by an actor by administering electric shocks in a study on learning. As the experiment progressed, the volunteer was expected to give the learner subject increasingly strong electric shocks—the volunteer was not aware that the shock was simulated. Most volunteers inflicted the shock without questioning the propriety of the undertaking, even when it appeared to cause considerable pain to the learner subjects. These were ordinary people, yet they followed the rules set down by the experimenter's authority without being constrained by the values they presumably held.

Milgram's sham experiment illustrated the degree to which individuals will comply with authority when its role in the management of a situation is assumed to be unimpeachable. His experimental setting was similar to the engagement ceremony in that both were managed by an authority figure who was sanctioned to set standards of behavior.

Cognitive dissonance theory is another body of research that can contribute to our understanding of the Moonie engagement. This theory has shown how individuals cannot easily dismiss a belief or attitude they hold, even when the attitude is directly contradicted by evidence or events. People will sooner adopt far-fetched ideas to explain events than relinquish their preconceptions.[33] In so doing, they avoid having to face the dissonance between what they see and what they have long believed. The dismissal of plain reality can happen when people are confronted by challenges to their ingrained patriotism, their prejudices, or their religious values. Under these circumstances, they may ignore cruelty, hypocrisy, or incompetence, or create elaborate rationalizations rather than challenge the principles espoused by their leaders. Thus, church members not only accepted the validity of Moon's deviant method of engagement, but also developed rationalizations to sustain it. For example, they took its peculiar nature as evidence of the divine inspiration of their leader, rather than as a reason to question his judgment. To have questioned it would have shaken the foundations of their religious beliefs.

The Marriage

After the mass engagement, time passed with no announcement of a marriage ceremony—with no clear reason announced. Three full years elapsed until Reverend Moon finally announced the ceremony that would bring together in a lifelong matrimony most of his American members. Madison Square Garden in New York was the site for the event. Thirteen hundred members who did not yet have fiancés but had been members for the requisite three years were brought together a week before the wedding ceremony and matched off by Moon. One hundred fifty Japanese women were flown in just days before the wedding to balance the number of mates in this group.[34]

When the day of the ceremony arrived, members who were to be married dressed in identical outfits, as if to flaunt their conformity before those who insisted that the church made automatons of its members. The 2,075 brides all wore Simplicity Pattern #8392 with the neckline raised two inches to preserve their modesty; the grooms wore dark blue suits and maroon ties.[35] In addition, 6,000 parents, friends, and guests were gathered in the vast auditorium to witness the ceremony. These people displayed a wide variety of attitudes: some smiled, some were bewildered, others were in tears. The assembled relatives were far from unanimous in their approval. A sister of one of the brides said of the wedding, "That man has caused more heartache in my family and everybody else's than anybody I can think of. My mother can't even talk about it without crying."[36]

Strains of Mendelssohn's "Wedding March" played serenely during the ceremony, and a triumphant note was struck at its close when participants linked their arms together after the Reverend's blessing and shouted, "Mansei!" (eternal victory). In ironic contrast to his role of heavenly matchmaker at this event, Moon had been convicted for tax fraud in federal court only six weeks before, and was facing sentencing in two weeks. The marriage epitomized many contradictions inherent in the rise of this new religious movement, but in terms of the sect's religious doctrine, it symbolized the fruition of Moon's messianic mission.

As the ceremony came to a close, members began a "separation period" during which sexual relationships were still not allowed, a period that would end a half year later, and then only if each spouse had brought into the church three new members. For most of those engaged in the original matching ceremony whom I had studied, the end of the separation was "only" six months away. For others matched later, it would continue for years. Yet most members adapted to the whole experience with relatively little difficulty, as the following examples indicate.

Ed was born in the Midwest and was thirty-seven years old when I interviewed him a year after his marriage. He had joined the Unification Church twelve years before while in graduate school at a large state university. Noreko, nine years his junior, was the woman he married. She had come to the United States several years before from her native Japan at the behest of the church, having joined the sect while working in a factory owned by one of its Japanese members.

At the matching ceremony Ed volunteered to be paired off with an Oriental member because he felt they best embodied the principles of the church; he recalled being "immediately fully pleased" with his fiancé when she was selected by Reverend Moon. The couple was separated right after the ceremony, however, as their church missions were located several hundred miles apart. They wrote to each other frequently, but only visited each other several times before the blessing. Ed did not find this unusual and stressed that he had busied himself with the work of the church during this period.

Ed's parents refused to speak to him when he first joined the sect, but after he had been a member for three years, they initiated some contacts, and there were more exchanges after the marriage. Ed explained:

> They were very negative when I joined and saw me as the black sheep in the family, as if I would amount to nothing, never working at a regular

job, never giving them any grandchildren. My sister and brother, on the other hand, had done nicely for themselves as far as my parents were concerned, and had all settled down not far from home. . . . My marriage softened my parents up. They seemed to think that maybe I will "do something" for myself now and become a family man. They didn't even seem to mind that my wife wasn't an American; I think they were just relieved.

The improvement in his family's response could be attributed in part to his participation in the sect's home church movement. After the separation period, several hundred members who volunteered for this movement began to live together, each couple in its own separate dwelling, generally not far from church centers. These couples would regularly touch base with the movement by attending church services and religious meetings, but were responsible for the management of their households. It was hoped that each of these families by way of example would interest nonmembers from their community in the church.

These members acquired a certain amount of autonomy in managing their affairs; nonetheless, the home church carried with it the monitoring function of the larger sect since important decisions were always made in close consultation with the couple's "central figure," the local religious leader who coordinated their religious and secular pursuits. A central figure would usually be the leader in a work setting, such as a fund-raising team, an administrative office, or a business establishment. Married couples were usually placed jointly under the leadership of the same central figure so that their mutual needs could be aligned with those of the church.

When Ed and Noreko turned to their central figure for consultation on the appropriateness of moving into a home church, there was an extended discussion of their ability to deal with the responsibilities they would have to assume. For the first time in more than a decade they would need to maintain an independent bank account, manage a budget for rent and groceries, and organize all their household duties. Ed admitted to a certain trepidation about leaving the fold, while at the same time expressing optimism about this new challenge.

Noreko, who spoke English well, described her reaction to this major transition, which entailed moving out of the church headquarters in mid-Manhattan.

> We were so happy at first to move into the World Mission Center after the separation period, and have our own home together. We had one room with a bath. It used to be a hotel room. We ate all our meals in the main dining room with the other brothers and sisters, but six months ago we asked our central figure if it would be wise to plan on moving into a home church, and he said we were ready. After we all discussed this, he suggested I take a job that would help Ed and me save for our own apartment and I began to work as a secretary. At first, I felt like a stranger at work because I was separated from my brothers and sisters

Charismatic groups that live communally go back in history. In the 1860s, elders of the Oneida Community in upstate New York dictated the marital choices of members. (THE BETTMANN ARCHIVE)

Fundamentalism persists as an influential, intense religious tradition in the United States. Rock music records are smashed here at the First Pentecostal Church of Saluda, South Carolina. (UPI/CORBIS-BETTMANN)

Contemporary awareness of the danger of cults dates back to 1969 in California when Charles Manson and his followers brutally murdered eight innocent people. Their small cult involved a mix of LSD and religious delusion. (UPI/CORBIS-BETTMANN)

Maharishi Mahesh Yogi initiated the popular Transcendental Meditation movement, and founded Maharishi International University in Iowa. His adherents claimed that TM lowered blood pressure, and that its practice could bring on world peace. (ARCHIVE PHOTOS/ EXPRESS NEWSPAPERS)

More than 900 people died in Jonestown, Guyana of cyanide poisoning. Jones ordered the mass suicide after members of his group killed a U.S. Congressman who had gone there on a fact-finding mission. (UPI/CORBIS-BETTMANN)

This picture of Jim Jones giving a Black clenched-fist salute was found in Guyana at the site of his cult's 1978 mass suicide. It was likely taken in San Francisco where he used to preach. (UPI/COR-BIS-BETTMANN)

Members of MOVE, a Philadelphia Black political sect, address a crowd in front of their barricaded communal residence in 1978. Days later, the police, unable to silence them, dropped percussion bombs on the house, causing a fire that killed 11. (UPI/BETTMANN)

Shri Rajneesh set up a communal cultic ashram in Antelope, OR. He was deported from the United States in 1985, and two followers were convicted of conspiracy to kill an attorney who had investigated their group. (REUTERS/SPIROS MANTZARLIS/ARCHIVE PHOTOS)

Richard Alpert (later Ram Dass), and Timothy Leary experimented with hallucinogen-induced altered consciousness at Harvard, and lost their faculty positions in 1963. (UPI/CORBIS-BETTMANN)

Leary later became a "high priest" of LSD use. He popularized altered consciousness within the cultural mainstream, and established it as a means of achieving transcendence. (UPI/CORBIS-BETTMANN)

The Guru Maharaj Ji was 6 when he began preaching in India, and came to the United States at age 13. He is pictured here with his American wife under the image of his father.

The author pictured here at the site of his first study on cultic groups in 1974 in Orlando, Florida. He worked out an agreement with the hierarchy of the Guru Maharaj Ji's Divine Light Mission.

Maharaj Ji's followers at the Orlando festival eagerly await his appearance. Surprisingly, they looked no different from most college-age youth of the time.

The Unification Church is led by the Korean-born Rev. Sun Myung Moon, who is pictured here with his wife. In the 1970s and '80s, his followers, "Moonies," recruited thousands into communal residences in the United States and overseas. (REUTERS/ARCHIVE PHOTOS)

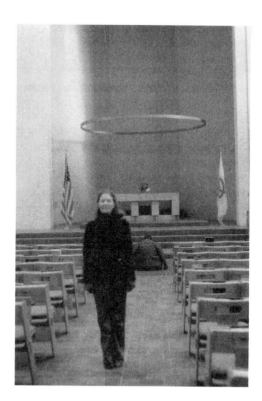

Moon's Director of Public Relations stands in the chapel of the sect's seminary in Barrytown, New York. After the author secured an agreement with the Church to conduct a research study, she was authorized to serve as liaison.

Moon arranged marital matches between his followers. The author studied their reactions after their engagement and then followed up a year after their 1982 mass wedding. (UPI/CORBIS-BETTMANN)

David Koresh, a Bible-quoting, folk-singing, high-school dropout, established tight control over members in his Branch Davidian commune in Waco, Texas. (REUTERS/HO/ARCHIVE PHOTOS)

In 1993, government tanks shooting tear gas broke into the Davidian compound after a 51-day stand-off. Over 80 died in the ensuing firestorm. (REUTERS/CORBIS-BETTMANN)

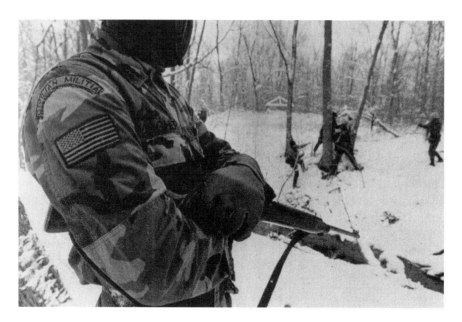

Many right-wing separatists believed that the Waco disaster portended a government attack on their own compatriots. Here armed members of the private paramilitary Michigan Militia train for an assault that they might suffer. (AGENCE FRANCE PRESSE/CORBIS-BETTMANN)

In 1995, two years to the day after the Waco firestorm, Timothy McVeigh bombed a federal office building in Oklahoma City, killing 168. He had visited the Waco standoff and was involved with the Michigan Militia. (REUTERS/JIM BOURG/ ARCHIVE PHOTOS)

Iran was consumed by charismatic religion under the Ayatollah Khomeini. In the 1980s his zealous nation sent unarmed children on suicide assaults against Iraqi heavy armor as a ticket to heaven. (UPI/CORBIS-BETTMANN)

Marshall Applewhite was a choir conductor and music professor. He met Bonnie Lu Nettles, a nurse, and she left her husband to join him on the road. They established the Heaven's Gate cult in pursuit of spiritual enlightenment. (AP/WIDE WORLD PHOTOS)

The Heaven's Gate cult used videos and a Web Site to recruit new members. After Nettles died, Applewhite had himself castrated in line with suppression of sexuality in the cult. (REUTERS/CBS EVENING NEWS/ARCHIVE PHOTOS)

The coming of the Hale-Bopp comet signaled the Heaven's Gate group to undertake mass suicide in 1997. Thirty-nine bodies were found on their rented estate outside San Diego, CA. Each was draped in a purple shroud and wore black Nike sneakers. (AGENCE FRANCE PRESSE/CORBIS-BETTMANN)

Shoko Asahara went from an arrest for selling fake herbal drugs to heading Aum Shinrikyo, a multinational cult based in Japan. The cult perpetrated kidnappings and murders while preaching Buddhist tolerance. (AGENCE FRANCE PRESSE/CORBIS-BETTMANN)

Japanese police wearing gas masks raided Aum's buildings after cult members killed 12 and injured hundreds in a 1995 poison gas attack at a Tokyo subway station. (AGENCE FRANCE PRESSE/CORBIS-BETTMANN)

L. Ron Hubbard, the founder of Scientology, was a science fiction writer. Here he is using the "E-Meter" to determine whether tomatoes suffer pain. The meter is now used for psychologically "clearing" the group's members. (ARCHIVE PHOTOS/EXPRESS NEWSPAPERS)

One type of spiritual recovery movement involves liberating oneself from one's hang-ups. Marianne Williamson, speaker and author, combines popular psychology and Twelve Step-related affirmations. (LYNN GOLDSMITH/CORBIS)

Eastern healing has been used to give Western medicine a spiritual complement. Deepak Chopra, M.D., a charismatic author and television personality, has attracted media figures like Demi Moore, Laura Day, and Donna Karan. (M. GERBER/CORBIS)

After a family encounter with cancer, Bernie Siegel, M.D. came to believe that "exceptional cancer patients" have the capacity to influence the course of their own illness. (LYNN GOLDSMITH/CORBIS)

Bill W., founder of AA, promulgated the concept that faith in God can help the alcoholic achieve recovery. Always respectful of a scientific approach as well, he is pictured here with alcoholism researcher E. M. Jellinek.

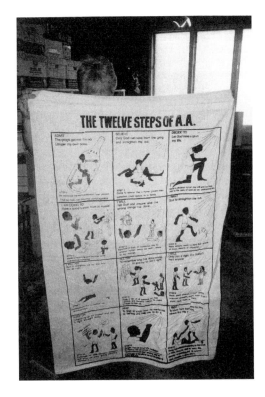

AA's success has gained it millions of adherents worldwide. A counselor in a health center in the Australian outback holds up a Twelve Step banner with pictographs and Aboriginal pidgin English.

all day, but this way Ed and I could save the money I earned to set up our own apartment.

We just now took a place on Staten Island about an hour from the Center, and we're trying to juggle the bills, relying on my salary and the small amount of money that Ed gets from the church for his work at the printing plant. It isn't easy, but our home is not just an apartment; it is a sacred part of the church. Our marriage there gives us a chance to belong to the perfect family. It is a very beautiful place for us both.

In this case, the expectations of the church and the natural inclinations of its members operated in concert. Both Ed and Noreko were comfortable with the mythology underlying the sect's marital ritual and also had no material difficulty adjusting to their marital relationship. Because of this, and because they saw their central figure understanding their needs, the structure binding them to the sect operated smoothly.

The home church movement represented one phase of the sect's evolution, reflecting a change in perspective on the part of Reverend Moon. During the period preceding the mass marriage, the church had become somewhat looser in its management of individual members, and tight coordination of daily habits became less common. Members living in the same residence no longer awakened each other for morning communal prayers; some began to keep their own checking accounts and acquire modest personal effects. The home church movement was part of this transition in which Moon was pressing members to complete their schooling or acquire a trade so that they might advance themselves. Many members were now trying to complete their college courses or continue the graduate training they had abandoned before joining.

Several months after the wedding ceremony, though, Reverend Moon announced a project for recruitment of new members, the International One-World Crusade (IOWC). Although such initiative had been mounted before, this one was to be conducted on a massive scale. Participants in previous campaigns were organized into teams of 25 for each state; in this new crusade 250 teams were formed, each with eight members, for a total of 2,000 participants, nearly twice as many as before. More than a third of the members married in the Madison Square Garden ritual joined the teams.

A call was made by Reverend Moon for all members to participate in the IOWC; those who complied were extolled for their commitment, while those who refused were expected by their central figures to have an acceptable excuse. The IOWC was mounted with great publicity among the membership, with articles in successive issues of *Unification News*, the church's nationwide newspaper for its members. Maps showing where mobile teams were located at any given time were published with updated reports on their activities. It soon became obvious that the numbers of new recruits hoped for in the campaign were not forthcoming, most likely because the country's youth, in a period of conservative good feeling and self-interest, were no longer so inclined to depart from the mainstream. The teams were redirected to fundraising activities in the streets, and many were later sent back to their old locales and expected to begin work and family life anew.

The entire undertaking was highly disruptive for the sect, and complaints were acknowledged even by the church. In the *Unification News*, descriptions of the IOWC written for other members by recruiters in the field reflected this.

> Have you ever experienced a situation that could only be described in accurate terms as "Hell"? The state of total absence of God's love, a place of secret enemies or complete dislike of another person? I am now confessing that I have had all these experiences during my time on IOWC.

This course of events was highly distressing to the members because they were dislodged from residential or marital arrangements they had earned, so to speak, by their long and faithful years of service to the church. They also had to accept a major upheaval in their occupational roles to solicit funds in the mobile teams. For those who had become ensconced in more comfortable positions, this was a difficult and embarrassing shift to make after years of advancement in the church hierarchy. Several married members became disillusioned and even left the church. The large majority, however, managed to regroup their energies of zealous commitment. Open criticism of the church itself was rarely expressed.

Sarah, a married IOWC participant with whom I spoke around this time, revealed the strength of the monitoring structure in resuscitating members' ebbing devotion.

> What was hardest about going on the IOWC was that I began to mistrust my husband, and even the sanctity of our marriage. I felt that he was rejecting me when he let me go off at the time. I ruminated about it for weeks as our team moved from city to city, at first recruiting, and later selling flowers on street corners. And it was hard to feel comfortable and secure, but when I came back, luckily we had an understanding central figure who was able to speak with Larry and me about my confusion. Over a few months he pointed out how my own problems in accepting my mission should not interfere with my understanding of the marriage as a sacred ritual, and not a secular project.

Sarah's counseling experience also suggests a similarity between the role of the sect's central figures and that of the mental health professional in stabilizing members' social adaptation. Both caregivers must interpret social values to troubled individuals, and both to some degree are given the prerogative of adapting these values to the individual's needs. When Sarah's central figure pointed out the way she must accommodate her feelings to the marital and fund-raising practices of the church, he wore the mantle of someone presumed to understand the broader social and religious issues underlying the needs of a troubled person. In like fashion, the contemporary mental health practitioner is perceived by clients as understanding general principles whose application will help resolve their own psychological conflicts. Faith healers, of course, are also accorded such roles within their cultures.

The central figure's importance in resolving conflicts related to the Moonie marriage is clear-cut in the case of Calvin, a member who was beginning to acknowledge his homosexual orientation before he joined at the age of twenty-three. His inclinations were morally unacceptable to the sect, and he ultimately adapted to the church's marital ritual.

When I spoke with him nine years later, Calvin said that his decision to join the church was prompted by the "idealism it offered, and the alternative it provided people to a constant obsession with sex." But it also appeared to offer him a release from conflicts over his own sexual orientation.

Calvin had not dated members of the opposite sex before joining but had been regularly preoccupied with homosexual fantasies. In addition, he had initiated several homosexual encounters with strangers, and recalled with distress that he knew he was "sure to move into a gay life, sooner, or later." When he first met members of the church, he was living in a neighborhood largely populated by single people whom he felt were more socially active than he. He was moderately depressed, and neither able to relate to the heterosexual community nor accept a gay identity. The anxiety caused by this conflict abated after his conversion because, as he said, "faith in Reverend Moon and the support of my brothers and sisters relieved me of these sinful ideas."

After several years of membership, Calvin had only occasional homosexual ideation. But then he experienced one distinct episode of attraction to a male church member, which made him anxious again. For solace and guidance, he turned to his central figure, discussed his concerns in depth, and accepted his mentor's religious homilies.

When the opportunity arose for members to apply for the matching, Calvin "decided not to worry" about the problems that might be raised by his history of sexual confusion, telling himself that Reverend Moon's involvement in the choice of his fiancé would help resolve this problem. He felt that the "strength of the church" would be bestowed on him through the blessing ceremony, thereby allowing him to live according to its creed.

The separation period that followed the engagement placed little pressure on Calvin with regard to a heterosexual relationship since his spouse was living several hundred miles away, but when the time came for the consummation of their marriage four months later, Calvin demurred, explaining that he felt the time for physical intimacy was not yet at hand. In fact, such requests were not uncommon among the newly married couples because a variety of interpersonal issues often had to be worked out before couples felt comfortable with each other. But Calvin was frightened by the thought of sexual relations with his wife, even though he felt quite warmly toward her, and was very enthusiastic about the marriage as a Unification Church sacrament.

He turned to his central figure several times over the next three months and on his advice moved into a room with his wife and began to share his bed with her. He recalled the experience a year later.

> It's not that I didn't want sexual relations, but the idea made me very uneasy. After I spoke with [my central figure], I learned to keep my mind on the church's idea that our union is part of our faith, and not a matter

> of outright sex, and soon the fear lessened. I think it worked out because
> I knew that we were part of a sacred family and not just partners in the
> flesh.

Calvin spoke of successfully completing sexual intercourse on several occasions in the following months, and added with pride that the couple's prayers for a pregnancy were soon met. He denied having any homosexual preoccupations since the time of the matching, over four years before.

Through the close collaboration between Calvin and his central figure, this charismatic group was able to produce a long-term change in behavior in someone whose natural sexual inclinations ran counter to church doctrine. Calvin's central figure shaped his individual needs, initially deviant in the church subculture, into a sexual adaptation that was acceptable to him and to the group. This change in sexual behavior is a striking example of the power of focused social influence.

Calvin's case highlights the difference between voluntary compliance in a charismatic group and coerced conformity in an authoritarian context. If Calvin had not been fully committed to the group's value system, his overt behavior might have been controlled but his fantasies and desires would likely have remained as before. The forces of intense cohesiveness and shared belief, rather than the overt threat of an authoritarian regimen, allow for such effective shaping of individuals' behavior within a cult.

Married Members: A Follow-up Study

The opportunity for a follow-up study of the engaged church members was extraordinary. For the social scientist, the entire sequence of engagement to strangers, waiting period, and marriage had the quality of a grand experiment of nature, as if a remarkable research manipulation had been carried out on thousands of unsuspecting subjects. An extensive questionnaire was mailed to all the original subjects who could be located four years after the original engagement survey and a year after the mass marriage. These members' responses provided further evidence of their tenacious commitment to the church: almost all were still active, and the large majority were currently married to a fellow church member (Table 8-2). Only a small number were either breaking up their marriages or had never been married at all.

Members' commitment to the church view of the marriage was still staunchly upheld. They were asked to evaluate the relative importance of fourteen assets in a fiancé, the same ones used in the original study. Again, the seven traits related to the church's religious values all ranked higher than the others that mirrored values held important in the common culture. Traits in a spouse such as "willingness to sacrifice personal needs and comfort for the church" still ranked higher than practical ones such as the ability to "contribute successfully to your economic support or to skilled homemaking."

The deviant nature of the marriage, evident in the couples' cohabitation practices, may help explain this finding. Most respondents (65%) were still in

Table 8-2. *The Original Sample of Engaged Members, Four Years Later*

Documented active in the church	93%
Married to a fellow member 85%	
Never married 1%	
Married and broke up 6%	
Dropped out	4%
Not located by mail, church records, or contacts	3%

the ritual separation period, and had yet to have sexual relations. In fact, many (38%) lived as far as five hundred miles away from their spouses, and less than half (48%) reported that they had spent a single night in the past two weeks in the same building as their spouses.

Not surprisingly, the role of the church was prominent in shaping members' plans for childbearing. Conception was encouraged among all those who had completed the separation period, and at the time of the follow-up a sizable number of couples already had a pregnancy or birth (24%). Since the separation period continues until both spouses have converted three new members, however, most remaining members (45% of the respondents) could not plan for children because they had not yet brought in a sufficient number of recruits.

The questionnaire had also been constructed to assess the impact of the church's control over members' psychological state. To this end, it included a list of experiences related to the marriage, all initiated by the church leadership. Typical experiences were "leaving your spouse for more than a week on church business," and "establishing a home church."[37] To assess the impact of these events on members' general well-being, the questionnaire asked if they had experienced any in a disagreeable manner. The questions were so framed because of recent evidence that life events with a perceived negative impact have a pathogenic effect on individuals' mental health.[38]

Did marital events determined by the church, if viewed negatively by members, also have a deleterious impact on their well-being? Furthermore, would members' affiliative feelings for the church mute this negative impact? An analysis of their responses revealed that an appreciable portion of the variance in their general well-being could, in fact, be predicted by the extent that they perceived church-related marital events as being undesirable (14% of the variance), and even more could be predicted by the combination of affiliative feelings and life event scores (32%).[39]

These statistical results suggested that specific life experiences engineered by this sect could produce a diminished sense of psychological well-being. Significantly, though, the members' commitment to the church buffers this distress by enhancing their well-being. Thus, one member of a newlywed couple might be sent off to a remote point on a fund-raising mission. The couple's faith in the church, however, buffers them from this church-imposed stressful event. These two phenomena, the creation of distress and its buffering, together create a *pincer effect* in the following way: The members implicitly sense that relief from distress is provided by their bond to the sect, and turn to the sect for solace when faced with disruptive life experiences. Ironically, their resulting compliance with the sect's dictates leads them to further conformity to its potentially disruptive demands. The sect thereby creates distress at the same time it relieves it—and at the price of further compliance.

Leaving the Sect

The way members leave a charismatic group can be as revealing as how they join. In a sect where the need to remain bonded is so compelling, departure entails rejection of the transcendent mission ascribed to the leader and carries a burden of soul-searching and guilt. As with induction, the full force of the charismatic group may be brought to bear on individuals.

Members left the Unification Church in two different ways: voluntary separations and deprogramming. Most people who left reached the decision over a period of time while continuing to live within the fold of the church. Deprogramming, or forcible removal, was much less common but received much more publicity.

Voluntary Dropping Out

A member's decision to leave the Unification Church reflects malfunction in the monitoring role of the church, as the member's disillusionment arises from the inability of member and sect to sustain mutual understanding. The members' experiences illustrate the complex circumstances that can lead to such a "failure" in the system's operation.

One member's ostensible motive for leaving was his loss of faith in the church and his own mission, but it can be seen how the monitoring system of the sect failed to sustain his commitment. Armand had been working for two years as a copy editor at *Newsworld*, a general-circulation New York newspaper operated by the church, and had taken great pride in his contributions to the sect's impact on the media, since he believed that the paper was doing an important job in conveying both the news and Reverend Moon's message. As frequently happened in the church, Armand was transferred to a new work setting, and stationed several hundred miles from *Newsworld* headquarters. The young man eagerly immersed himself in his new assignment of witnessing, since he felt that bringing new members into the church was also of utmost value. The recruitment methods practiced in this region were open; potential converts were informed from the outset that they were being introduced to the Unification Church. Within a few months, though, a new central figure, a native Japanese, was appointed to the team, and its mission changed from recruitment to fund-raising. Armand found that this new leader was less open in his dealings with the public, as was common for Oriental-born church functionaries. Unlike previous central figures, he was a person Armand could not fully respect. Furthermore, "heavenly deception" was now a prominent theme in conducting the team's affairs, wherein it was acceptable, even laudable, to mislead nonmembers when necessary to promote the church's goals.

Armand soon found himself quarreling with the team's leader about matters of strategy. He insisted that the degree of deception practiced ran contrary to the principles of the religion to which he was committed, and that a straightforward approach would be more effective in raising funds. In particular, he balked at not revealing fund-raisers' identification with the Unification Church and their aggressive door-to-door sales techniques.

On one occasion Armand went so far as to telephone the central figure to whom he had reported while working at *Newsworld* and voice his reservations about the team's operation, hoping for a sympathetic hearing. Much to his mortification, he was told that it was not for him to question the principles of the church.

Armand recalled:

> I was made to feel like a bad person for speaking honestly. He even said that God would not be with me, and here I had trusted him and was sure he would understand. But I wasn't about to go on sneaking into stores, lying about the permits we were supposed to have, and believing that the ends justify the means. . . . I was angry and hurt, but I also began to feel very guilty, as if I were abandoning the church. I began losing sleep, not caring what happened.

A month after the telephone exchange with his former mentor, Armand, in a state of disillusionment, moved out of a church center where the group was temporarily staying and returned to his parents' home, which he had left five years before when he had joined the sect. Ironically, he had ignored numerous pleas made by his parents that he leave the church because of its alleged abuse of its members.

Armand's parents spoke with me at this point and reported with distress that he was now removing himself from social contact and spending all his time in his room, lying in bed. Furthermore, they said that he had lost much weight in the few weeks since his return, that his mind was "always somewhere else," and his gaze "vacant." They feared he would not be able to manage on his own and thought he might best go to a hospital. Armand, however, refused, although he did agree to one psychiatric consultation with me.

A year later Armand called and asked to come by. He had begun to resume an active life and appeared in good spirits. He was working full time as a sales representative and had moved into an apartment with two friends, one of whom had also left the sect. His feelings about the movement were ambivalent.

> As for myself, I still respect the Reverend Moon and the *Divine Principle;* he is a very important religious teacher. On the other hand, how could I have continued to place my faith in a group that preached God's word

but could also mislead people at the same time? The contradiction was
more than I could live with when I left.

The moral dilemma Armand had faced and the ensuing soul-searching and
depression were quite common; it was reported by about half those interviewed. In Armand's case, we may use systems theory to clarify how circumstances coalesced to shake his faith. All religious groups confront contradictions when their members are forced to live in a community where contrary
values are espoused and must then rely on protective operations at the system's boundary. For a small charismatic religious group, the resulting conflicts
are more intense because contact with the surrounding society forces the
group to deal regularly with an inhospitable, even hostile, world. Unpleasant
collisions with this world highlight the differences between the two ideologic
systems. Often members must dismiss the society's broader values by systematically denying the humanity of outsiders and even subjecting them to
abuse. In the case of the Unification Church, this aspect of boundary control
often took the form of "heavenly deception." Armand, however, found himself
unable to do this.

In his work at *Newsworld*, Armand was exposed to the values of the broader
society, but only when transferred to the IOWC did he experience difficulties
in assuming the necessary protective stance. In this setting, he was ill prepared to assume the defensive posture of the group since he had been
wrenched from a relatively protected position at *Newsworld* and placed into
direct confrontation with a hostile public. His daily face-to-face contacts at
the newspaper were nothing like his dealings with the targets of the group's
"heavenly deceptions." Armand also came into conflict with the monitoring
personnel of the sect, both his original and his new central figure, and this
occurred as he experienced an unexpected loss of autonomy and decline in
status.

These difficulties loosened the ties binding Armand to the system. He began
to relinquish his grip on the church's shared belief system, its model of right
and wrong, and adopt the values espoused by the general society. At this point,
he was no longer effectively maintained within the group's boundary and
ceased to be a component of the system.

Although Armand said he left the church because of a loss in commitment
to the values it espoused, many members expressed their reasons for departure
in more mundane terms. Doris, for example, was a temperamental young
woman who had been a vocalist with a professional singing group sponsored
by the church. She described her departure in terms of disappointed love.
Her story shows that no matter how strong the hold of a charismatic sect on
its members, it cannot fully expunge the romantic feelings some may feel,
however great their desire to live up to the standards of their adopted religion.

Two years after leaving, Doris related her experience with a measure of
bitterness, and acknowledged that even during her later years in the church
she felt less positively about it than most members and was often unhappy
about her circumstances. In discussing the mass engagement, she pointed out

that she and other long-standing members were "strung along for five or ten years with the carrot of the [eventual] matching dangled in front of us." She said that members were constantly told an engagement and marriage would soon be forthcoming, only to find it repeatedly deferred. She sometimes wondered whether the requirement that members enlist more recruits was not a form of blackmail they had to pay for a marriage. Doris rarely hinted at her feelings and then only to a few trusted friends who were not sympathetic to such misgivings.

Doris also admitted to being attracted to a co-worker during her years at the performing arts department of the church, another sign of her alienation. In time, this attraction became a grave problem for her since she secretly hoped that he and she might be matched. Under unusual circumstances, some members would be considered by the blessing committee for a prearranged match, but Doris had no precise notion as to how such a pairing might be granted. The church disapproved of the discussion of any romantic interest between members, which made it inappropriate for her to make such a request based on her own attachment.

As the matching date approached, Doris hoped that her secret affection for her co-worker might somehow be requited, and also assumed that his apparent friendliness actually reflected his desire to be her spouse. After Reverend Moon called for volunteers to be assigned by photograph to Korean and Japanese women, however, this co-worker turned to her one day at work and said that he hoped to participate in a Kodak match, since he saw these Oriental women as the finest in the church. Doris became deeply resentful over what she regarded as a rejection and also grew anxious, fearing that Moon would assign her to someone with whom she would not be happy. Only after she had been out of the sect for a year, however, did she realize that her expectations of being matched to her co-worker had been ill founded, as was her assumption that he had wanted to be her mate.

At the matching ceremony, the young man whom Moon selected for Doris seemed personable enough, but Doris was not comfortable accepting him as her spouse. She now became obsessed with the fear that she could no longer find a satisfying marriage in the church, and discussed the matter at length with her central figure, an older Korean woman with whom she previously had a good working relationship. Doris was assured by the woman that she could break off the engagement if she wished, but she came to feel that any match at all within the church would end up being problematic. Unlike other demanding church edicts she had agreed to accept in her eight years of membership, this one was threatening and unpalatable.

Doris hoped to gain support through proximity to her family, which had previously been accepting of her membership, and sought permission through her central figure to take a new work assignment in the city where she had grown up. Her request was granted and while there she met a man she had known who had left the church only a year before. Within a few weeks, a romantic relationship developed, one that Doris felt could be permanent. He told her he would rejoin the church for her sake, but only if she would present their union as a fait accompli since he believed it would otherwise be abrogated by the church elders.

Doris agreed to his terms but feared that the entire situation would be unacceptable to the church. Once again, she turned to her trusted central figure at the performing arts department since the woman was well connected in the higher echelons of the church. The woman was distressed to hear the story, but agreed to intercede on Doris's behalf with a senior church figure. She returned, however, saying that Doris would have to reject her new lover immediately to remain in the church. Doris had not wanted to leave the sect, but now felt she had no alternative. She established a home with her new mate outside the church and got a job.

The matching and wedding produced real difficulties for several members, but through its monitoring function the church was able to draw on their strong commitment to help them get through the situation. With a major disruption like the matching, however, it is not surprising that some loss in members did result, as in Doris's case.

Other members left the church after realizing that they could no longer sustain its arduous lifestyle. A great amount of work was expected of them. Respondents to my initial survey, for example, reported devoting an average of 67 hours a week to tasks that would have been recompensed by wages outside the sect. The members rarely questioned this expenditure of time and effort; and there were unusual occasions when a combination of circumstances might put the work in a less favorable light and even undermine a member's commitment. This sometimes happened when there was a sudden shift in work assignment.

Alec, for example, had been working in one of the church's semi-independent businesses, a Korean restaurant, for two years when he was transferred to a mobile fund-raising team. He later told me he had probably become "spoiled" by having his own room and schedule during that period. Furthermore, in his office job of overseeing a small work force, he viewed himself as a manager rather than a line worker.

Initially, Alec had hoped that his efforts in his new position would give him something of a spiritual renewal. He had served on a fund-raising team for two years after first joining the church, and generally had not minded the work. At this point in his career, though, it turned out that Alec could not help feeling the activity was beneath him, an indignity; he could hardly suppress his feelings of dissatisfaction as his team worked from early morning until late night peddling flowers on city streets.

What Alec found least tolerable was the faceless anonymity imposed on members of the team. They were herded about in a van as they traveled through their territory and spent their nights bedded down in sleeping bags in cramped quarters, "lined up like a bunch of sardines." To save time and energy, clothing was pooled and team members got back different garments after each washing.

Soon Alec began to feel confused and rebellious. To retain "a shred of identity," he acquired a small suitcase and began to launder his own underwear and other clothing, his first abrogation of church standards. As he later made clear, this was a sign of doubt about his place in the church.

> Nothing was my own. I had no space. Even the clothing I wore was a challenge to my identity. I asked myself, "If you need to keep these few shirts away from your brothers in the church and don't really want to go along with this terrible schedule, then what are you doing here?" I started asking myself this and couldn't come up with enough of an answer to keep it up. Then I got frightened that I didn't have what it takes to support the others who were on the mission with me. Maybe I thought I was letting them down.

Alec's disillusionment slipped into depression and anger at himself. He consulted with his team leader, who, after realizing that Alec's concerns could not be resolved in his present setting, suggested a change of place. In his new position, Alec worked on special assignments for one of the church leaders, but still could not recapture the sense of commitment he once felt. His disaffection from the church was sharpened when he found to his surprise that the leader's wife was herself disheartened because the church hierarchy was pressing her to keep her toddlers in a full-time communal nursery. Alec sympathized with her and began to see the church as an oppressor. He also started to think seriously of leaving the church, having decided that its lifestyle no longer "made sense" to him. For days he was tearful and ruminated over what seemed to be an inevitable rift between himself and the principal commitment he had made in life. The leader's wife became his confidante and tactfully encouraged him. One day he bade her farewell and set off for the town where he had gone to college, his last link with the world outside the sect. After his turmoil, he felt relief in leaving.

Whatever their reasons for leaving, members who departed voluntarily prepared for this task in deliberating over their choice; they felt the decision was essentially their own. In contrast to those abducted and forced out of the group, they thought through their own rationales for leaving and somehow reconciled them with a remaining affection for the group. For those who were deprogrammed, however, the experience was quite different.

Forced Departure

Deprogramming refers to the use of physical restraint by a family or its representatives in an attempt to dislodge a member from one of these zealous groups. The degree of coercion exercised varies from parental observation of a child in the family home to physical abuse by strangers behind locked doors in remote settings, and the legalities involved in such interventions are complex. Deprogrammers generally draw on state conservatorship laws that allow a family to intervene when one of its members is judged mentally incompetent, but their practices were often found to violate members' First Amendment rights of free speech and free religion. Conflicting views of deprogramming were held by different legal authorities. Richard Delgado, for example, pointed out that a meaningful distinction should be drawn between the constitutionally protected right of traditional religious practice and the affiliative ties arising from coercive induction into certain cults. He asserted that "religious cults expose their indoctrinees to a greater variety of classic brainwashing techniques and with greater intensity," and therefore, "two essentials of informed consent—knowledge and capacity—are not present simultaneously."[40] This position served as the basis for curtailing the autonomy of certain adult cult members.

In contrast, the American Civil Liberties Union, in a number of cases, defended the rights of cult members to maintain their affiliations and espouse whatever beliefs they held, pointing out that absolute free choice and even risk are inherent in the privileges associated with the First Amendment. Jeremiah Gutman, president of the New York Civil Liberties Union, expressed this view in saying that "all religions are equally good or bad. That's what the First Amendment says."[41] Many a heated argument involved these distinctions, in court and outside.

The courts generally upheld the rights of sect members to resist the forcible incursions arranged by their families[42] and well-known, normally "professional" deprogrammers such as Ted Patrick and Galen Kelly lost crucial legal battles in cases where they had forcibly intervened. Even though "professional" deprogramming procedures left their practitioners vulnerable to legal charges, families of some cult members still sequestered relatives in an attempt to reverse their conversions.

In examining the psychology of these circumstances, we will consider two types of forced departure from the Unification Church: one "professionally" organized and one family directed. Both cases also demonstrate different ways in which a mental health professional can be drawn into these forcible removals.

In the first case, a representative of the Unification Church asked me to assess the mental competency of Michelle, a twenty-five-year-old who had joined the sect five years before, had been abducted by deprogrammers, but then escaped and returned to the sect. A conservatorship had been issued alleging that she was not mentally competent to care for herself.

Three weeks after Michelle returned to the church she appeared in my office. She was accompanied by a husky male church member, as she and the sect's officials were fearful of another abduction. My interviews with Michelle, as well as a full battery of psychological testing, were conducted in private and the results were confidential. The evaluation showed that her mental competency was unassailable, and I gave her attorneys a brief statement to that effect.

Michelle gave me a revealing account of her failed deprogramming. Eight weeks before, she and three other church members were returning to their headquarters from a recruitment meeting when their car was stopped by three unmarked vehicles. A police officer stepped out of one of them, demanding the driver's license of the church member who was driving, and Michelle's brother stepped out of another car and identified her to the police. At this point the parties present, some in police uniforms and others in civilian clothes, asked that she leave her car, as they wished to serve a conservatorship on her. Michelle became frightened and refused, but was then dragged out and forced into one of the police cars. Once inside, she was handcuffed and brought screaming to the local police station where her father had been waiting. From there, she was driven to a nearby motel and placed in a room by two uniformed guards.

During the next week Michelle was kept in seclusion, with the door of her room locked and shades drawn. Her watch was removed and she soon had little idea of what time of day it was. She became fearful that she might be physically tortured or even raped, despite being reassured by her captors, strangers to her, that this would not take place.

All exchanges during that week were intended to turn her against the sect. The only visitor with whom she spoke at any length was an apparently experienced deprogrammer who repeatedly told her that the Unification Church was violating the rights and liberties of its members, and then pressed her to agree that the church's activities were ill conceived. He repeatedly played recordings of persons who had allegedly left the Unification Church and segments from television shows on unsavory aspects of the sect. The deprogrammer told her over and over that she had been brainwashed by the church, but she felt that it was only now that this was happening.

After about three days of this treatment, Michelle concluded that it would be to her advantage to act as if she accepted the deprogrammer's point of view, so she started speaking as if she had begun to agree with the endless tirades against the sect. Toward the end of a week, as she estimated the time, her brother appeared and took her for a walk outside her room, perhaps, she surmised, to test her acceptance of the deprogramming procedure and to see if she would try to escape. Michelle decided that running away from him was not feasible, since the deprogrammers apparently had the cooperation of the local police. She had heard stories of other members being taken to mental institutions after attempting to flee. Her brother now told her that she would be flown that night to another city to stay at a different center, and that evening he accompanied her to the airport along with the deprogrammer and other persons involved in the undertaking.

The new center, where she stayed for a month, was housed in a converted motel with a staff of a dozen or so people. At any given time, about eight "residents" were undergoing deprogramming from a variety of groups, including the Unification Church, Hare Krishna, and some lesser-known religious sects. Here Michelle was subjected to repeated questioning and extensive defamatory talks on the Unification Church. She commented on their imposition on her strong religious feelings.

> First, all of my moral convictions and feelings about the Bible and the [Divine] Principle and just about everything in life were open to discussion. There was always pressure for me to conform to their way of thinking, and what they presented was considered proper morality. Then the

pressure was always intense to decide that if you're righteous, you will get on the bandwagon of deprogrammed people and see the Reverend Moon as the Devil. But it was easier for *them* to talk about being righteous than it was for *me* to get to church; that didn't seem to be something they liked. After I insisted, though, I was able to attend church only once out of five Sundays, even though I was taken out half a dozen times to bars and dance halls.

Along with the other residents at the deprogramming center, Michelle was expected to review both scholarly and popular material on brainwashing, on the assumption that she would realize the mistreatment she had undergone in the church and would turn away from her beliefs. The imposition of these ideas was ironic according to Michelle, since she was subjected to verbal assaults and implied threats of coercion in a way she had never experienced while in the Unification Church.

Despite the overt oppression she was exposed to, there were limits on the demands made on Michelle. Staff at the center accepted her refusal to give the names of her church associates, and they did not use physical force to keep her and others at the center, as far as she could see. But she did think they would pursue her if she tried to escape. As in the charismatic groups themselves, the line between voluntary compliance and coercion was not always clear. In any case, Michelle reported that after a month at the center, she was asked to speak with a reporter writing about the deprogramming practices there and told him that she wanted to reestablish contact with the Unification Church. According to Michelle, he helped her by providing her with an excuse to leave the compound, and she successfully escaped.

In a series of interviews, Michelle revealed a modest psychological residue from the deprogramming experience. She initially spoke of the great fears she had experienced when she was first abducted, but acknowledged that she was generally comfortable while at the deprogramming center. On returning to the church, she was tense and had trouble sleeping at first but then attended a two-day workshop that apparently constituted the sect's attempt to "reprogram" her. She spent a lot of time preparing the defense for her conservatorship hearing. Michelle stayed in the company of church members at all times and insisted that she had no qualms about remaining affiliated with the church. She seemed to be stabilized by these activities and by the close support she received. When I met with her, however, she still felt uneasy about her own safety and was anxious sometimes while alone at night.

As a victim of forced departure tactics, Michelle had been dragged across the boundary of a sect's social system and was then able to return. This provoked strong feelings and perhaps distorted perceptions. So it is wise to refrain from drawing definite conclusions about Michelle's experience during the five weeks she was held for deprogramming. For instance, she may have been more swayed by her captors for a time than she could admit to herself after she returned to the sect. Nonetheless, based on my own psychiatric evaluation and on independent psychological testing, she was clearly mentally competent at the time of the interviews and capable of deciding for herself whether to stay in the sect or leave. She seemed a calm, deliberate, and thoughtful young woman.

Reasons for exercising caution in drawing conclusions about events at the border of a charismatic group become more evident in the case of Kim, a relatively unstable young woman of twenty-one who was removed from the Unification Church by her parents. Details of what happened to her were obtained from multiple sources, including the young woman herself, her family and, later, from an active member of the Unification Church. It became clear that none of these sources could have independently provided a full and coherent reconstruction of what had taken place.

For four months, Kim attended workshops and social activities of the Unification Church on an intermittent basis, while living with her parents. During this time, she had led her parents to believe that she was involved with a mainstream Protestant sect, and only after she moved into a Unification Church residence did they become aware that she had entered a cult-like group. After two months of uncertainty and distress, Kim's parents contacted Dennis, a young man who had been in the church for several months the year before and was removed by his parents. With some advice from him, they planned to take their daughter back and sequester her at home. They hoped she could be persuaded to abandon the church with assistance from both Dennis and Kim's recently estranged boyfriend.

The father now managed to get a phone call through to Kim at the church residence and convinced her to meet him outside the building, whereupon he, along with her mother and boyfriend, urged her to come into their car for a moment and then sped away with her. Kim spent the next week at home. She later told me she had not wanted to stay, but was also reluctant to resist the demands of her parents, whom she still cared for. Dennis, the family's youthful consultant, came to visit her for an hour every day or two. Kim was hesitant to speak with him, but they did discuss her views on the church as he tried to point out to her its pernicious influence.

After several days, Kim told her parents of nightmares in which church members, in the form of ghost-like figures, came to menace her. She also began to fear abduction by church members in roving vans when she went out for short walks with her parents, but could give no examples of such abductions having been carried out on other ex-members when I later asked her about this. She was unable to fall asleep unless in the company of one of her parents or her former boyfriend. When her parents were no longer able to leave Kim alone at night at all, they contacted me for a consultation. I explained that I could address her symptoms but was not prepared to pressure her into staying out of the church.

Kim was quite defensive when I spoke with her, and did not want to discuss in any depth her feelings about being a church member or leaving. Although she expressed anxiety over her nightmares, she discussed them only briefly. She was probably fearful that an extensive examination of her conflicts would threaten her fragile adjustment. A week later, Kim began to go out for an hour or two a day with her boyfriend. She was now able to fall asleep without someone nearby and complained less of nightmares. She also expressed a desire to stay out of the church but was still unwilling to examine her feelings about the entire affair.

Kim appeared to be a histrionic and rather dependent young woman who had entered the church in part because she did not want to continue living with her parents and working in the family business, but had trepidation about an independent existence. Also important was her rocky relationship with her boyfriend. The sect provided an alternative object for her dependency needs and a way of coping with her disinclination to set out on her own. She showed no evidence of disordered thinking and had no prior history of paranoia, so her fears of abduction were probably no more than a situational reaction.

After she was spirited away from the church, Kim became involved with her parents again and regressed to the point of needing someone by her side at night for fear of nightmares. But her emotional state was improving. A month after my contact with the family, Kim's mother called to say that her daughter had been on the phone with people she feared were acquaintances from the Unification Church. By now, Kim was spending a good deal of time by herself and was supposed to be looking for full-time work, but she displayed little interest in that, exacerbating her mother's concerns about what might happen to her over the long term.

A month after her mother's call, Kim left the family's apartment one morning and did not return. Her parents notified the police, who issued a missing persons bulletin. I tried to reassure the parents that Kim was no doubt physically safe, but must have found her way back to her friends in the church. Since her parents had no idea how they might reach her, they were understandably frightened. The police contacted me and, at the parents' request, I gave them a description of Kim's psychological state.

Two weeks later, Kim's parents received a call from the police in a nearby city informing them that their daughter had appeared in a station house saying that she had no money and wanted to return home. They had put her on a bus and expected her to arrive home shortly. When Kim did arrive, she explained that she had been kidnapped by a church member driving a van and had been held by the sect for the last two weeks until she was able to escape. The story did not ring true since no such abductions had been reported before, and any action of this kind could have serious grave legal consequences for the sect. I suggested to her parents that they support her apparent desire to leave the church.

The parents themselves placed little stock in their daughter's tale of abduction, but since they were willing to accept Kim on any terms, they went along with what she said. Dennis, the ex-member, on the other hand, began to press the family to secure the services of a private investigator to look into the supposed abduction, and was soon drawing Kim into a project of retribution against her "kidnappers." The parents now became worried that Dennis was a destabilizing force who would only encourage her to persist in the confabulated tale. Increasingly, they saw him as an irritant and finally told him that his assistance was no longer welcome.

I did not meet with Kim again until several months after her reappearance, although her parents spoke with me intermittently. She now seemed committed to staying with her family and had returned to her situation before joining the church by involving herself once again in the family business and resuming the relationship with her boyfriend. She was still reluctant to give details about the period during which she had disappeared, but did not depart from her original story.

As is common with events occurring at the boundary of a charismatic group, several questions remain unanswered. Had Kim indeed returned voluntarily to the church after being at home for three months? If so, how long had she been harboring plans for this during her stay at home? Was she lying intentionally about this, or could her behavior be attributed to an unconsciously mediated denial of reality? Some time later I found that a Unification Church member whom I knew well also knew Kim. He told me that she had returned willingly to the church from her parents' house and, with her agreement, was then brought to a center for the management of disturbed members in another city. Within two weeks, however, she began to express misgivings about remaining with the group and vanished from where she was staying, much as she had left her family two weeks before.

Kim's experience is a variation in the theme of conflict for individuals torn between a charismatic sect and a close-knit family. Often such conflicts cannot be resolved smoothly, and the troubled person is compelled to create a credible enough tale to repress the conflicting motives. Like others who cannot reconcile their divided feelings, many who leave the church come to believe their own stories and cling to them because they provide respite from unmanageable conflict.

A Study of the Departed Members

It is difficult to obtain objective observations on the psychiatric status of ex-members, given the heavily biased information provided by participants, especially while they are still enmeshed in the immediate circumstances of the departure. In an attempt to arrive at a balanced view of the dropout phenomenon, I sent structured questionnaires to those who had left the Unification Church some time before.

There were two sources for this study: the follow-up on the Moonies who had been engaged and married and a separate survey of dropouts contacted after they had left the church. Both groups provided valuable insights.

The engaged members were followed up after three years, one year after they were to be married. Of this sizable number (314), three subgroups are relevant here. The first consists of engaged members who *had left the church* by the time of the follow-up study (14). The initial questionnaire allowed me to examine what their attitudes had been three years before. On measures of psychological well-being, affiliativeness toward the church, and satisfaction with their fiancés, they had not differed from other members at that time.[43] When they completed the first questionnaire, these members had indicated no dissatisfaction with the church that would have predicted their eventual flight.[44]

A second subgroup (9 persons) *were considering leaving the church at the time of the first survey* and in contrast had shown significant psychological distress then. Surprisingly, only one of them actually dropped out in the subsequent three years, and the scores of the rest were not different at follow-up from those of the other respondents with regard to either psychological well-being or affiliative feelings toward the membership. Clearly, the desire to leave can be transient, albeit accompanied by considerable distress.

A third subgroup of respondents (14) indicated *at the time of the follow-up* that they were thinking of leaving the church. None of them had expressed this inclination three years before. These members now had much lower affiliative feelings toward the church and diminished psychological well-being relative to the balance of the group.

In light of these findings, little relationship seems to exist between a member's actual dissatisfaction at a random point and the person's eventual departure from the sect. Members who contemplate departure at a given time are clearly depressed, probably at the thought of severing ties with the church and reestablishing a new identity. In the end, however, few actually leave. Apparently, certain relatively acute circumstances lead persons to leave these groups, ones not necessarily evident a considerable time beforehand. The expression of a strong inclination to leave is likely measured in weeks, or months at most, rather than years.

The unreliability in predicting possible dropouts in this population prompted me to study dropouts who had clearly committed themselves to leaving. My previous work with Unification Church members offered the chance to make contact with several people in different parts of the country who for varying reasons had chosen to leave the sect. Eight former members agreed to cooperate as a project team for the study, largely out of a desire to assure that both the public and they themselves get a clear picture of the consequences of departure. Many felt that everyone who had ever joined the Moonies was viewed in a stereotypical way, as if permanently altered by the experience.

This core group gave me lists of all the ex-members whose locations they knew. Altogether, the project team contacted sixty persons, and all but two agreed to take part in the study, yielding a sample of sixty-six who lived in twenty-one different states. All answered a structured questionnaire anonymously and sent their responses to me for computer coding. These participants had left the church after an average of four years and were evenly divided among men and women. Their average age was twenty-nine, almost all were white (96%), and half were college graduates.

On the whole, they had adapted well in their respective communities according to standard measures of social adjustment. For example, only three had been married before leaving the church, but most (52%) were married now, and none was living with parents or relatives. In addition, the large majority (79%) were either full-time students or engaged in salaried work.

Only a few members (6%), all of them married women, were not employed at all. Furthermore, their level of emotional adjustment appeared to be good. The general well-being scores for this group were no different from those of the general population.

Nonetheless, the experience of departure was difficult. Over a third of the respondents (36%) reported that they had experienced "serious emotional problems" after leaving. An appreciable number (24%) had "sought out professional help" for these problems and two had been hospitalized.[45]

Comparisons could be drawn with the responses of active members to determine what changes had come about in the dropouts' psychological adjustment and views on the church. Although some years had passed since respondents had left the church, they still indicated a surprising degree of positive feelings toward the members who had *not* dropped out. Thus, the majority (62%) still "cared strongly" for "the ten members they knew best," a figure not so different from the portion (89%) of active members who had answered the same way in our previous survey. These affiliative feelings were not necessarily confined to the persons they knew best in the sect. A small but notable portion of the respondents (20%) indicated that they still "cared strongly" for "all church members the world over," compared with 38% of active members who had answered this way.

The religious beliefs that persisted among the dropouts were also similar to those of active members. Thus, a large portion of ex-members maintained that they still strongly felt "a close connection with God" (40%), albeit less than the portion of active members who felt the same way (76%), and almost half the ex-members (41%) still avowed a strong acceptance of specific church tenets such as "The kingdom of Heaven can be established on earth if all other people fulfill God's desire for man."

A large majority of the ex-members agreed either moderately or strongly that they "got some positive things" out of membership (89%). Yet this sign of a relatively benign disposition toward the church was balanced by the response of a majority (53%) who felt that "current members should leave the Unification Church."

In examining these findings further, a telling distinction emerged. Differences in perceptions of the church rested in large part on the way members had left the group: those who had been coerced expressed a much more negative view toward the church. To learn more about the role of coercion in relation to members' attitudes, I arranged to have the project team designate which respondents had been deprogrammed, based on their knowledge of each one. Ten of the sixty-six dropouts were identified, and the deprogramming was corroborated by their own reports.[46]

The deprogrammed former members showed a greater alienation from the church, scoring lower on loyalty toward the members they knew best and on their relative acceptance of church creed.[47] Significantly, all eight respondents who later participated in deprogramming other church members had themselves been deprogrammed. Thus the process did have a lasting effect in sustaining animosity toward the sect.[48] This latter finding was most revealing, because it showed how influential boundary phenomena are in generating aggression between a cult and the general society. The battle for a member's allegiance may come to represent the group's survival to both those inside and those outside. This applies not only to continuing efforts at deprogramming, but also to the protective response to any assault on the group. We have seen the profound consequences of this with Jonestown and MOVE.

9

THE MILLENNIUM APPROACHES

During the past decade, three cultic movements ended in disaster: the Branch Davidians, Aum Shinrikyo, and Heaven's Gate. Each received enormous press coverage and alerted or alarmed the public about the potential for suicide and murder in charismatic groups. To clarify how such movements can come to a tragic end, we will consider what led these three groups to their fatal outcomes, and how the psychology of the charismatic group can nullify the basic human value of preserving life.

Waco and Antigovernmental Paranoia

In physics, action produces reaction, and this law of nature can apply to charismatic groups as well. The intensity of feeling in such a group can generate an equally zealous response of fear and anger among those who see themselves wronged by them or threatened by their strongly held ideologies. Even worse, the clash between a cult and police authorities can end in tragedy and provoke a vengeful reaction by others. This is what happened after a federal assault on a small cultic group in rural Texas. Two years later, domestic terrorists bombed a government building in an apparent act of revenge, killing more than eighty adults and children.

An armed confrontation took place outside Waco, Texas, in 1993 between the federal government and a small cultic offshoot of the Seventh-Day Adventists. The episode left the credibility of the American justice system in question for many people and played a role in an even greater tragedy.

The sequence of events began with a raid on the Branch Davidians' compound by the Bureau of Alcohol, Tobacco, and Firearms, acting on evidence that the sect members had accumulated a large cache of weaponry. An exchange of gunfire left four federal agents and six cult members dead. A day later military vehicles were brought in to surround the complex, and David Koresh, the group's leader, released ten children. Some members of the group left the compound and were arrested, and Koresh pledged to surrender after he received an appropriate "message from God."

After three weeks FBI agents began what they considered to be a psychological intervention, broadcasting deafening rock music and Tibetan chants over loudspeakers. Koresh continued to say that he would surrender in response to the appropriate divine message. On day fifty-one of the standoff, the Department of Justice ordered army tanks on the perimeter of the Branch Davidian properties to break through the compound's walls and fire tear gas grenades in an attempt to flush out the cult members. Fires soon broke out all over the compound, apparently set by the Davidians themselves, producing a firestorm that took the lives of almost all residents of the compound, including Koresh.

The Branch Davidians Emerge

How did this cultic group move toward mass suicide? The original Davidians, established in the 1930s as an offshoot of the Seventh-Day Adventist Church, were led by a zealot named Victor Houteff, who believed that the return of Christ was imminent. From the outset, the group's social organization was distinguished from that of other religious sects as their charismatic founder moved a core group of members to an isolated communal setting outside Waco. This isolation provided fertile soil for a pattern of leadership set by the will and idiosyncrasies of a single individual. After the leader's death in 1995, his mantle was passed on to his widow, Florence, who proclaimed a date for the arrival of the Kingdom of God and encouraged adherents of the Davidians around the country to give up their possessions and join her in Waco. Like so many prophesies that fail, hers led to a dispersion of some of the group's adherents, while a core group remained and redoubled their commitment. The control over this group of about fifty, now called Branch Davidians, later passed on to a new leader, Ben Roden, who was succeeded on his death by his widow. On the heels of this series of successions, Vernon Howell, a twenty-eight-year-old who had proselytized for the Davidians, arrived at the Waco compound from California with an entourage of followers.

Howell was born out of wedlock into a Seventh-Day Adventist family. He was religious in his youth, and devoted much time to his church and to solitary prayer. Although he suffered from a learning disability and dropped out of high school, he had skills that would later serve to establish him as a leader of people. He could readily commit passages of the Bible to memory and string them together to make a point. He had enough talent for playing the guitar and singing to engage an audience, and he could seduce and manipulate women with remarkable facility. These skills came into play when he moved to southern California in his late teens, joined the Branch Davidian movement, and brought together a circle of female converts. He had regular sexual relations with members of this small circle, and even married one fourteen-year-old among them.[1]

In the Waco compound, Howell focused his attention on Roden's elderly widow and succeeded in seducing her and assuming the reins of power. Her son, who had hoped to rise to lead the group, was no match for Howell's wiles and began carrying a gun. Howell, however, later effectively ceded control of the group to the Rodens' son. He decided to act on the revelation that he was an agent of God who would bring on the Armageddon in a confrontation with nonbelievers, and then establish the New Jerusalem. He left for Israel, but to his disappointment met with no success there.

Howell then returned to Texas and reconfigured his prophesy. He changed his name to David, representing himself as head of the biblical house of David and to Koresh, for Cyrus, who had allowed the Babylonian Jews to return to Jerusalem. He assembled a group of disaffected Davidians, told them to buy guns, and led a guerrilla-like attack to retake the Branch Davidian Waco compound, a siege that ended in an exchange of gunfire. As a result of the assault, he and seven members of the sect were indicted on charges of attempted murder, but their trial ended in a hung jury. Now the possibility of an armed assault on the group was prominent in Koresh's thinking, feeding his paranoia and leading him to stockpile more armaments.

Koresh's remarkable control over the sect and his grandiosity were evident as he formed the compound's women into a harem and breeding ground for his next generation. He was reported to have designated nineteen women as his wives, one of them a mere ten years of age.[2] Each wore a Star of David, a sign that they had been chosen by him. The women concealed the common paternity of their children from local authorities by not providing a name for the birth father on their birth certificates.

These events may well be viewed as an aberration of individual behavior, but we need to look at them from the perspective of how forces in a social system can shape and distort behavior in groups—from the perspective of the charismatic group. A key issue is the role of the group's operative philosophy and *beliefs*. In shaping his group's ideology, Koresh drew on both the millenarian vision of the Adventists and the long-standing American reverence for bearing arms. He also used the idea of direct communication with God to serve his purposes. When his compound was ultimately surrounded by federal agents, he presented them with a "letter from God" signed "Yahweh Koresh" that said, "I am your God and you will bow under my feet."[3] By the time this was written, close to the end of the standoff, Koresh had likely slipped into a more gravely pathologic state, as his messianic view of the group clearly reflected his own delusional grandiosity.

To assure its integrity as a social system, a charismatic group has to maintain control over its physical and psychological *boundaries*. Such control is needed to protect the group's ideologic base, to retain its members, and to ward off outside incursions. This aspect of the sect's operation contributed to the siege mentality promoted by Koresh, his need to acquire armaments, and the construction of a fortress-like residence for the sect's members. It also allowed him to assert an increasing degree of control over the behavior of the group's members. Attempts by federal agents to undermine the group's boundaries by intruding on the compound with loud musical broadcasts only bolstered the intensity of the members' reactive commitment to self-defense.

Koresh's role also illustrates the remarkable degree of behavioral control seen in cultic groups, as reflected in the *monitoring* function of such a system. As we have seen, compliance with the leader's expectations is promoted by a series of operant reinforcements that produce a relief in depression and anxiety to the degree that a believer accepts the group's creed and its rules of behavior. By virtue of this relief effect, a member's mood becomes dependent on the degree of his or her commitment in the group. This emotional dependence on the group and its beliefs left the Branch Davidian sect members fully responsive to Koresh's demands. It provided the basis for his ability to make many of the sect's women his sexual partners, who would bear him children, while the sexual behavior of other members of the cult was tightly regulated. Individuals and couples who could not comply with such demands had already left the group by the time the confrontation with federal authorities had begun, and in the remaining distillate of the most committed members there was little likelihood of anyone voicing dissent over Koresh's views. His control and the associated collapse of conventional social norms were further illustrated by his abuse of children. He often beat young boys and engaged young girls in sexual activity.

At the same time, Koresh became increasingly unstable as the adulation of his followers promoted his grandiosity. His loss of consensual moral standards led to a collapse of the perspective that might have made him exercise common sense and respect for human life. The group came to be governed by his unfettered baser instincts.

The leader of the Davidians now needed to avoid the intrusion of an outside perspective at any cost in order to avoid a disruption of his absolute control. This goal came to predominate even over an instinctive inclination to protect his own life and the lives of his followers. In the case of religious martyrdom, the need to protect a group's ideology can lead to the demise of its members on an issue of "principle." Some members of the Waco cult accepted this fate willingly. Indeed, one member had to be restrained by authorities when she tried to run back into the compound as it was burning to the ground. Others were trapped in the conflagration and could not have escaped.

Koresh and the Branch Davidians embarked on a course that led to self-destruction, but the federal government also contributed to the tragic ending of the cult. After the initial raid by the Bureau of Alcohol, Tobacco, and Firearms resulted in the death of federal agents, the Department of Justice brought in heavy armaments to ensure that federal firepower would be unquestionably superior if a second raid was needed. As the standoff wore on, hostage negotiators had no backup team, although they were on full alert throughout the protracted and fruitless negotiations. They were operating under intense media attention and were increasingly fatigued and angered. A mood of confrontation emerged among the agents involved, as seen in the words of the assistant director of the FBI Criminal Division, who said angrily of the Davidians that they "had thumbed their noses at law enforcement."[4]

There was no ambiguity about how law-enforcement officials viewed the Branch Davidian survivors. After their trial in federal court, five received forty-year prison sentences, and three others got five to twenty years plus fines. As a harbinger of the misdirected revenge that would follow these events, a visitor in the courtroom called out, "Give me liberty or give me death"[5] while the defendants were led away.

Federal authorities learned a lesson from the loss of life in Waco, and from the paranoia it generated in many right-wing groups fearing a similar assault. The tactic of waiting and watching without provoking a group's need to protect its boundary, and without adding to the paranoia of a group's leader, has been adopted as a wiser policy for dealing with such confrontations.

Right-Wing Militias, Armaments, and Oklahoma City

In 1995, Timothy McVeigh, an alienated army veteran on a mission of vengeance against the government, drove a truck filled with homemade explosives up to a federal office building in Oklahoma City. He left it to be detonated by a time-delayed device, committing the worst terrorist attack in the nation's history, with a death toll of 168. This tragedy sheds light on society's response to the Davidian cult itself and the reaction of cult-like right-wing militias to governmental intervention.

McVeigh had been intrigued by weaponry for many years. He worked as a guard in an armored car after high school, and his co-workers recalled that he owned a variety of firearms. He was not a stable person. At one point while in the service he claimed that the Army had planted a computer chip in his buttocks.[6] Later, while living in Arizona, he frequented a shooting range, and as another patron there recalled, he would fire hundreds of rounds at random targets: "He pretty much went crazy, emptying on anything—trees, rocks, anything there."[7]

McVeigh traveled to Waco in April 1993, at the time of the Branch Davidian standoff, and was said to be angry at what he saw. He later attended meetings of the Michigan Militia, a militant antigovernment group whose members spoke of taking action against the Bureau of Alcohol, Tobacco, and Firearms and the FBI in response to the Waco siege. The cultic separatist subculture of the militia was central to McVeigh's violent course of action. Members of such "militias" espoused a paranoid view of the federal government, as well as anti-Semitic and anti-black attitudes. Among these groups were The Order, which operated in the Pacific Northwest and whose leader was killed in a shoot-out with government agents in 1984. The Covenant, the Sword, and the Arm of the Lord was another such group. One of its members was sentenced to death and executed in Arkansas for the murder of a Jewish businessman and a black police officer; McVeigh's bombing in Oklahoma City took place on the same day that member's execution was scheduled, and two years to the day after the Waco conflagration.

Means to the Wrong Ends

Charismatic groups may have strange ideologies, but it is the *means* they adopt to achieve their ends that are most likely to determine their actual impact. For the Unification Church, a zealous recruitment technique was the vehicle for bolstering the validity of its message; a furor among parents followed. For the small, politically motivated group MOVE, it was the broadcasting of its propaganda on loudspeakers onto the streets of Philadelphia; the police were called in. The means of carrying forward a movement's mission typically heightens its conflict with the broader society, often leading to an overt clash. Moon was investigated, and eventually indicted and jailed; MOVE members were attacked in force by the police after they refused to relent in their noise-making.

As events that led up to the tragedy in Oklahoma City unfolded, weaponry was the means used by both the Davidians and the militias of the right. But this is a sanctioned part of American culture, which supports the use of guns for self-protection. Firepower was the option chosen by Koresh to retake his group in a guerrilla attack early on, by the ATF to investigate stockpiles of weapons, by the FBI to "protect" children allegedly subjected to sexual abuse, by the right-wing militias to save their land from minorities, and finally by Timothy McVeigh, deluded into an act of senseless retribution. In each of the steps in this sequence of events, the acceptance of weaponry as a valid means of action raised the level of danger.

Aum Shinrikyo

The attack was well-orchestrated, to say the least. During a morning rush hour in March 1995, two five-man teams converged on the Kasumigaseki station, the hub of Tokyo's underground transit system, and a short walk from the Japanese Parliament. They carried plastic bags of sarin, a liquefied poison gas, along with their umbrellas. Already protected by antidotes to the poison, they punctured the bags with the umbrellas, releasing vapors from the liquefied gas, and fled quickly. Sarin, which was developed in Nazi Germany, attacks the central nervous system and is deadly in the smallest quantities. In this case, the attack killed twelve subway riders, and many others were temporarily blinded and collapsed on sidewalks as they tried to run for safety.

Aum Shinrikyo was a religious sect that claimed to have 10,000 members in Japan and 20,000 abroad, mostly in Russia. It had been previously suspected of wrongdoing by the Japanese police, and was now presumed to be responsible for the subway poisonings. After the subway attack, more than

2,500 officers raided Aum's various offices, while hundreds of Aum priests continued to meditate and pray at its headquarters. The public's anxiety was only heightened when statements of the group's leader, Shoko Asahara, were beamed to Japan by radio from Vladivostok and Sakhalin in Russia, statements such as "Let us face death without regret."

At the cult's main compound in Kamikuishiki, a small farming village in the shadow of Mount Fuji, riot policemen entered warehouses carrying caged canaries, a means of alerting them to the presence of toxic fumes. They found some five hundred metal drums containing deadly poisons like sodium cyanide. The discovery of huge stocks of the chemicals used to make sarin was particularly startling, because even minute quantities of the poison are extraordinarily lethal.

An investigation by Japanese authorities revealed that Aum's leadership had managed to acquire or build a vast, diversified arsenal, including computer-controlled laboratories and remote-controlled machinery for sealing plastic pouches. They had recruited large numbers of university science graduates, who were conducting research into botulism and other biological weapons. The police seized raw materials that could have been used to cultivate viruses. Aum operated three companies of its own to buy chemicals, and in Moscow, where the group claimed a considerable following, there were reports of members having met with Soviet nuclear specialists, indicating Aum's interest in acquiring nuclear weapons. There was also evidence that the group had purchased a large Russian military helicopter and had priced Russian tanks, submarines, and military aircraft.

Previous investigations into Aum had been hampered by strictures in Japan on the conduct of police work that had been established in response to the country's experience before World War II, when police were able to detain and even torture suspects and crush religious expression.[8] Unlike their counterparts in the United States, Japanese authorities were not allowed to infiltrate suspicious organizations, conduct wiretaps, or even plea-bargain in any formal way. Although Aum was immediately suspected of perpetrating the poisonings, arrests of members of the group were made only on minor charges like trespassing and traffic violations during the initial stages of a protracted investigation.

Limitations on police action were all the more significant in light of events that preceded the Tokyo attack and that should have led authorities to act. Matsumoto is a modest town known for its large wooden temple. It has little in common with Tokyo, but six months before the Tokyo attack, sarin from an unknown source wafted through a residential neighborhood of the town, killing seven people and sending forty-four to local hospitals. The police dropped their investigation into this event before a conclusion was reached but later found that Aum was the culprit.

In 1989, agents of Aum had murdered lawyer Tsutsumi Sakamoto, along with his wife and infant son. Sakamoto had represented families of cult members who were trying to get their relatives back from Aum Shinrikyo, and had appeared on television to present his case shortly before. Police found the bodies only when they undertook a search after the Tokyo attack six years later. Cult members testified that the victims had been injected with a drug, struck with a hammer, and then strangled.

Aum leaders had even considered releasing nerve gas in the United States, a country thought by Asahara to be inimical to his group.[9] Dr. Ikuo Hayashi, who had served as medical director of Aum, said that attacks were planned for June 1994 but were suspended. The intelligence director of the group had instructed him to go to the United States to pick up a package of sarin that was to arrive in a shipment of ornaments. Hayashi, by the way, a respected cardiologist who had worked in an American hospital before joining the cult, is illustrative of the talent that was inducted into the group.

Asahara as a Cult Leader

In his pamphlets, Shoko Asahara urged people to join his program of "Death and Rebirth," pointing out that "as we move toward the year 2000 there will be a series of events of inexpressible ferocity and terror"; that "Japan has been unjustly deprived of the concept of death and life after death"; and that he would teach people about both.[10] Japanese newspapers estimated that Asahara's chemical stockpile could have created enough nerve gas to kill between 4.2 and 10 million people.

However, Asahara was described by followers as an intelligent, soft-spoken married man with six children. He had a long beard, a beatific smile, and wore oriental robes. He was the sixth of seven children born to a maker of tatami mats in a small Japanese village. One of his older brothers was almost completely blind and had to attend a school for children with limited vision. Shoko's parents decided to enroll him there as well, as his vision was also limited, but because his sight was better than that of the other students he became a leader among them. He later experienced a string of failures during his school years, including unsuccessful runs for student body president in elementary, junior high, and senior high schools. After failing his college entrance exams, he moved to a Tokyo suburb to work as an acupuncturist.

In the early 1980s, Asahara opened a shop selling concocted Chinese medicines and was arrested and fined for marketing drugs of unproven effectiveness. He later launched a company called "Aum," which ran a yoga school and operated health-related activities. He traveled to Nepal and India and came back with photographs of himself with senior Tibetan lamas, even the Dalai Lama. He promoted his school with some success, using these pictures to present himself as an internationally respected religious leader.

By 1987, Asahara had acquired a small following and had founded Aum Shinrikyo as a religious sect. It was a time when a number of similar Buddhist- or Shinto-oriented sects were emerging in Japan and attracting young people who were disenchanted with the country's materialist orientation. Aum appeared to offer a clear alternative. As though to prove its special power, it promised its members the ability to levitate, and would present recruits with photographs of Asahara poised inches above the ground in a yogic position.

It also provided recruits with headgear containing batteries and electrodes designed to align their brain waves with those of their leader. Asahara had a knack for recruitment, and Aum began to attract many bright, discontented university students, particularly those trained in the sciences. As his sect grew richer, he developed a paunch and began to drive around in a Rolls-Royce.

The group's tactics for securing members reflected many of the worst aspects of other cultic groups. These included *alterations in consciousness* and sensation, as the recruits were sometimes starved and given psychotomimetic drugs. In one account given after the sarin attack, a woman described how she and her daughter were locked inside a dark, windowless room shortly after joining the sect and were forced to watch a continuously running tape of Asahara. Furthermore, when police raided the cult's training compound in Kamikuishiki shortly after the subway attack, they found fifty people in an advanced state of malnutrition and dehydration, some barely conscious; remarkably, they eschewed the medical attention offered them.

Intense *cohesiveness,* bolstered by physical isolation, was also a vehicle for sustaining members' involvement. Asahara demanded that many of his followers live in communes, cut off from relatives and family. There was a striking inconsistency between the activities of Aum's leadership and the Buddhist-derived philosophy maintained by the large majority of its members. Most members knew nothing about the criminal activities of the group's leaders, a fact that reflects the profound discrepancy between the means employed by the core leadership and the pacific attitudes shown by members.

As is typical of many charismatic sects, recruits were often told to sign over their property to the group, and Aum went so far as to murder one person who opposed the expropriation. The relative of a recruit was kidnapped in the street after protesting that his sister had been required to give away all her assets, and later, police unearthed evidence that the man had been murdered by Aum members.

Surprisingly, the Tokyo disaster made only a modest impression on most members of the cult. A few weeks after the event, one graduate student reported that he was urged by his family and friends to leave the group. He insisted on staying, and said, "I've got to do this, and that's all I can say. I'm sorry, Mom. Sorry, Dad. . . . If I were head of the public security commission in Japan, and if I were thinking of what group is the most dangerous for the present social system in Japan, it would be Aum . . . because Aum has such incredible potential for the future."[11] A disaffiliated member, questioned about his experience in the group, had eaten only root vegetables that were often rotten and caused diarrhea. Nonetheless, he said that even after leaving Aum, he often found himself singing Aum songs and recalling his experience with the group fondly.

Fumihiro Joyu, a thirty-two-year-old spokesman for Aum, was something of a media star in Japan and an idol of many teenage girls and young women. As a monk in the movement, Joyu said that he shunned wine, women, and sex. Even after the Tokyo attack, he attracted a bevy of young girls in front of the sect's headquarters waiting to see him emerge. Some of them were college students belonging to a Joyu fan club. He continued to deny the cult's responsibility for the gas attack months after the event.

The sustained commitment of members, as exemplified by the graduate student and the group's spokesman, flew in the face of reality and reflected a need to retain fidelity to a failed movement even when it was proven unworthy. This is very much what Festinger found among members of a doomsday cult. Who remained committed even after their leader's prediction of the world's end came to nought; many simply rationalized this failure and retained their fidelity to the movement.[12] Similarly, Moonies who dropped out of the Unification Church often sustained an affection and commitment to the movement; they could not fully relinquish their intense belief in the sect and their emotional attachment to its members.

Heaven's Gate

In March 1997, police in Rancho Santa Fe, California, found thirty-nine bodies neatly laid out in bunk beds in a rented mansion. All had died by drinking a mixture of vodka and barbiturates in anticipation of leaving their physical bodies, their "earthly vessels," in order to ascend to a heavenly destination. This event brought an end to the Heaven's Gate cult and its leader, Marshall Applewhite.

During the previous year, the group had been operating a computer business for clients in the San Diego area but had accepted the appearance of the Hale-Bopp comet as a sign that the time for their ascent to heaven had come. They were not alone in attaching cosmic significance to that astronomical event; the comet was said by some outside the cult, and was touted on the Internet as well, to trail a spaceship in its wake. As this story of the cult emerged, the public was once again startled to see how deranged leaders could bring their followers to an unthinkable end. The intense nature of commitment within this group was further underlined by the suicide six weeks later of two men who had previously left the group. They killed themselves in the same way, wearing the black Nike sneakers and purple shrouds similar to those that had been worn by the other thirty-nine, and left notes behind that they were going to join their deceased compatriots.

Marshall "Bo" Applewhite was the surviving member of a pair of cult leaders who had begun to attract a following twenty-four years before. The son of a Presbyterian minister, he had been an opera singer of some talent, a choirmaster, and a successful voice teacher at a college in Houston, Texas. By the early 1970s, he was apparently having emotional problems. His father had recently died, he had left his teaching position, and he was deeply in debt. Around this time he began looking into the teachings of mystics and reading science fiction. He came to believe that UFOs were objects that had been mistaken for angels.

Applewhite met Bonnie Lou Nettles, a nurse who believed that souls of the dead could be called up through mediums, and that flying saucers made visits to the earth. She did an astrologic reading of him and found that their stars were in alignment. The two decided that they were destined to fulfill a supernatural mission and took to the road; Nettles's husband was left behind with three young children. The two found little support for their ideas, though, and alienated even their one would-be follower, overspending on her credit card. When confronted by the police, Applewhite was driving a car he had rented long before and had left unpaid. He was arrested for auto theft and ended up in jail for six months. While there, he became convinced that people, like caterpillars, must go through a preparatory stage for the "next level." He came to understand that he and Nettles would be killed, only to be resurrected in a "cloud of light," one that "humans refer to as a UFO."[13]

When reunited, the pair embarked on a decade-long attempt to recruit people to their perspective on the afterlife. Perhaps a few hundred people passed through their group during this period. Most left quickly, but a few dozen remained.

The pair struggled with uncertainties over what to do with the followers who stayed with them and how to maintain the idea of a UFO that would take them to the afterlife. For a time, they all slept in tents in the Rocky Mountains during warm months and in Texas in cold weather. "The two," as Applewhite and Nettles called themselves, dispatched followers on road trips cloaked in secrecy, in the hope of recruiting more members to their cause, but these efforts met with limited success. They appointed teams of adherents to work as stargazers and watch for the arrival of a spaceship that would fulfill their prophecy. There were some false alarms of anticipated arrivals based on Nettles's telepathic predictions, but she made explanations for them. While the members lived indoors sometimes, they rarely stayed in one place for more than six months. Some would get jobs to help support the group. Work was generally done under assumed names; members concealed their identities by producing fictional job applications and by driving without licenses. These acts of concealment were dictated by the paranoia and seclusiveness generated by their leader's fear of external assault.

Regimentation was severe, and the group's activities were spelled out in a detailed "Procedures Book." Daily functions, from the ingredients of the dishes members cooked to their patterns of sleep, were prescribed to the finest detail. They shared clothing, even underwear. They maintained bizarre diets, including drinks of water, lemon juice, maple syrup, and cayenne pepper. Enemas were sometimes used for purification. But despite all these oddities, members presented themselves in a congenial and bland manner to the outside world. Many were involved in computer consulting and Web site construction toward the end, and were remembered by their clients as well-behaved and quite likable. As with so many other cults, a deceptively unremarkable facade was maintained to avoid the intrusion of outsiders.

Since the "next level" was a place without sex, celibacy had to be strictly enforced, and sleeping arrangements were made accordingly. For example, gay men slept in rooms with women. Sexual thoughts were also prohibited, and lengthy confessions couched in euphemisms were expected from adherents when carnal thoughts arose. Some members of the group fell prey to sexual relationships and marijuana smoking, and they were asked to leave.

The group's sexual practices took another turn after Nettles died of cancer. Applewhite explained that "her vehicle slipped through the transition . . . to the next level," and he now remained close to women in the group to stifle his own homosexual impulses. One male member who was attracted to him convinced him that castration would solve their problems. After an unsuccessful attempt handled crudely in Mexico, Applewhite and seven others were surgically castrated by a more competent professional.

In time, Applewhite made clear that he was waiting for a "demonstration" that the group's ascent to heaven was impending. One possibility was an assault on the group by Christian fundamentalists or by government agents, which would end in the members' deaths and their journey to heaven, but this did not take place. Applewhite soon began to discuss suicide and repeatedly queried members of the group on their willingness to commit this act, expecting them to indicate that their reservations were subsiding, which they did. He needed a sign, however, and the first appearance of the Hale-Bopp comet provided just that, as the tail of light behind the comet was thought by many UFO buffs to conceal a spaceship. Now Applewhite led the group to believe that ascent to this spaceship would allow them to outlast their own mortality, and he gave them the signal to move ahead on this belief and carry out their final act.

An Elaborated Folie à Deux

The leadership of Applewhite and Nettles was distinctive in that "The Two," as they called themselves, seemed to feed on each other's delusional commitment to a set of outlandish beliefs. Such behavior is also seen in the psychiatric syndrome of *folie à deux*, in which one partner draws the other into a shared system of delusion, be it persecutory, grandiose, or simply foolishly misguided. Although Nettles's life appeared stable while she was working as a nurse and living with her husband and children, she apparently persuaded Applewhite to accept her long-standing claim that she communicated with the dead and saw flying saucers. Applewhite brought an emotionally needy state to their emerging *folie à deux*. It was precipitated by his father's death, his loss of a job and identity as a college teacher, and his unmanageable indebtedness. In this respect, he was like many of the unhappy, displaced people who respond to the appeal of zealous religious sects.

The Two developed their cultic movement because of a need to find adherents to bolster their beliefs; it coalesced around the idea of an ascent to a material heaven. As with other emerging cultic groups, their shared delusions were launched with ideas drawn from the common culture. It is significant that 72% of Americans have been found to believe in angels, 22% in reincarnation, and 45% in UFO visits, beliefs not far from those of Applewhite and Nettles.[14] Even so, their elaborated *folie à deux* did cause recruitment difficulties, because at times they sounded and acted unreasonable, like a single, unstable, and deluded person. They had lost their first disciple, a Texas housewife, by misusing her financial credit and provoking her husband. Another woman who hosted a speaking engagement for them in Los Angeles shortly after Applewhite was released from prison found them entirely unconvincing because of the bizarre quality of their presentation, but recalled that their message of ascending to heaven produced a positive response from the audience.[15] The message was not unlike the vision of the Rapture, the Christian concept of a person's transport to God in a material heaven.

With time, each cultic group evolves in a way compatible with its leader's style of operating. Charles Manson was a gravely unstable man whose psychopathology was fueled by psychotomimetic drugs, and he attracted only a small group of followers. The gurus Maharaj Ji and Shri Rajneesh were eloquent and shrewd, and they were able to draw together a large following by virtue of their charisma. Reverend Moon was a capable organizer and businessman, and he established a structured group that was highly successful in recruiting and retaining members. Applewhite and Nettles, with their limited charisma and penchant for nomadic movement, had only a modest ability to recruit and organize. With persistence, however, they picked up a few interested parties at each of their presentations. Eventually, they acquired a coterie of a few dozen adherents whom they actively manipulated.

The two developed the structure of a viable charismatic group, in that they sustained the system functions we have attributed to these movements. They adopted the function of *transformation*, converting raw material from the common culture—such as belief in a material heaven and UFO ideas—into a belief in ascent to a celestial site. They *monitored* the group's internal activities by exercising tight control over members' daily routines; they required members of the group to report sexual thoughts, enforced in elaborate confessionals. *Boundary control*, protection of the group's perimeter from outside intrusion, was practiced by means of secretiveness, as in falsified job applications and concealment of their identities in other official documents. Overall, "Bo" and "Peep," as they came to call themselves, succeeded in developing a fairly well-structured charismatic group, one whose operation allowed them to manipulate their adherents and prepare them for a flagrantly irrational final act.

Suicide, Murder, and Immolation

Suicide, murder, and immolation: any one would be a terrible outcome for a single individual's life, but they are even worse when they involve members of a large group. The three cults discussed in this chapter carried no constructive message, no theme of martyrdom our culture could recognize. For a better understanding of the dynamics of these groups, consider the following circumstances:

ISOLATION

A group can remove or distance itself from the values of our common culture, even the importance of preserving life. This can take the form of geographic isolation, as when Jim Jones moved the Peoples Temple to the interior of Guyana, or when David Koresh sealed off the complex in rural Texas. Shoko Asahara established an isolated compound in rural Japan; he also maintained a gulf in communication between his inner circle and his widely dispersed adherents, and assured a chasm across which communications would not easily pass. A group can become isolated when it becomes nomadic, when ties with outsiders are continually severed by repeated moves; this took place with Heaven's Gate during its many resettlements across the western United States. MOVE, in Philadelphia, effectively walled itself off in a row house by blasting its propaganda over loudspeakers into the surrounding neighborhood and allowing no messages to come back.

To stabilize its identity and to sustain its members' zeal, a charismatic group needs to transform ideas and human energy into material of its own making. It needs to convert recruits to its ideas, to shape new behaviors in them, or to color their feelings and thoughts with its own ethos. But isolation has a characteristic effect on this systemic function: When outsiders' presence or ideas are lacking because the group has severed its ties with the general society, the system's *transformation function* turns in on itself. This sharpens the members' focus on the group's idiosyncratic ethos and ideas, which is no longer tempered by contact with the social norms and realities of the surrounding culture. The group culture becomes increasingly removed from an externally validated reality and intensifies its commitment to its own idiosyncratic philosophy.

PARANOIA AND GRANDIOSITY

An isolated cultic group provides fertile soil for the emergence of paranoia and grandiosity in its leader, and will aggravate these traits in the leader who already sees himself as espousing a philosophy of absolute truth. Koresh could cite the Scriptures to his own purpose, since he was accepted by a group that believed him to be speaking the word of the Lord. In reflex fashion, this strengthened his sense of divine connection. When Applewhite got his followers to undergo castration, could he not feel that he had unlimited influence?

Grandiosity generates paranoia. A person who needs to sustain full control over his flock will inevitably begin to suspect others of trying to take it away. He fears that the government—the FBI in the case of Waco, Congressman Ryan in Guyana, the police in the case of MOVE—or even parties inside his own sect will envy his powers and try to obstruct his mission. This sets up a siege mentality and leaves the leader awaiting the moment of assault. Jones had his followers practice suicide drills because he preferred to see them dead rather than taken from him by an outside force. Applewhite spoke of an Armageddon brought on by governmental assault. McVeigh and the right-wing militias interpreted Waco and the separatist standoffs with federal agents as evidence that the government was ready to launch homicidal attacks on them.

The interweaving of grandiosity and paranoia sets the stage for thinking that a fight to the death, or mass suicide, or martyrdom following a confrontation with the government is legitimate. Who knows? If the cause is so true, the mission so absolute (whatever outsiders may think of it), the group might win out in the end. The group would emerge as a vanquishing party (Aum), as martyrs (MOVE), as denizens of the heavens (Applewhite), or perhaps just free of the enemy's intrusion (Jones).

ABSOLUTE DOMINION

Isolation, grandiosity, and paranoia all set the stage for a leader to establish absolute dominion over his followers. This can be achieved through the intensification of the system's *monitoring* of members' behavior—that is, observation and regulation of members to ensure that the group's tasks are carried out as the leader's control continues. Applewhite and Nettles prepared a detailed "Procedures Book" specifying each aspect of their adherents' daily activities, from their mode of dress to the particulars of food preparation. Koresh, like other cultic leaders, from John Humphrey Noyes of the Oneida Community in the nineteenth century to Reverend Moon more recently, decided which of his followers would become sexual partners. He had several women bear his children, thereby seeding his group with progeny of his own; he maintained control over the group's armaments as well.

Certain circumstances can serve to moderate the concentration of power in one person's hands, and protect against the juggernaut of his or her unlimited control. A group may have an administrative structure that constrains the idiosyncratic and destructive use of authority by its leader, as did the Unification Church. A leader may be hampered by being absorbed in his own mental world; many Hindu-oriented cultic leaders, like Maharishi Mahesh Yogi, followed their own meditative path. Some leaders, like the Guru Maharaj Ji, may simply come to appreciate the benefits of affluence and family life, tiring of the various means they have used to exert control over their following. But others establish increasingly centripetal controls over their adherents' mental and physical resources, and are seduced by their own ability to manipulate the minds and bodies of their flock.

THE GOVERNMENT'S MISMANAGEMENT

A society that respects religious freedoms will not exercise control over individuals' beliefs, even if they make little sense to the broader public. It should, however, apply its legal code to each of its citizens in a clear and equitable manner, and in the case of charismatic groups, this is particularly important. The laws of taxation, contract, firearms control, and protection of individuals' bodies and property are all vital to preserving the balance between the idiosyncratic behavior of cultic groups and the obligations of individuals to respect the legal rights of others. Reverend Moon was indicted and later convicted for nonpayment of taxes on his personal income. His subsequent imprisonment for eleven months was determined by a fair application of federal law, as implemented by the American jury system. This served as a clear message to his church and to other groups as well that the tenets of religious freedom cannot be used to shield its practitioners from the requirement to abide by the law. The fact that many mainstream religious leaders protested Moon's indictment does not mean that it represented a compromise of our judicial system. Instead, their concerns reflected an atmosphere of healthy debate over the boundaries of religious activity in an open society. Was Moon indicted to set an example? Perhaps. But many of the actions taken by the Internal Revenue Service are also designed to use public example for making clear the importance of compliance with the law.

The law apparently was applied differently in an investigation into the taxation practices of the religion (legally so designated) of Scientology. This well-organized group gathered large sums of money from its members by "auditing" them, applying a sequence of drills for mental purification, and charging a great deal for this practice. The Scientologists were pursued and investigated by the Internal Revenue Service for tax evasion from 1967 through 1991, after which the investigations were apparently called to a halt. A *New York Times* report six years later[16] revealed that Scientology negotiators were apparently able to compromise the IRS by threatening to reveal inappropriate activities of some IRS agents. The investigation was dropped as a result.

When a society ignores illegalities among a cult's members, it may suffer the consequences. In the case of Aum, the Japanese police were apparently fettered by a variety of historical constraints that kept them from actively pursuing the group for flagrantly illegal actions carried out by that group. And a society can also overreact. In the case of Koresh and the Branch Davidians, armed assault, later acknowledged to have been misguided, left the impression of a federal government guilty of the needless killing of its citizens. This became the focus of rage for certain armed fringe groups, and later helped precipitate disaster.

Religious freedom must be respected when the government intervenes, but certain options should be pursued in order to protect a free society from abusive charismatic groups:

Legal Action. Laws relevant to a group's illicit activities must be applied early on, as soon as violations by cult leaders and their followers become clear, as in the areas of physical abuse, firearms regulation, and taxation.

Intelligence Coordination. Although we do not want to see the federal government violating established procedures for surveillance, it is quite appropriate for it to coordinate the gathering of information on movements that are suspected of violating the law. This applies to splinter ideologic groups that may be engaged in crimes just as it does to criminal groups organized for monetary gain.

Education. We live in a time when techniques of manipulating group psychology have been developed into workable procedures for engaging the unsuspecting, when sects can move across great distances and effectively disguise their harmful activities, when young people and adults are increasingly removed from the guidance of family and traditional religion. Therefore, it is important that the public be educated to understand how they can be drawn into movements whose covert agendas they may not understand. This responsibility falls on the schools as well as the media.

THE IDEOLOGIC THEME OF DEATH

Death and murder are themes that may lie buried in the unconscious mind or just below the surface of polite behavior. A handshake can disguise murderous intent; disappointments can arouse secret thoughts of suicide. Psychosis can bring such impulses to the fore, but so can the deranged thinking that is often evident in charismatic sects. A grandiose mission can be understood to justify murder if it is perceived as means to a sanctioned end, and suicide can be seen as the portal of salvation.

A natural death leading to spiritual redemption is a venerable theme in religions around the world, from the eventual achievement of nirvana in the Buddhist tradition to the reunion in heaven of Christians with past generations. Religious zeal can hasten this process through an earlier demise, through martyrdom, or through Christian rapture. In the silliest form, heavenly ascent can be seen as a real and immediate option for members of a group when UFOs are thought to ply the heavens and a body can be reconstituted by signaling "Beam me up, Scotty." Sadly, Applewhite and his followers took the notion of access to a spaceship hidden in the tail of the Hale-Bopp comet all too literally.

Death may result from a group's implementing *boundary control* to excess, as with Aum's proclivity for murder as a means of dealing with dissidents and adverse publicity. Boundary control may also lead to death in response to the clear threat of outside intervention. Koresh and his adherents precipitated their deaths by conflagration. Jones told his flock to "take the potion . . . because we are not committing suicide—it is a revolutionary act."[17] Are these options entirely alien to a civilization that led Jewish martyrs at Masada to choose death rather than capture by the Roman pagans, and Greek soldiers to fall on their swords when battles were lost?

THE HERALDED EVENT

These last examples illustrate the role of a triggering event, a spark that ignites the tinder in groups that carry within their ethos the themes of suicide, killing, or sanctified death. We know that Applewhite anticipated suicide as a means of achieving ascent to the heavens; that Jones repeatedly schooled his followers in the technique of poisoning themselves; that Koresh stockpiled weapons to fight a battle against outside assault to its very end; and that Asahara was expecting his group's mass murders to produce some cataclysmic result. The tinder was there in each case.

The thoughts or emotions that trigger a final course of action often die with the group or lie behind the silent mask of its captured leader. They are fairly clear in the case of an outside assault, as with Jones and Koresh, but in the case of anticipated redemption, they may be tied up in motives known only to the deranged leader himself, or in psychological needs beyond his understanding. Why did Applewhite decide that Hale-Bopp and not an earlier or a later celestial event was a signal for his group's suicide? Why did Asahara take the plunge into mass murder when he did? Was a fear of their own physical mortality triggered by some experience or insight, or an anticipated loss of control over the cult structure itself, or perhaps just the fatigue of bearing absolute power for too long?

IV

SPIRITUAL RECOVERY AND ALTERNATIVE MEDICINE

If the disenchanted, the displaced, and the unhappy are drawn to charismatic groups, so may those suffering from actual illness. People who are sick want to know that they can recover and that death or debility can be averted; many healthy people also struggle to escape the fear of death. But modern medicine, with its strong technologic orientation, often provides little support and reassurance, so where do they turn? Alternative medicine, representing a variety of healing movements outside the medical mainstream, is a common choice.

Some alternative-medicine movements have a spiritual or ideologic orientation and are not taught or practiced in our major teaching hospitals. The beliefs they embody are embedded in an emotionally supportive structure that lends meaning to illness and recovery. They are like charismatic groups in that they operate from a base of spiritual (or pseudoscientific) ideology, and may be fueled by the alterations in consciousness and sensation associated with pain, suffering, or addictive drugs. But the beliefs they espouse encompass the lives of their followers less than do those of the charismatic cults. They may target a limited group of people who suffer from a particular illness or provide a more generic philosophy for ensuring good health. They are usually called "alternative" therapies, but for those who accept them, they are often *the* alternative, the hope they need.

Some of these spiritual recovery movements are meditative, others rely on herbal cures, and still others advocate self-realization. These movements reveal how our society struggles to deal with the less rational needs of its members for succor and certitude in an era when scientific medicine cannot address all the emotional needs of those who are ill. For this reason, it is important to understand their interface with contemporary empirical medicine: how they may complement conventional care in a positive way, and how they may sometimes undermine it.

185

10

THE NATURE OF
HEALING MOVEMENTS

Finding a Perspective

I considered the study of religious cults an avocation and pursued it along with my day job as a psychiatrist in the addiction field. While the Moonies were making headlines with their aggressive recruitment techniques, I was learning about the remarkable effects of the spiritually oriented group Alcoholics Anonymous. AA was clearly a zealous and cohesive movement, a charismatic group of sorts, one that worked very well as a worldwide treatment program for alcoholics. Its success suggested that there might be a benefit in applying some of the group techniques observed in both AA and in the cults to mobilize patients in alcoholism clinics so they could accept the idea of sobriety more fully, and become more effectively committed to their own recovery.

Around the time I began to look at cults, I was asked to head a treatment program for indigent and poorly socialized alcoholic patients at the city hospital affiliated with the Albert Einstein College of Medicine in New York. This was an opportunity to persuade the more stable outpatients in the clinic to take an active role in managing the program and in engaging newly admitted patients. The approach allowed the seemingly "dead-end" patients in our detoxification ward to identify better with the goals that their abstinent compatriots were espousing. Perhaps they could support each other in their struggle for recovery. This format drew on the same principles of shared ideology and cohesiveness—and the "in-group" mentality—that energized the members of the charismatic groups. To justify this innovation on economic grounds, we operated the program with half the staff of the traditional, professionally directed program, and found that it actually yielded results that were as good as or better than those of conventional care.[1]

The municipal authorities who governed the hospital were at first concerned that "deficient" patient-run care with "poor staffing" would be foisted on our clientele, whom they assumed to be helpless in managing their own affairs, but over time they saw how the approach could be beneficial. A decade later we took the same approach on a larger scale at Bellevue Hospital and New York University Medical Center, and it came to be accepted by the city as a progressive model for care, and was given an award for innovative treatment by the American Psychiatric Association.[2]

This experience seemed to demonstrate that the principles observed in spontaneously generated charismatic groups could be modified and applied in medical settings. Along with colleagues, I later examined the roles of cohesiveness and spiritual belief in the recovery patterns of severely addicted physicians who achieved abstinence while attending AA, and in two other recovery-oriented programs, one for mental illness (Recovery, Inc.) and the other an addiction-treatment movement (Rational Recovery).[3] Neither Recovery, Inc. nor Rational Recovery was spiritually oriented, but both maintained an intensive engagement of their members based on ideas adapted from behavioral psychology. They generated intense mutual support, corrected attitudes associated with target symptoms, and avoided the circumstances that can trigger relapse. In this respect one can see the underlying psychological similarities between these movements and AA. Whether they espoused an overt spiritual philosophy (AA) or an apparently rationally-grounded one, all three relied heavily on a deep commitment to the group's philosophy and on the mutual supportiveness of their members in achieving healing.

Each group also undertook its mission of relieving pathology by using a cognitive and behavioral framework to get its members to think and act differently. That is to say, each group has a characteristic set of ideas for its members to accept, like avoiding thinking about drinking or about stressful experiences. This then helps to structure the way members view their lives, so that they can conform to the recovery-oriented behaviors expected of them by the group. And the vehicle for implementing this framework is the ideology and the social engagement engineered by the movement and its leadership. In this way, these movements parallel the charismatic groups we have studied so far.

Spiritually oriented *alternative medicine movements* became popular in the 1980s and '90s. They were directed at a host of different illnesses and they espoused a variety of remedies. There were many earlier healing groups and quack cures, but this new wave of movements included meditative approaches of Asian origin, domestically grown holistic medicine, and self-realization groups. Like charismatic groups, each was characterized by a shared ideology, and each generated a pattern of social cohesiveness among its adherents.

The widespread commitment to spirituality in American culture is certainly clear in surveys of the overall population, where 87% report that religion is important in their lives.[4] This attitude also has parallels among family physicians, the large majority of whom report that they believe in God.[5] In one study of primary-care physicians, two-thirds said that praying with patients would be appropriate behavior for physicians, and a relatively small number of physicians also said they apply Christian prayer directly in medical practice and clinical research.[6] More than half of psychiatrist members of the Christian Medical and Dental Association said they would prescribe prayer as a treatment for depressed or alcoholic patients.[7]

Indeed, the United States and other industrialized countries have witnessed a growing interest in spiritual and religious matters in recent years, and the messages of allied healing movements are being disseminated more readily because of advances in communication technology in our "global village." This trend received official acknowledgment when the National Institutes of Health were authorized by the U.S. Congress to establish an Office of Alternative Medicine to study these generally unproven techniques, many of overseas origin, which were gaining wide acceptance among the general public. I decided to apply what we had learned from the charismatic groups to these spiritually oriented recovery movements, since their group psychology often seemed more potent than the actual practices they prescribed.

Defining the Movements

Although contemporary health researchers set high standards when they evaluate new medical treatments, many patients adopt unconventional approaches to treatment that are not based on evidence from controlled studies. In fact, one recent national survey revealed that a third of Americans had turned to therapies outside the medical mainstream in the previous year.[8] It is important that people be aware of the nature of these therapies so that the medically ill can be assured effective care. The need for this awareness is highlighted by the fact that the federal government has overseen pharmaceutical preparations since early in this century but has no comparable monitoring of nondrug treatments. This leaves the public without clear standards for understanding and evaluating recovery movements that are spiritually oriented.

The term *spirituality* is generally associated with the search for transcendent meaning in life. It has been distinguished from movements that focus on physical and psychological problems on the one hand, and from many sectarian religious practices on the other.[9] This distinction is also compatible with the way the term has been used in various professional health settings, like primary medical care, gerontology, and pain management.[10] We can thus define *spiritual recovery movements* in the following manner: (*a*) they claim to provide relief from disease, (*b*) they operate outside the channels of established empirical medicine, and (*c*) they ascribe their effectiveness to metaphysical or nonmaterial powers. Nowadays, in industrialized countries, they may be subsumed under what we call "alternative medicine."

The appeal of these movements derives partly from the fact that most contemporary physicians depend increasingly on medical technology and have little time or inclination to attend to the spiritual needs of their patients. This is evident in the output of major medical journals, where only 1% of articles in general medicine and 3% of articles in psychiatry even mention religion.[11] In contrast, alternative movements draw on a variety of spiritually oriented traditions.

Christian tradition understandably serves as the basis for some spiritual recovery movements. Americans' strong religious orientation is highlighted by the fact that 94% of respondents in national surveys avow a belief in God or a universal spirit, and 42% attend church in a given week.[12] One example of our appetite for religion is the success of psychiatrist M. Scott Peck's book *The Road Less Traveled,*[13] which combines psychotherapeutic and religious inspirational approaches. The book was on the *New York Times* paperback best-seller list for over six hundred weeks, a publishing record. Peck draws on his interpretation of Christian belief to explain how mental illness results from deviating from the will of God. Biomedical researchers, urban blight, and overcrowded mental hospitals do not impose themselves on the spiritual model that he evolved while practicing in a rustic corner of western Connecticut. He creates this perspective by wedding his theology to the psychoanalytic thinking of Freud and Jung, and to the thoughts of pop-culture icons from John Denver to Kahlil Gibran.

This religious orientation is also seen in general medicine. Cancer patients often turn to religious healing, and many books, like *A Medical and Spiritual Guide to Living With Cancer,*[14] offer a Christian potpourri for dealing with grave illness. One survey revealed that 19% of cancer patients who went for conventional medical care had also resorted to spiritual or faith healing, which included prayer, laying on of hands, or other means of achieving divine intervention.[15] Among professionals, the 8,000 members of the Christian Medical and Dental Association avow that their religious faith is "absolutely critical to [their] personal and professional lives" and actively apply that faith in their clinical work. Of the psychiatrists among them, 96% said that they were born again, and a like number acknowledged having encouraged someone to accept Jesus as a savior.[16]

Eastern spiritual approaches have been adopted by various groups in the West. They have been popularized by their devotees and by the media, and have fanned the expectation that treatment options will emerge outside Western, scientifically based medicine. Transcendental meditation, a simplified form of its Eastern counterparts, has gained popularity among many westerners for achieving mental and physical relaxation, and perhaps decreased blood pressure as well. Acupuncture is associated with some exotic Chinese practices that are less known in the West, such as moxibustion and cupping.[17] Many of its contemporary uses in the West go far beyond any applications that have been demonstrated scientifically to be effective.

Having read accounts of alternative medicine and spoken with its adherents, I assumed that practices derived from folk medicine were integrated into China's medical mainstream. Not so, said Dr. Shen Yucun, Director of Mental Health at Beijing University. In 1993, she showed me her extensive facilities, which included computerized EEGs, epidemiologic research, and contemporary psychopharmacology. She looked at me quizzically when I mentioned acupuncture and herbal medicine, and spoke dismissively about them, saying that they were used by despairing people with chronic illnesses seeking temporary comfort. Other doctors I met in established medical programs in China said the same thing.

I then visited The Tibetan Hospital, a large facility for traditional healing in Lhasa. Dr. Chowong Lhundup, its vice director, claimed no working relationship with Western-style medicine, and was affiliated only with the Men Dzekhang Medical College, a school for traditional Tibetan medicine. His program was supported by the Chinese government in a system independent of their Western-oriented hospitals and clinics. For him, physiology was explained by humors like those described in medieval times: wind moving within the skeleton, bile in the blood, and phlegm in the flesh. Anatomical charts lining his walls depicted elaborate nerve pathways that bore no relationship to the ones in standard medical school texts. He said acupuncture, herbal pellets, and bloodletting were the modalities they used—not the typical medical pharmacopoeia. It was clear that if Dr. Shen at Beijing University and I were practicing scientifically grounded medicine, Dr. Lhundup was articulating his static system of belief. He was a scion of a spiritual movement that could engage the commitment of sick people in Lhasa, and perhaps in the West as well; his movement had been influential enough to raise the issue of how it had secured a measure of acceptance back in the United States, acquiring credibility well beyond its proven value.

Ayurvedic medicine, an ancient healing practice from India, has also gained media attention in the United States. In this system, different parts of the body are understood to be linked by humors, and by spiritual factors as well. Health is conceived as a state in which these forces within the body are in balance, and therapeutic measures, like traditional Indian medications, massage, and meditation, are employed by the spiritual practitioner. Medicines are prepared from a variety of herbal materials. This system has acquired considerable appeal. A recent appearance on the Oprah Winfrey network television show of Deepak Chopra, one of its physician advocates, helped spur sales of 400,000 copies of his book in one month,[18] and Eastern spiritual traditions have also spawned considerable public interest in herbal preparations. These preparations have spread among networks of people with AIDS and cancer, but they have often come under sharp criticism from members of the established medical community.[19]

Deepak Chopra and some of his colleagues recently published an article on Ayurvedic medicine in the *Journal of the American Medical Association*. The authors were later severely criticized by physicians who pointed out that their paper was contrived to promote commercial herbal products that they were marketing for profit, a publication practice contrary to *JAMA* policy.

To see what ideas Chopra himself was putting forward, I read his book, *Perfect Health: The Complete Mind/Body Guide*,[20] along with related articles. He pictured the human body on a "quantum level," a term adapted from physics that has no clear meaning in medical science. His quanta are basic units of matter or energy that take the form of "intense but invisible vibration," and then coalesce into particles that underlie the body's function. This pseudoscience was new to me.

Chopra gave an example in the book of a physician suffering from chronic leukemia who, in his fear of death, agreed to "try anything." The physician later achieved a measure of inner peace when Chopra had him trained in meditation in his clinic, a "stately, sixty-five-room Georgian mansion" in Massachusetts. The doctor's commitment to meditation seemed to me to emerge from his anxiety over his poor prognosis, reminiscent of "conversions" to cultic movements born out of depression and loss—and also of many religious experiences of the suffering throughout history, for that matter. According to Chopra's lab report, the doctor sustained a moderate decline in his white-cell count after a week. Chopra writes that "we think he has turned the corner," but then gives no further follow-up.

Advocates of *holistic medicine* generally apply this term loosely, but the concept has become important to some physicians and to contemporary alternative medicine.[21] It has been called "an approach to the whole person . . . appealing to lay people who feel their lives and health care are fragmented," and has been credited for "its gift of spiritual wholeness [as] the crux of the health and vitality of creation."[22] Practitioners of the holistic approach tend to focus on psychosocial and nutritional issues, and may encourage the use of unconventional therapies like macrobiotic diets, meditation, or body awareness.[23] They promote active communication between physician and patient but may suggest that love or religious conversion can resolve serious illness, as described by the academic physician and popular author Andrew Weil.[24]

Weil illustrates the breakthrough of New Age alternative medicine into the professional mainstream. Even before his graduation from Harvard Medical School, he had carried out a number of highly credible studies of marijuana and published them in major medical journals. He later traveled among native Indian tribes in Colombia and took his share of indigenous psychotomimetics. Weil emerged from the counterculture era with the idea that the need for altered consciousness was inherent in human nature and elaborated this in his 1972 book *The Natural Mind*.[25]

As Weil became involved in nontraditional healing, he validated his growing belief in natural cures with anecdotes and conjecture rather than controlled studies. He tells of a man with severe rheumatoid arthritis who could not find gloves to fit over the painfully swollen joints of his hands. One day, the sting of a bumblebee left the man tender and swollen, but his arthritic pain subsided. A few weeks later the swelling in his joints was gone, and his arthritis did not return over decades of follow-up. Weil implies here that nature can give us cures without recourse to modern medicines. He also recounts the experience of a nineteen-year-old girl close to death from a terminal blood disease. She began a regimen of diet and psychic healing, and miraculously overcame her affliction, again with no return of her illness. Another man recovered from ulcerative colitis after responding to a therapist who manipulated his skull, allowing his digestive "impulses" to begin flowing again. Such stories complement Weil's belief that many conventional medicines are too strong, even toxic, and that better cures can often be gained from natural sources.

But Weil has also found for himself a creditable place as a professor of medicine at the University of Arizona, practicing what he calls "integrative medicine" aimed at combining the best of alternative and mainstream theories. He has a clinic that embodies these practices, where doctors are said to have enough time to attend to patients' subjective concerns, ones that are often lost in the rush to provide inexpensive treatment in the era of managed care. In this respect, his ideas address a sorely felt need. Weil reaches a broad if diffuse audience through best-selling books like his *Eight Weeks to Optimal Health*,[26] and a Web site that receives thousands of hits each day. His appearances on public television parallel his role among other New Age gurus. Like Doctors Deepak Chopra and Bernie Siegel, who make appearances among their own followers, he has moved alternative medicine and spiritually oriented healing from the fringes into the popular mainstream. Whereas the cultic charismatic groups establish a community through face-to-face contact, these gurus sustain a diffuse but often committed community through the electronic media.

Self-liberating approaches are another form of spiritual movement. They derive their popularity from the assumption that mental and medical illness can be overcome by an ill-defined power of healing that lies within us, according to such popular figures as Maryanne Williamson and Bernie Siegel.[27] This self-actualizing power is thought to offer the means of releasing innate, spiritual "energies" that can change the course of physical disease or emotional distress. Techniques range from healing through "creative visualization" of diseased organs to confronting memories of childhood abuse.[28] The ways that relief is achieved are described by some advocates in nonspecific expressions of enthusiasm, and by others in terms drawn from biologic disciplines like neuroscience and immunology.[29]

These self-liberating approaches are not necessarily constrained by the usual norms of medical practice. Bernie Siegel, an accomplished surgeon on the Yale University faculty, came to label himself a "clergeon," wedding the spiritual and the scientific, despite the skepticism of his colleagues. He states emphatically that love can heal illness and that visualizing a healing change in one's body can bring about changes in diseased organs. How accomplished physicians can reconcile such unproven and questionable concepts with their scientifically grounded training remains an open question.

Twelve Step movements derive their spiritual message from the steps toward recovery developed by Alcoholics Anonymous, drawing on "the care of God as we understood Him." With over a million members in the United States, AA has contributed greatly to relieving the burden of alcoholic illness and has inspired other groups to adopt the same Twelve Steps for a variety of problems associated with health risk, from narcotic addiction to eating or sexual disorders. But some members of these groups have enlarged this perspective by focusing on recovery from a wide range of interpersonal problems, from "co-dependency" with troubled spouses to recovering from one's "dysfunctional" parents. Ubiquitous workshops and coverage by the mass media have yielded sales in the millions for Twelve Step–type books such as *Codependent No More* by Melody Beattie and *John Bradshaw on the Family*.[30]

Authors and lecturers in this movement often disparage the anonymity of AA and instead present their own troubles as the basis for a philosophy of bootstrap self-redemption. Author Melody Beattie, for example, had a spiritual experience at a state hospital where she had been taken to address her un-manageable problems of depression and alcoholism. She later moved on to counseling spouses of alcoholics, and freed herself from the need to save her husband from alcoholism. Divorce led her to the conviction that codepen-dency with an addicted spouse had no place in her own life or that of others, and she went on to write best-sellers about the same issue. Her books enu-merate literally hundreds of traits found among victims of codependency, a term that could characterize almost anyone who has ever had a close rela-tionship. Problems of clarity aside, Beattie seems to have helped many people take charge of their troubled relationships and reshape them.

Impact of the Spiritual Recovery Movements on Health Status

A religious or spiritual orientation has proven to be effective as *a buffer against psychiatric symptoms* in a variety of settings in the general population, in spe-cific subgroups like the bereaved and the medically disabled, and also in the cultic sects we have examined.[31] A spiritual orientation can apparently reduce the likelihood that stressful life events like physical illness will produce de-pression, anxiety, or pain. Significantly, 25% of the American population re-port that they turned to prayer for aid with illness in the previous year, and 4% turned to "spiritual healing."[32]

Supportive relationships also contribute to *health-promoting behaviors* among sick people who have sought out psychiatric and medical care,[33] and they can serve as a medium for conveying vital information to patients and for engaging them in appropriate medical self-care. For example, researchers found a sizable decrease in mortality among patients with hematologic cancers when they gave them an educational program designed to improve their com-pliance with medication regimens,[34] and AA members are more likely to follow medical regimens for abstinence than are non-AA members.[35] Didactic ma-terial and instructions on self-care, delivered in a socially cohesive setting, can be coupled with a philosophic view that gives some redeeming meaning to illness and recovery. Bringing alternative healing and its practitioners in as collaborators in some health-care settings might thus enhance compliance with treatment and morale.

Social support can be beneficial in itself, as demonstrated by studies of its relationship to mortality rates. Interpersonal support through marriage and community ties is correlated with lower rates of mortality in large samples of the general population and in cancer patients as well.[36] Smaller, controlled studies, like one by David Spiegel and colleagues, have made a similar point. Spiegel and his co-authors found that metastatic cancer patients who received group therapy lived appreciably longer than matched controls who did not.[37] Similar results have since been reported for patients given group therapy after being diagnosed with malignant melanoma.[38]

While engagement in a supportive network can increase the likelihood of complying with medical care, it may also have direct physiologic effects. In both laboratory studies[39] and assessments of changes in people's life circumstances,[40] it has been found that psychosocial factors affect cardiovascular and immune responses. The sympathetic nervous system, subject to influence by psychosocial stress, has long been known to have direct effects on cardiac function, and providing cancer patients with a supportive group program may enhance immunologic function in the form of natural killer cell activity.[41] Much needs to be done, however, before the impact of life events on neuroendocrine status and medical illness is clear.[42]

Negative or nonexistent effects of alternative medical approaches have also been reported. In some controlled studies, they have shown no benefit at all compared with conventional medical care. For example, two studies were carried out at large urban alternative clinics prescribing a mystifying array of cancer treatments.[43] In both studies these treatments produced no improvement in survival. Poorly conceived alternative therapies such as encounter groups and toxic herbal preparations have proved to be useless or even harmful in a number of studies.[44] The encounter group studies are relevant because some encounter group leaders were found to be overly intrusive and controlling, causing emotional casualties—not unlike the practices of some of the cult leaders we have considered. It is important that practitioners of alternative care who are lent credence by society or by authorized caregivers do not convey a message that undermines patients' faith in conventional care they need. This is particularly true now that some health insurers are underwriting alternative medical treatments.

Another problem is that sick people involved in alternative healing approaches may not seek conventional care as soon as it is needed. Among the general public, 10% of those surveyed had sought a provider of unconventional therapy in the previous year for a major medical condition, and almost a third of them did not see a physician.[45] Of cancer patients who undertook "questionable" alternative treatments, 17% did so before obtaining conventional medical care.[46]

A Cross-Cultural Perspective

Spiritual recovery movements usually do not have as much of a hold over the lives of their adherents as do charismatic cults. Their philosophies are also less at variance with that of the general culture, and they do not isolate their adherents from the community in the way cults usually do. Their acceptability of a spiritual recovery movement to sick people depends instead on whether it is compatible with the values in their culture.

In preindustrial societies, established healing practices and spirituality are generally intertwined and derive from the same value system. In many types of shamanism, for example, divinely inspired healers provide meaningful care and relief of physical symptoms, if not an actual cure. Arthur Kleinman studied *Tâng-ki* healers in Taiwan and evaluated their impact on psychosomatic problems, transient illnesses, and pain associated with disease. He found that their credibility was reinforced by indigenous Confucian concepts of the healer and the healed that served as the basis for their acceptance and influence.[47]

Traditional spiritual healing and scientific medicine can also coexist or even support each other. Contemporary obstetric "faith clinics" in Nigeria combine Yoruba rituals that ward off demonic possession with the divine healing practices of the Christian Apostolic Church, but they also provide medically grounded midwifery.[48] Many Puerto Ricans in New York seek conventional care for mental and physical illnesses from local hospitals while at the same time using Espiritismo healers.[49]

But there is also a history of antagonism between religious and secular healing systems in Western society; Christian Science is a good example of this. In 1875, Mary Baker Eddy defined illness as an illusion that her church would address, to the exclusion of conventional medicine.[50] With its emphasis on individual freedom in religious and other matters, our legal system has acquitted Christian Scientists of criminal charges even when they have denied their children needed treatment for fatal illness, but conflicts continue to come up in the courts.[51]

The Psychology of Membership

Acquiring a Spiritually Oriented Perspective

The likelihood of a person joining the Unification Church, as we saw in Chapter 3, was directly proportional to the degree of distress he or she was feeling upon first encountering the group. If the need for emotional relief motivates people to affiliate with zealous groups, then those suffering from illnesses are likely candidates for joining. This is particularly true if they are unsure of the ability of conventional care to cure their illness.

In order to understand how engagement in such groups takes place, we can turn to the social psychology of group influence and consider the way people attribute meaning to their experiences. Research on *attribution theory* suggests that people are most likely to accept a new or unusual explanation for any given situation—such as a sickness—under certain circumstances: when they encounter problems they cannot solve, feel they are not being given sufficient support, or have lost confidence in themselves.[52]

Consider the experience of Marianne Williamson, a New Age guru, who achieved prominence after making her own commitment to spirituality. She served as a consultant to Bill and Hillary Clinton in their search for meaning after heavy Democratic losses in the 1994 congressional election, and was spiritual companion at the marriage of Liz Taylor and Larry Fortensky, who had become a couple after they were patients together at the Betty Ford drug clinic. Williamson's own experience of spiritual recovery shows how a diffuse philosophy of healing may be acquired at a time of stress. When she was twenty-four, her life was in turmoil on the heels of a number of broken relationships, hard drug use, and a nervous breakdown. She came upon the three-volume *A Course in Miracles*,[53] a self-study program on spirituality, written by a psychologist but supposedly channeled from Jesus himself. Upon reading it, she experienced a personal awakening and embarked on a journey that led her to espouse its philosophy of Christian-oriented spiritual belief.

Williamson came to define health as "inner peace" and healing as "a return to love." The latter phrase serves as the title of her best-selling book, which has had sales of over two million. She is a charismatic speaker, presenting her ideas in heavily attended lectures and "Centers for Living" in Los Angeles and New York where support is provided to people with "life-challenging" illness.

We considered in Chapter 3 how some inductees to the Moonies had wandered into one or another of the group's social settings and then had become engaged in a "front" philosophy, such as support for world peace or meeting the challenge of ecology. Only later did they become aware that they had slowly become committed members of the Unification Church itself. A diffuse philosophy can lead to identification with a group and then to full affiliation with its subculture, both in cultic religious groups and spiritual recovery movements. Williamson's *A Return to Love* illustrates such a diffuse philosophy. It contains a grab bag of ideas about healing from a range of sources, including Carl Jung, Deepak Chopra, and the Holy Spirit. The reader can become his or her own healer by learning to act on the ability to love. Cancer patients who gain a healing dose of love by attending support groups are said to live twice as long. Williamson reports that this is due to a psychoimmunologic factor that in fact "is love, or God." She writes that recovery rates among patients choosing holistic medicine and traditional medical treatment "are roughly equal." These are leaps to generalization, at best.

Williamson's talk-show level of appeal is evident in *A Return to Love*, where she recalls suffering a "serious sore throat" on one occasion. She ordered a drink at a bar to salve the pain, and noticed a man looking at her flirtatiously. Overcoming her distaste for an encounter, she spoke to him and found to her surprise that he was a physician who then told her, "I can get you some erythromycin." She answered, "practically jumping up and down, 'This is a miracle! I [had] prayed for healing.'" For the reader, she then draws the lesson that "the Holy Spirit finds ways to express His power through vehicles we can accept. Medicine is such a vehicle."

Creative visualization, as well as barroom miracles, has a place in her world of healing. She tells the reader to imagine the AIDS virus as Darth Vader, and to unzip his suit to let an angel out, transforming darkness into light. She then reflects that when the cure for AIDS is found, millions of prayers will have helped it happen. It is not hard to see the parallels between the spiritual appeal of a vague ideology in some cults and the engaging quality of her diffuse philosophy of healing.

A culture of healing may come down to what the sick person *believes,* not what is scientifically proven. You can believe what you hear about biomedicine from your doctor, or you can believe that *pranayama,* or balanced breathing, can soothe your nervous system and cure depression or even cancer. It is the seeming credibility of the practitioner, and the social context in which he operates, that largely determines which view will appear most credible. Spiritual recovery movements can be bolstered by their ties to a non-Western healing philosophy, the trappings of a quasimedical alternative health care clinic, the fervent endorsement of others who underwent treatment, the enthusiasm of a television talk-show host, or the fanfare surrounding a bestselling book. A similar group psychology also plays a role in the acceptance of new, scientifically validated treatments. Doctors implicitly instill hope in their patients whenever they offer a new treatment option. Spiritually oriented recovery movements differ from biomedicine, however, in that they are hardly ever submitted to controlled studies and objective validation.

The experience of Annette, a woman in her early thirties, illustrates the casual entry of many people into a healing culture. She told me how she had suffered a painful back injury six years before. She reported that a radiologist told her at that time that she had a "fracture at T12," but her doctors provided no relief. Some time later, a friend introduced her to a practitioner of Chinese medicine who gave her considerable relief from pain through acupuncture. Annette's interest in Eastern healing practices and their spiritual meaning grew, and she began attending meetings of a committed group of followers led by the practitioner. She also began practicing meditation, "breathing deeply and focusing the energy on a series of organs, starting at the face, moving through the internal organs, and clearing the body." Two years later, she developed a severe cough accompanied by "chills and a fever of 102." Although told by a physician friend of hers that she might have pneumonia and should be examined in his office, she "took ginger baths, and was in bed with probably five quilts for a couple of days. I meditated and recovered."

What happened here? While experiencing distress, this woman was exposed to an explanation of her pain associated with an unconventional medical treatment. Feeling relief, she attributed her recovery to a spiritual philosophy that she later began to practice in an enthusiastic group setting. Importantly, she also felt a greater sense of personal control or self-efficacy by virtue of adopting this spiritually oriented approach. She then applied it to another illness, potentially unwisely.

A sense of *self-efficacy,* the conviction that one has the ability to actively master a challenge, can help patients mobilize themselves when they need to address their illness.[54] It has been shown that constructive interventions made to improve patients' sense of self-efficacy, by engaging them actively in framing their own treatment, can enhance compliance with conventional care.[55] An enhanced sense of efficacy, however, can also have a negative effect if it moves a person toward a conversion to ineffective alternative care and/or to shun needed conventional treatment. This concept of self-efficacy certainly helps to explain why many people are attracted to an active role of choosing alternative medical treatments and self-care.

Consolidating the Belief System

Affiliation with a zealous movement can offer considerable emotional relief to a sick person. As we saw with cults, this *relief effect* can also serve as the basis for operant reinforcement of involvement in a spiritual recovery movement over the course of membership. That is to say, the relief from uncertainty when a person accepts a new perspective can provide ongoing reinforcement of his or her commitment to the group and its views. The tie to the movement is reinforced by the relief from malaise that a sick person feels and attributes to involvement in the group. The movement then serves as a buffer against distress, much the way religion can help people deal with adversity by providing the comfort of a supernatural rationale for their difficulties.

This emotional support can be important in conventional care as well. Most psychological therapies relieve distress by systematically replacing a perspective of disillusionment with a newer, more hopeful outlook. Professionally conducted cognitive therapy is designed to do this by reconstructing a depressed person's understanding of the circumstances that make him or her view the world in a bleak way.[56] It constitutes a therapeutic "ideology" of sorts but is delivered without a value-laden belief system. Self-help groups like Rational Recovery for alcoholics also take a cognitive approach by teaching members to suppress thoughts related to their craving for a drink. Such groups make a consistent effort to take steps to transform a patient's initially hopeless outlook, just as a spiritual recovery movement tries on every occasion to overcome the pessimism and helplessness people feel because of their disease.

Spiritual recovery movements, however, add the dimension of faith in a new explanatory philosophy to sustain sick persons in their cognitive restructuring. This transformation takes place by instilling belief in the transcendent quality of the movement's philosophy and approach to therapy. For example, the physician Bernie Siegel tells patients with cancer that by changing their attitude and getting in touch with their inner strengths, they can become what he calls "exceptional cancer patients." Siegel believes that this enhanced strength and awareness produces physiologic changes that can alter the course of disease.[57]

Achieving Compliance

Spiritual recovery movements expect their adherents to comply with certain ritualized "healing" activities such as herbal diets, meditation, or spiritually oriented meetings. Since acceptance of the movement's credo is supposed to yield relief from illness, a new recruit will be inclined to go along with the suggested regimen rather than violate the beliefs that are a source of comfort. Whether this helps improve health status clearly depends on the nature of the rituals themselves and whether the sick person is encouraged to seek conventional medical care when it is needed. In the case of AIDS treatment, for example, where medication regimens are complex and onerous, compliance can be a problem. If alternative care is not supportive of medical treatment, the patient is likely to suffer greatly.

Many people will comply with instructions cloaked in the credibility of "scientific" or "medical" authority, even if they are asked to do things they would usually consider unacceptable. As we saw in Chapter 8, Milgram found that research volunteers would administer shocks to a seemingly innocent person when they were given a specious rationale by a sham researcher who was supposedly carrying out a psychological experiment.[58] In another study, psychiatrists prepped to participate in a sham treatment study telephoned their hospital with orders to administer seemingly toxic doses of a supposedly new drug. Almost all the nurses who answered the phone complied with the orders given, even though they ran counter to hospital procedures and the nurses had been alerted to the drug's potential toxicity.[59] Such findings help explain the harm done to recruits in some dubious spiritual movements like Scientology. Once members accept the authority of a supposed healing program, they may comply with its demands even if they are inflicting harm.

The intensity of belief in spiritually based healing is sometimes accompanied by a denial of reality if that denial is necessary to sustain the credibility of a movement's effectiveness. In one study, people affiliated with fundamentalist churches who participated in faith healing for medical illness were found to believe that their illness had improved in an objective way, although in fact there had been no measurable change in their physical status.[60] Psychological testing revealed that they were denying the reality of their illness. The healing ritual had apparently provided them with a basis for coping with illness that was in direct conflict with reality but was comforting to them and was supported by their belief system.

11

ALTERNATIVE HEALING IN THE MEDICAL MAINSTREAM

Two recent developments illustrate how spiritually oriented recovery movements are entering into medical settings. One is religious, the other secular. They show how ideologic commitment can introduce an alternative medical technique into established medical settings. In the first, an organization of fundamentalist Christian psychiatrists has drawn on their beliefs to treat patients who share the same faith. The second is quite different: zealous alcoholic patients have co-managed a hospital-based clinic with its medical staff, promoting stronger engagement of new patients and greater cost efficiency. We will see how accepted standards for health care can be modified by such developments, where the forces observed in charismatic groups play a role in conventional medical care.

The Christian Medical and Dental Society

A few years ago, I began a study to see how religious spirituality can play a role in professional mental health care. My colleagues and I used a model of charismatic groups to examine the role of shared belief, altered consciousness, and social cohesiveness in this form of healing, and the question of how these forces affected conformity to the behavioral norms of fundamentalism. We surveyed 145 psychiatrists who were members of the Christian Medical and Dental Society (CMDS)[1] and not surprisingly found that they shared a strong religious commitment. Almost all said that they had been born again and that they had encouraged someone to accept Jesus as a savior (96%). Their religious orientation colored their views on sexual behavior. The great majority felt that homosexual relations between consenting adults are wrong (88%), as well as sexual relations before marriage (86%) and abortion on demand (99%).

How did such beliefs affect the behavior of these psychiatrists? We solicited their views on introducing religious practice into their care of patients by asking about their belief in the therapeutic effectiveness of the Bible and prayer in treating mental illness. They scored Bible and prayer as more effective than medications and psychotherapy for many nonpsychotic syndromes, such as suicidal intent, grief reactions, and alcoholism. They discriminated between believers and nonbelievers with regard to the suitability of prayer as treatment. Over half reported that they would use prayer as a "therapeutic approach" for depressed patients (52%) and alcoholics (59%) who were "committed to Christian beliefs." Few said they would use it with those patients if they were from a "nonbelieving Christian background" (14% and 20%, respectively).

To examine how the Christian psychiatrists' involvement in religion affected their own emotional state, we used the scale for emotional distress from my studies of religious cults. The psychiatrists' self-reports indicated a marked decline in distress during the period immediately after they had "been born again or [had] an intense religious experience that changed [their] outlook on life."[2] This is illustrated by a decline of more severe mental health problems among some of the members; whereas 19% felt very anxious before their born-again experience, only 1% reported that they felt that way in the month following their religious experience. This decline in malaise, reflected in a number of items queried, suggested the psychologically reinforcing nature of the religious experience, one that paralleled the relief effect typically observed in the new religious movements. These psychiatrists felt that they had been relieved of unhappiness by means of a religious experience, and they maintained a stronger religious orientation in their daily professional lives after their spiritual awakening.

They also felt very close to their fellow members. We had them apply our cohesiveness scale to two different groups of psychiatrists: the ten CMDS psychiatrists they knew best, and the ten psychiatrists they knew best who were *not* members of that organization. They were much closer to the Christian psychiatrists than to the nonmembers.[3] For example, when asked, "Do you like being part of their activities?" 61% responded affirmatively for the ten fellow members, but only 15% did so for the ten nonmembers.

The experience of one of the members shows how a period of emotional distress had a critical influence on his later career, a course typical of many participants in the study. His experience also shows how Christian psychiatrists often draw on biblical passages as an aid in treating patients. Dr. North came from a churchgoing background but had grown up with little interest in religion. In college he decided to participate in a Bible class to find solace during a period of depression, and during the closing prayer of that class one day, he suddenly felt intensely that he was being born again in Christ. From that point on, he embarked on a plan to combine his religious commitment with his plans for a career in medicine. This course was not without conflict, though, as he was reprimanded during his psychiatric residency for engaging a patient in prayer as part of his treatment.

At the time of the study, Dr. North was admitting patients to a private psychiatric hospital where many of the staff were "Christian-oriented." He said that his therapeutic approach was conventional but when appropriate he went further and brought Christian beliefs into the session, though he had refused to lay on hands when occasionally asked to do so by a patient. Although he was not promoting himself as a "Christian psychiatrist" per se, many of his patients were referred to him because of their strong religious persuasion and desire to be treated by someone with similar beliefs.

When asked to give an example of his work, Dr. North described an experience with Joan, a forty-one-year-old devout Christian, who suffered an episode of severe depression and delusions, apparently precipitated by the suicide of her teenage daughter. Dr. North hospitalized her and prescribed antidepressant and antipsychotic medications, but in their therapy sessions in the hospital, Joan was unable to express her feelings of sadness and anger. She asked to bring her Bible into their sessions, but he refused to let her, fearing that she would find a passage like the one about Judas hanging himself, and do the same. After Joan's psychosis abated, though, he felt that it was important for her to fully express her grief and anger over the loss of her child, so he read passages from the New Testament with her which showed that God allows justified anger and that a bereft person should go through a period of grief. The citations carried an authority for this devout woman that the doctor's support alone could not, and they helped her accept his message of the validity of expressing her feelings and putting her grief behind her.

Although the introduction of Bible reading moved the therapy away from the psychiatric mainstream, it was consistent with the culture that the doctor and patient shared and did not (at least in Dr. North's view) undermine the medical treatment. Furthermore, Joan had done well on her medications, so the doctor did not resort to a risky religious intervention out of desperation.

Not all patients can be treated effectively, though, and psychiatrists must often make difficult clinical decisions subjectively, sometimes with a considerable sense of conflict over how to best address their patients' needs. In another Christian psychiatry case, intense religious belief apparently compromised the physician's good judgment. Sheila, a forty-two-year-old woman with a long history of heavy drinking and depression, was referred to Dr. Lawrence by the local mental health center. Her problems had contributed to the breakup of her marriage several years before and to her estrangement from her family of origin. The other family members were churchgoing, devout Christians who expressed great displeasure over her drinking and her transient relationships with men she met in bars. Dr. Lawrence admitted Sheila to the hospital for detoxification and encouraged her to become involved in Alcoholics Anonymous. She did attend AA meetings and stopped drinking after she was discharged. She also began to express an interest in the religious commitment that she knew Dr. Lawrence espoused, and asked him to pray with her, which he did briefly at the beginning of each of their sessions. But Sheila still hadn't recovered from her depressive symptoms after a few months, despite a variety of medications. She stopped going to AA and began drinking in a limited way. She did, however, stay in therapy and would appear early in the doctor's waiting room before each scheduled session. Around this time, according to Dr. Lawrence, Sheila had an intense religious experience and her mood and drinking problem improved for a few weeks. She then began to pray "even more intensely."

Dr. Lawrence was called out of town on family business rather suddenly but was available to his patients by phone. He did not hear from Sheila for two weeks when, to his great distress, he was informed that she had made a serious suicide attempt and had been admitted to the hospital. Before he returned from his trip, however, she signed out of the hospital against medical advice. When he returned to the hospital, he received a note saying that she had left him and that she retained her strong religious feelings and "cared for him greatly" for what he had "given her"; but the note did not say why she had left and disappeared without a trace.

Dr. Lawrence was clearly very touched by Sheila. He felt that her outcome was positive because she had found in religion the means of moving toward a resolution of her problem and toward "salvation" from her troubled life. When asked, he acknowledged that he did not know whether she had stopped drinking, gotten over her depression, or made any major changes in her lifestyle after she left the hospital. From what Dr. Lawrence said, there was actually no reason for believing that Sheila was achieving a resolution of her psychiatric problems, alcoholism, and depression. In addition, it appeared that she had developed a dependent relationship on him before he left town, which he interpreted as mutual religious commitment. In fact, he may have inadvertently left her in a vulnerable position, feeling rejected when he left town, and this might have contributed to her suicide attempt.

In maintaining a reasonable balance between religious belief and medical management, Dr. North is more typical of the Christian psychiatrists I interviewed. Dr. Lawrence's case, on the other hand, illustrates that such balance is not always achieved. Lawrence's reliance on a religious perspective led him to seriously misread his patient's vulnerabilities. This can be true of practitioners in spiritually oriented healing movements as well.

The Unmet Need and Its Relationship to Alternative Medicine

The emergence of an organized group of fundamentalist Christian psychiatrists can be considered in light of the popularity of alternative medicine. This is evident in the disparity between most psychiatrists' religious views and those of the general population of the United States. Whereas 95% of the general public believes in God or a higher power, most psychiatrists (56%) are agnostics or atheists.[4] Psychiatrists' lack of attention to the religious and spiritual concerns of their patients is evident in their psychiatric journals, where only 3% of published articles include a measured religious variable.[5] This limited attention to religion is striking, considering the ubiquity of religious belief in America and the way in which religion can affect mental and emotional states.

My colleagues and I found similar discrepancies in attitude between our indigent, typically homeless, addicted patients at Bellevue Hospital in New York and the medical students who participate in their treatment. The students ranked a belief in God among the *least* important of the factors they thought the patients themselves considered important to their recovery. They felt that creature comforts like better food and housing would be seen by patients as most important to their own rehabilitation. The patients, on the other hand, rated belief in God as most important to their recovery.[6] These findings point to a need for religious sensitivity and support that the Christian psychiatrists respond to in their patients. They help explain the emergence of nonmedical movements like AA as a way to address spiritual needs that are ignored by medical practitioners.

The incorporation of religious belief into psychiatric practice, however, is a large step beyond the expression of sensitivity to patients' beliefs. By merging the medical with the spiritual, physicians must change the standards of treatment they learned in standard specialty training. One thing that can promote such a change is an intense religious experience like being born again, which yields relief from emotional distress and serves to focus commitment. The organized Christian psychiatrists espouse a set of strongly held beliefs, rooted in the Bible and promoted by evangelical Christians; these shared beliefs gave legitimacy to their adoption of new standards of behavior, which include a religious orientation in their therapy. Responses to our survey indicated that the converts became engaged in a cohesive group that sustained their acceptance of these beliefs. As in other spiritual healing movements, they turned to an explanatory system of beliefs that shaped their conception of illness as a spiritual malady, and how it should be addressed. This view was clearly sought out by a number of patients who wanted spiritual solace in the face of mental distress.

The Self-Help Clinic: Impact on Institutional Care

Modern health care bureaucracies can be oppressive, denying patients the support they need to cope with illness and leaving them isolated from any human relationship with their treatment providers. The spiritual recovery movements raise important questions in this regard. Can the zeal they generate be introduced into the treatment systems of our large medical centers? Can they be adapted in some form in order to create a sense of community in medically run, conventional treatment settings? This may suggest alternative approaches to established medical care for the future. To address the questions raised, I drew on my specialty experience in addiction treatment and designed an experimental program for alcoholism rehabilitation in a large hospital. Over time, my colleagues and I developed an approach that we have continued to use for the last twenty years.

One premise in our undertaking was that the chronic alcoholic's commitment to abstinence is essentially an ideologic one. Rationality alone does not succeed in addiction recovery because the idea of abstinence runs counter to the compulsion and the impulses that dominate the alcoholic's thinking. Abstinence must be sustained by an abiding *belief* in its worth and an emotional commitment to it. After years of being addicted, a person is always doing battle with the alcoholic's usual logic—that one drink, or even an evening's drinking, won't really hurt.

To counter this alcoholic logic, we started a program in which the treatment community as a group espoused a belief in not drinking, based on intense affiliative ties among the patient members. These alcoholics were welcomed into a close-knit mutual-aid network of cooperative self-help at the outset of their hospital treatment in order to mitigate the impersonal nature of institutional care in our large municipal facility and to provide an opportunity for shared commitment to the ideology of abstinence. I had been impressed by the ability of both the charismatic religious sects and Alcoholics Anonymous to bring about a reduction in the use of alcohol among their members by similar means.

Such an undertaking would have little value in the long run if it did not address an unmet need for cost-effectiveness. In financial terms, the overall cost of alcoholism to American society in lost work and medical treatments is remarkably high, $162 billion a year by one estimate,[7] in large part because many alcoholics go without needed care. We thought the appeal of alcoholism rehabilitation could be enhanced by integrating some of the characteristics of spiritual recovery movements into medically based institutional care and having patients assume the bulk of responsibility for the operation of their programs. This might generate greater commitment and optimism and cut back on the amount of professional staffing needed to run treatment programs.

Two aspects of charismatic group psychology were important in developing our own program: the remarkable degree of social cohesiveness that marks AA groups, and the system of shared beliefs in abstinence. We tried to incorporate these elements into our hospital-based program by generating mutual dependency among patients: developing a set of small, interrelated patient-run therapy groups, each around ten members, where leadership no longer resided exclusively in the professionals who govern as authority figures. Instead, it fell largely into the hands of a network of stabilized, abstinent patients who had themselves confronted the same problems as the new patients—"co-converts," as it were. This approach stands in contrast to the typical format of institutional treatment, where a clear distinction is drawn between the healers and the healed. The professionals in most medical institutions effectively place the patients in a passive position by prescribing and dispensing therapy without affording them an opportunity to assume an active role in managing their treatment structure.

Implementation

We set up this experiment within the alcoholism program of the Bronx Municipal Hospital Center, a large public facility affiliated with Albert Einstein College of Medicine. This program, established to treat poor patients, consisted of a twenty-bed ward and a large outpatient clinic. Most of the patients were black or Hispanic, unmarried, unemployed, and high school dropouts. Alcoholics of this background generally have a poor prognosis for continuing with an addiction treatment program, and the need to sustain their morale and commitment in a large public hospital is acute. On admission, those who had the most severe problems withdrawing from alcohol went directly to the inpatient service for an average of ten days and were then discharged to the ambulatory clinic; less disabled ones began their treatment as outpatients.

For the purposes of comparison, we divided the clinic in two: the conventional program, entirely professionally run, and the experimental program, based on peer support. In the conventional program, therapy groups were conducted by social workers or trained alcoholism counselors, and were supplemented by individual counseling. In the experimental program, the management of treatment was placed largely in the hands of the patients; both the orientation and long-term therapy groups were led by a cadre of senior patients who had established sobriety and demonstrated a measure of social stability over the several months since they had been admitted. These senior patients monitored the progress of each of the patients entering the program. The program's professional therapists would drop in on the therapy group meetings occasionally, and would meet with the senior patients in a consultation group to help them manage more difficult clinical issues. It was made clear to the self-help patients that their first line of support in the clinic was to be their peer group, not the professional staff.

Upon entry into the experimental program, patients also joined the patient-run "Self-Help Club," which was given responsibility for many of the functions that would have been carried out by professional therapists in the traditional program. The club's purpose was to help patients keep in touch outside the clinic, to enable them to reach out to patients who did not return to treatment, and to provide each other with support while they were away from the clinic. Established members showed newer ones how to navigate the welfare system, since most were on public assistance. A club member was also assigned to each of the inpatients to acquaint these newcomers with the program's operation and to encourage a smooth transition into ambulatory care. In this way, the program was personified by a cohesive peer group with consensually supported beliefs, rather than an impersonal hospital bureaucracy.

A redefinition of the role of the counseling staff was also essential to the experimental model. Therapists were assigned *twice* the number of patients as was the case in the traditional program. This fit their role as facilitators of the self-help process rather than traditional managers of care for each individual patient. The staff promoted the program's "self-help philosophy," whereby patients worked with their peers when they encountered problems rather than relying on members of the hospital's bureaucracy.

We had learned from the charismatic sects and the spiritual recovery movements that the support of a zealous group culture with a shared mission helps maintain members' consensual ideology. It was therefore important that communication take place not only in the smaller therapy groups but also in meetings that involved the entire population of the experimental program, to enhance group cohesiveness and commitment to the shared ideology. A number of patient-run activities, such as a steering committee, recreational activities, outings, and a monthly meeting of all the program's members, were used for this purpose.

This treatment approach entailed a considerable shift in relations with the rest of the hospital. For example, staff from other services were sometimes puzzled to find a recovering alcoholic patient escorting a newly admitted one for general medical care, rather than seeing the patient accompanied by a staff member. These peer escorts, however, allowed a new patient to experience the trip as a protected entry into the alien culture of the hospital.

Raymond's experience was typical of our "self-help" patients. He had been an outpatient for eight months, abstinent for the last four until he took a drink after a family argument. Within a few days he was drinking heavily and fell down a flight of stairs, bruising his head badly. The next morning he came to the clinic for help without an appointment and asked to speak with his group leader, the senior patient whom he knew well. The senior patient along with another patient who was there at the time pressed Raymond to go for a medical evaluation for his head injury, hoping to use this to help him terminate his relapse. The two peers spoke with Raymond's staff therapist, who saw him briefly with the clinic nurse and wrote a referral note for medical assessment. After a supportive exchange with Raymond, the two patients prevailed on him to seek further help and to go with them to the emergency service. They later took him to an AA meeting at a chapter the three had previously attended. With their assistance, and with further contact from another member of his peer-led therapy group, Raymond was able to maintain abstinence until his next group meeting at the clinic. At the meeting, an additional member offered to spend time with him during the next few days to provide encouragement and support.

Raymond's fellow patients were able to collaborate with the staff and make use of the cohesive ties within the group as well, as they had been socialized to the program's norms for helping each other and making use of the hospital facilities. Without the strong supportive network afforded by these social ties and the abstinence ideology promoted by AA, Raymond might not have been reengaged in the program and returned to abstinence. In this respect, these interactions were similar to those in the charismatic sects; they embodied an intimacy and intensity felt for anyone identified as a member of the group, and allowed for a great deal of mutual support.

Evaluating the Program's Effectiveness

We carried out two studies to compare the effectiveness of the experimental and the traditional programs. In an era of cutbacks in financial support for alcoholism rehabilitation, we were attentive to the economic criteria, to ensure that we could continue to treat all the patients whom we hoped to serve. Our first consideration was to see how each program dealt with the high rate at which patients dropped out of care after leaving the ward and entering the clinic.[8] There was a significant difference between the two programs: 84% of the experimental patients who had been exposed to their outpatient peers while on the hospital ward moved on to the clinic after discharge, while only 52% of the inpatients treated in the traditional program did so. For the patients who began in the outpatient clinic right off, there were no significant differences in dropout rates between the experimental and the traditional treatment programs, though the experimental program was operating with half the counseling staff of the conventional program. The self-help format apparently enabled counselors to effectively treat much higher numbers of patients, so the program was more efficient on economic grounds.

In a second study, we evaluated patients who continued in therapy for a full year and compared the self-help patients with those who did not have the peer-led model but instead had twice the counseling staff.[9] Of all the patients, only a small minority (18%) had been free from alcohol for a month at the time of admission. At the end of a year, a clear majority (74%) had not drunk for at least one month, and half (53%) were attending AA, with no difference between the two groups. The number of patients who had active relationships with their families had increased over the year (from 37% to 56%), as had the number who were working at least part-time (from 15% to 31%). Similarly, the number without a stable residence had declined by half (from 20% to 10%). At each month of treatment, patients who were in the experimental program performed as well as those in the traditional one.

These findings came as a surprise to many psychiatrists who assumed that usual standards for professional staffing could not be compromised without a loss in therapeutic effectiveness. Success in allowing indigent, addicted people to have a hand in program governance was unexpected by many professionals as well.

The viability of this program suggests that a zealous self-help model can be used to increase the effectiveness of other kinds of health care. And we have adapted the approach to treat patients with combined mental illness and drug addiction,[10] in a form recognized by the American Psychiatric Association[11] for its effectiveness and acceptability within the medical mainstream.

Alternative medicine places emphasis on treaters outside the professional mainstream, and patients' initiative in framing their own care. The idea of adapting the spiritual recovery idea and peer support to institutional care is quite promising in this regard. It offers a chance to motivate patients for self-help, since health care bureaucracies are poor candidates for motivating people to move toward recovery. In time we may find the compassion seen in the alternative-medicine movement introduced into the medical mainstream. With sensitivity and a good dose of common sense, this can be done without compromising the scientific foundations of contemporary medical care.

12

THE AA EXAMPLE

A contemporary charismatic healing group such as Alcoholics Anonymous provides a model of an effective, inexpensive social instrument that can be used to treat certain psychological problems, and the operation of this group can be understood by comparing it with charismatic religious sects. Members of AA healing groups are highly cohesive; they maintain a system of shared beliefs and their behavior is strongly influenced by the group. Despite these points of similarity to religious sects, however, important differences emerge. For example, the behavioral demands of such a healing group relate only to the recovery from illness, not to unrelated aspects of their members' lives such as the occupation they should pursue or how they should manage their family relations. Religious sects generally have a universalist philosophy and a code of behavior touching on all aspects of the lives of their adherents.

The two types of groups also differ in the target of their efforts. The healing group directs its emphasis primarily at change in its own members, while the religious groups promote an ideology ostensibly intended to transform the world. Insofar as AA does not impinge on the values of the broader society, it is less likely than religious sects to generate conflicts at its boundary. Indeed, its ideology is compatible with mainstream attitudes and often gets support and encouragement from nonmembers.

Alcoholics Anonymous (AA), founded in 1935, is an excellent illustration of how a charismatic healing group can develop from its origins in intense personal leadership through to its establishment as a stable, albeit zealous, institution. Although AA is now a worldwide organization with over one million members and a stable administrative structure, new recruits still recapitulate the zealous experience of its founder in some fashion as they become engaged into the group. We will consider the evolution of AA in three stages, each with counterparts in the development of other charismatic groups whose success has allowed them to follow a path of maturation—using a model originally developed by Max Weber.[1]

The Charismatic Gift of Alcoholics Anonymous

Alcoholics Anonymous had its origin in the transcendent religious experience of its principal founder, Bill W., whose tale, like those of so many other leaders of charismatic groups, was one of protracted distress—in this case from alcoholism. He is referred to by his first name only, in accordance with the AA tradition of anonymity, but his history is well known.[2] He was born in East Dorset, Vermont, in 1895, into a middle-class family. Bill began studies in electrical engineering while in reserve officer training in college, but also began drinking heavily. He recalled later that he used liquor to override the inhibitions he felt in dealing with people, particularly his "social betters." By the time of the Great Depression, Bill was drinking gin around the clock, while living off his wife's meager income.

In the course of Bill's deterioration, an old drinking friend named Ebby came by to visit him and described his own experience in the Oxford Group, a zealous religious sect. Ebby averred that his involvement in this sect allowed him to overcome his problem with alcohol and achieve sobriety. Meetings of the Oxford Group were characterized by open confessions and guidance from the members in the assembled group.

At the time of this encounter, Bill's situation was grave—he had been hospitalized for detoxification four times during the past year. Wearied and shaken by his drinking, he was struck by his friend's good grooming and attractive appearance and by the influence that might be exerted when one alcoholic shared with another his own struggles to control his drinking. Not long after, he had a revelatory experience.

> All at once I found myself crying out, "If there is a God, let Him show himself! I am ready to do anything, anything!"
>
> Suddenly the room lit up with a great white light. I was caught up on an ecstasy which there are no words to describe. It seemed to me in my mind's eye, that I was on a mountain and that a wind not of air but of spirit was blowing. And then it burst upon me that I was a free man. Slowly the ecstasy subsided. I lay there on the bed, but now for a time I was in another world, a new world of consciousness . . . and I thought to myself, "So this is the God of the preachers!" A great peace stole over me.[3]

The very intensity of this transcendent experience made the episode a turning point in his achieving sobriety, and Bill began preaching to alcoholics at the hospital where he had been admitted many times.

But this in itself had little impact. So, influenced by the Oxford group, he established a network of mutual aid and discovered the effectiveness of social support when there is a commitment to a common goal. By 1937 Bill and a co-founder could count forty alcoholics with whom they had struggled, who had themselves experienced the intensity of spiritual recovery and its attendant abstinence.[4] Within two more years their group had grown to one hundred, and they published the book *Alcoholics Anonymous,* which was to become the movement's bible. From the start, AA displayed characteristics of a charismatic sect: strongly felt shared belief, intense cohesiveness, experiences of altered consciousness, and a potent influence on members' behavior. New adherents also pursued an apostolic mission of converting despairing alcoholics, imbued with the charismatic zeal and proselytizing urge of its founder Bill W.

The Routinization of Charisma

The sociologist Max Weber defined the role of the charismatic leader in terms of the ability to galvanize people into pursuing a transcendent mission, but he pointed out that such a leader could only be successful in the long run if he created a structured social order and an attendant body of tradition. Alcoholics Anonymous has indeed evolved from the zealous ideal of its founder into an effectively managed organization. By the time of its fiftieth anniversary in 1985 it had 58,576 chapters in over ninety countries with more than one million members.[5] Harrison Trice,[6] who has closely followed AA's evolution, suggested that its expansion illustrates the manner in which it conforms to Weber's conception of the routinization of charisma. Through historical study, Weber observed that the powers of a charismatic leader persist as they become invested in a successor's organizational roles and the ritual trappings of their movement.

THE DEVELOPMENT OF RITUAL

The transcendent mission of a routinized charismatic group is expressed in its rites and rituals. Using these behavioral prescriptions, the group establishes standards of how its members should conduct themselves in their own lives and in their joint activities, in conformity with the group's mission. Although few rites and rituals are rigidly defined by AA, members across the globe adhere carefully and zealously to the ones that are.

As in the Oxford Group, AA meetings exhibited from the outset ritualized open confessions of prior transgressions and the acceptance of a "Higher Power" for guidance. Of the Twelve Steps of Alcoholics Anonymous, ten are based on the creed of the Oxford Group. The other two, the open acknowledgment of helplessness before alcohol and carrying the message to other alcoholics, are unique to AA.

A central ritual in membership is the regular attendance of AA chapter meetings. Inductees are expected to come to "ninety meetings in ninety days" when they first join, so as to bolster their abstinence and commitment to the group and after this they attend meetings at least once or twice a week, often daily. The meetings vary in format only slightly in different chapters, and their rites are therefore immediately recognizable in settings separated by thousands of miles. For example, all who speak at a meeting begin by saying "My name is _____, and I am an alcoholic," symbolizing their rejection of the denial of their illness typical of alcoholics. Such well-known sayings as "One day at a time" and "Easy does it," drawn from the writings of Bill W., are part of the verbal exchanges. They appear on posters and signs at meetings, and are even popular as bumper stickers. This ritualized use of language binds people together and reinforces the conformity requisite to committed membership. It represents an acceptance of myth-building and the "loading" of language with the group's own connotations.[7]

Specific meetings are also given their own ritualized meaning, such as those celebrating members' achieving ninety days and then a year of sobriety. On these occasions, the celebrants relate the story of their alcoholism and recovery to date. Each typically portrays the descent into alcoholism, his or her abject state during that period, and eventual transformation by means of engagement with Alcoholics Anonymous. The litany of sin and redemption by each speaker, heard in different variations many times over, is compelling for the sincerity and weight of personal testimony. Even the casual observer cannot help being swept up by the intense commitment of the speakers. One patient whom I referred to an AA meeting was skeptical before going but returned enthusiastic.

> I can't tell you how remarkable it was. I sat quietly in back, almost hiding from anyone who would acknowledge my presence, but each speaker drew me in. There was a magnetism and passion in their tales, and I felt moved by them as people who had just then become important to me. It was personal in a way I never expected.

As in most charismatic groups, the pursuit of new members is an important component of ritual. It supports members' commitment by underlining the credibility of the movement, since the testimony of new members provides further validation of the group's ideals. The mutual assistance inherent in the induction process also helps established members sustain their sobriety, as they themselves identify with the struggle of new members to overcome the denial of their illness and withstand their craving for alcohol.

Emphasis on induction has been an essential theme running through the group's evolution. It was a central aspect of Bill W.'s charismatic mission, from the time he began to preach to hospitalized alcoholics. His subsequent work with Dr. Bob, the next convert to Bill's emerging model, was prototypical of the later ritual of "Twelfth-Step" recruitment activities carried out between a member and a new recruit. This role has been transmitted in an apostolic manner to subsequent generations of members; all inductees are expected to establish a formalized relationship with a long-term member who can serve as their sponsor in the arduous process of recovery.

The sponsorship ritual illustrates the value of the formalized induction format within the charismatic group, as the fledgling member chooses a mentor from long-standing members. The relationship is a rather demanding one for both parties, and entails daily confessional communications from inductee to sponsor for many months. Members are thus introduced to many of the group's practices, such as the Twelve Steps, and engaged in a continuing dependency. These roles have their counterparts in most other routinized charismatic groups, such as the central figures of the Unification Church.

One study of the exchanges between sponsors and inductees revealed the evolving relationship between the two.[8] As the recruits' length of sobriety increased, a shift occurred away from morale building and specific instructions for achieving abstinence toward personal change and spiritual growth. As in other charismatic movements, the new member first picks up the rudiments of conformity and later moves on to a deeper restructuring of psychological adaptation.

The sponsorship ritual is important to the sobriety of the sponsor who derives strength from providing advice and serving as a model. One study of a sample of AA members revealed that a majority (66%) of those who successfully achieved abstinence had served as sponsors, while only a minority (19%) of unsuccessful members had played this role.[9]

As in all other charismatic groups, involvement in newfound rituals creates conflict in the members' preexisting relationships, since major changes in commitment and lifestyle do not come without a disruptive effect. The nature of induction to AA and the conflicts it may raise can be seen in a patient I treated for alcoholism and referred to AA. Harry consulted me because of increasing difficulties at work. As an executive in a large corporation he was under the scrutiny of his superiors because of several episodes of intoxication on the job, particularly while on business trips. When he and I reached an understanding that his problems were caused by alcoholism, we agreed that his treatment plan would include attending Alcoholics Anonymous and taking disulfiram (Antabuse), a medication that deters the alcoholic from drinking since it precipitates physical discomfort when alcohol is consumed.

Harry did well at first, but his commitment to AA was modest and on two business trips he skipped his disulfiram and drank immoderately. With my encouragement, he sought out a sponsor and began speaking with him each day. Despite reservations, Harry became increasingly involved with his sponsor and started to attend meetings on a daily basis. His "conversion," as it were, became evident in one of our psychotherapy sessions when I asked him how he felt about some problems he had been having at work. He responded with a look of calm determination that "I know now that everything will be all right as long as I follow the program because the alcoholic in me isn't speaking anymore. I take it one day at a time." The program was *the* program, AA, and "one day at a time" was one of its unmistakable catchphrases.

Harry and his fellowship had connected. He decided to follow the AA regimen and maintain sobriety, and continued to use AA catchwords and interpret many of his problems in terms of AA rhetoric. Actually, the language of AA served him reasonably well in expressing himself in therapy and probably in daily life.

Harry's strong bond to AA caused two problems in his ongoing relation-ships. His wife did not have the same enthusiasm for the fellowship, and his frequent absences from home while he attended meetings made her feel iso-lated and resentful. Despite Harry's attempts to convince her to attend Al-Anon, AA's counterpart organization for family members, she was uninter-ested in this group. As with members of charismatic religious groups, he had trouble empathizing with the reservations of a reluctant family member. In-deed, like those groups, AA instructs its members to cut off a spouse, sibling, or parent if they jeopardize one's commitment to the goals of membership. Harry was applying a ritualized AA solution to a family problem: send the spouse to Al-Anon. But it wasn't working.

Another conflict arose over Harry's taking disulfiram. Like many AA mem-bers, his sponsor was opposed to all psychiatric medications, viewing them as "crutches" whose use detracted from a full recovery through AA. Like other zealous groups, AA tends to see the world in black and white and sometimes eschews professional and scientific thinking alien to its ideology.

Both of Harry's conflicts demanded resolution. I met with him and his wife several times to aid her adjustment to his commitment to AA and help them work out some issues in their relationship. With Harry himself, I dealt only gingerly with the issue of disulfiram and AA, not wishing to come into direct conflict with the group. After a while, Harry saw less of his sponsor and continued taking the disulfiram in large part because he had chosen to avoid a conflict with me. But his commitment to AA remained strong. When dis-cussing his problems in organizing a division of the corporation where he worked, he commented about a competitor at work:

> I was going to get into a grand confrontation with Carter but you can't afford resentments if you're an alcoholic [an AA catchphrase]. I thought of Bill W. and of his setting up the General Service Board to succeed him. If he could work that miracle, I could certainly handle this problem of mine without a battle.

Harry was integrating the amorphous philosophy of the group as well as the experiences of its founder into his everyday life.

THE DEVELOPMENT OF WRITTEN AND ORAL TRADITIONS

A second component of the routinization of charisma is the emergence of traditions in which the sanctity ascribed to the original leader and the group is invested in fixed codes of behavior. The Twelve Steps, a written tradition, have a hallowed position in AA literature and are repeatedly reviewed and studied by members as they become more deeply involved in the movement; they are the group's Ten Commandments. Much of the success of AA is attributable to how the Steps deal specifically with alcoholism and do not form a general code for behavior. They are therefore applicable to diverse segments of society with very different lifestyles. Their narrow focus also serves to undercut the abuse of members for financial or personal gain, and minimizes the fears of new recruits that their lifestyles will be materially compromised by membership.

Consider the role of the first three Steps in supporting an abstinent lifestyle.

1. We admitted we were powerless over alcohol—that our lives had become unmanageable.
2. Came to believe that a Power greater than ourselves could restore us to sanity.
3. Made a Decision to turn our will and our lives over to the care of God, *as we understood Him.*[10]

In the Fourth Step, initiates are asked to undertake a protracted confession that, in Lifton's terms, acts to heighten their self-surrender.[11] In AA this is called a "fearless moral inventory," in which the member reviews individual failings and attempts to make amends. One other vital tradition, that of prosyletizing, is embodied in the Twelfth and final Step, in the words "We tried to carry the message to alcoholics." The Twelve Steps therefore serve as written guidelines for the personal conduct of members themselves.

THE ESTABLISHMENT OF AN ADMINISTRATIVE STRUCTURE

For a social system to sustain itself over time, it must have an internal organization that creates new initiatives, keeps order, and resolves everyday conflicts. Thus, a final component of the routinization of charisma is the development of an administrative apparatus to assure that the leadership functions are carried out over time. Here, too, Bill W. may be credited for having passed on his mantle of inspired leadership to a stable and effective organization, and the success of this accomplishment alone may well warrant the praise that Aldous Huxley gave him as "the greatest social architect of the century."[12] The well-organized but democratic hierarchy of AA bears his influence. While tradition is preserved by this organization, numerous devices prevent an ossification of leadership ranks and allow for the lively expression of the group's original charismatic mission.

Consider the ritual of sponsorship, the first rung in the group's leadership ladder. A sponsor is chosen by each new recruit and is then responsible for inculcating the new member in the lore of AA and helping the person follow through on the Twelve Steps. Because the choice of sponsor is essentially a free one, the institution prevents rigidity in this important managerial stratum.

At the next level of administration, in the chapters, formal and informal discussions define the proper relationships between members, and deliberations among chapter officers provide governance over local administrative issues. Chapters elect their officers at meetings open to all members and conduct their business by parliamentary procedure.

The Twelve Traditions define norms for behavior at higher administrative levels in a way that assures both the preservation of the group's charismatic role and the disavowal of personal gain or profit. They stipulate that members "need always maintain personal anonymity at the level of press, radio and films," thereby preventing the use of the affiliation for personal gain. They state further that "each group has but one primary purpose—to carry its message to the alcoholic who still suffers. . . . The name of AA ought never be drawn into public controversy," thereby preventing the development of off- shoot causes and enterprises that could vitiate the group's function. Feminist issues, for example, have attracted considerable attention among AA members in recent years, but they did not become established as institutional prerog- atives because of this constraint.

In her study of utopian communities, Rosabeth Kanter observed that those communes that achieved stability for the long term had succeeded in dis- persing charisma throughout the corporate group.[13] The establishment of the General Service Board of Alcoholics Anonymous, which Bill W. had desig- nated as the permanent successor to the fellowship's founders, made this possible for AA too. Operating through an annual General Services confer- ence attended by elected delegates from ninety-one geographic areas, the Board promulgates guidelines on issues of concern or controversy.

One further characteristic of the group's administrative function is dictated by the Traditions' injunction against accruing assets and power within the organization. Members pay no dues, but instead make small contributions of no more than a few dollars at each meeting. Even at the national level, large donations are not accepted, and no contributions at all are accepted from nonalcoholics. The fellowship's central offices are manned by a volunteer staff. The wisdom of this policy becomes apparent when comparisons are made to other charismatic groups in which leaders have been able to take advantage of members for their own financial advantage.

The Fully Evolved Healing Group

Alcoholics Anonymous is a good example of an institutionalized charismatic group with a narrowly defined goal. To learn more about such well-delineated groups, we will consider first AA's strengths and weaknesses, and then look at how some related groups, offshoots of AA, have fared. A comparison be- tween certain aspects of AA and charismatic religious groups will highlight how the format of the charismatic group may be adapted to specific focal goals.

AA's Success in the Community

In a careful review of studies on the outcome of AA participation, Chad Em- rick and his associates concluded that drinking problems abated in about two- thirds of AA members during their period of participation; they consumed either less alcohol or none at all.[14] Almost half of those who improved re- mained abstinent for a year. On the whole, AA proved superior to professional treatment in helping alcoholics maintain total abstinence, although organized professional care without AA membership was somewhat more effective than AA in helping alcoholics to reduce their drinking without total abstinence. AA therefore compares very favorably in outcome with more elaborate and costly professional management for those who turn to it for aid.

How did AA achieve success when there was little public appreciation of the needs of the alcoholic? In answering this question, we must examine the social context in which AA arose and then its psychology as a charismatic group. As a social movement, AA had a considerable advantage in gaining acceptance. Unlike the charismatic religious sects, no changes of the broader society were necessary to achieve its goals. Cooperation was expected only from its own participants, and they themselves were forewarned that they should anticipate little help from those close to them. The family and friends of AA recruits usually were pleased to be relieved of their burdens of so many years now that these alcoholics were attempting to help each other.

Response to AA in the press was quite positive too: reports heralding its success appeared soon after its inception. One early article in the Cleveland *Plain Dealer*, for example, led to a growth in the membership of its local chapter from fifty to three hundred in only twelve weeks. Another in the *Saturday Evening Post* brought 6,000 letters of inquiry from readers who wanted help.[15]

Alcoholics Anonymous also succeeded in developing a good working relationship with the medical community. Many hospitals now host AA chapter meetings, and AA inter-group offices maintain working relationships with detoxification centers, thereby assuring ready access to medical care for both new recruits and relapsed members. In fact, few if any medical facilities designated for alcoholism treatment in the United States today do not have on-site meetings integrated into their programs. Furthermore, the American Medical Society on Alcoholism and Other Drug Dependencies, the principal medical organization in this field, actively supports AA as a primary form of treatment. Indeed, the Society counts among its members a good number of recovering alcoholic physicians who recovered through AA. When it is successful, the battle that AA fights against an inner opponent, the craving to drink, enhances the beliefs of new members and draws them into close ties with their fellow members, strengthening their commitment to the group and its mission. AA members are very much bound together by their struggle against a common enemy.

AA Psychology

The psychology of AA as a charismatic group is of course central to its success. Alcoholics are most likely to turn to AA when they have "bottomed out," or reached a nadir of despair, which opens them to alternatives. In this they resemble recruits to religious sects, who tend to be distressed as well as alienated from those closest to them at the time of their induction.[16]

Recruitment into AA occurs in a psychological context that allows communication to be closely controlled, so as to assure that the group's ideology will be sustained in the face of uncommitted active drinkers. As in the Unification Church workshops, most of those attending AA chapter meetings are deeply involved in the group ethos, and the expression of views opposed to the group's model of treatment is subtly or expressly discouraged. A good example is the fellowship's response to the concept of controlled drinking, an approach to alcoholism treatment based on limiting alcohol intake rather than totally abstaining. Some investigators and clinicians have reported success with this alternative to treatment.[17] The approach, however, is unacceptable within the AA tradition, and the option is therefore anathema to active members. It is rarely brought up by speakers at meetings and suppressed when it is raised. As an inductee becomes involved in the group, the sponsor monitors the person's views carefully, assuring that the recruit adheres to the perspective into which the sponsor was drawn; any hint of an interest in controlled drinking is discouraged. Similar constraints would be applied if a recruit questioned the importance of any of the Steps or the need to attend meetings regularly.

The issue here is not the relative merit of controlled drinking: in the United States it is not a viable treatment approach for the large majority of alcohol-dependent people. Rather, it is the way communications are managed in AA. As a charismatic group, AA is able to suppress attitudes that could undermine its traditions. Indeed, deviance from the abstinence norm is regarded as a serious "slip." As David Rudy points out, by rigidly defining the limits of acceptable behavior, the group strengthens and reaffirms its own boundaries.[18]

AA generates an intense personal involvement in the group, one comparable to the members' previous dependency on alcohol, and thus provides them with "an alternative dependency." Over 80% of members invite fellow members to their homes, outside the meeting format.[19] In his studies of the life histories of alcoholics, George Vaillant has found that recovery from alcoholism most commonly happens when an alternative dependency is substituted.[20]

The emotional impact of this dependency on AA is apparent in the experience of many members whose equanimity is closely tied to their stable relationship to the group. One of my patients, a successful lawyer who regularly attended AA meetings, spoke of his irritability in dealing with his wife and partners after returning from a long business trip.

> Missing meetings while I was away was a big problem. I didn't get to one for five days last week and I just couldn't take to that old "button-pushing." I kept barking at Jennie and was unpleasant at work. I knew something was unsteady inside of me that was making me more irritable at every turn. But getting back to a meeting made me feel like my old self again. I'll have to make a meeting every day on the next trip.

Charismatic groups tend to divide the world into the good within their groups and the evil lodged in their enemies. AA also relies on this psychological defense of projecting outside themselves the evil that members fear from within. It personifies unacceptable evil in the form of alcohol itself and the alcoholic disease process. This breeds the typical Manichaean outlook in which the world is divided into good and evil. It leads members to avoid all persons who may again entrap them in drinking and affiliate even more strongly with others in the fellowship. As Margaret Bean points out,[21] the initiate is usually encouraged to give up social contacts outside AA, for the express reason that the person is endangered by these people, since they are the ones amongst whom he or she fell prey to alcoholism in the first place. This strategy works well in promoting the alcoholic's recovery at the cost of some friendships.

For a few potential members, AA's appeal is limited by its sectarianism, recently reflected in more elaborated dogma.[22] Agnostics and atheists may react aversely to chapter meetings, which are often begun with the Lord's Prayer and may dwell on the idea of a Higher Power. In Eastern cultures, the Christian orientation of the group also presents problems for recruitment. On a visit to Thailand I found that attempts to establish AA chapters had met with success among Western-born Christians, but were poorly received by the Buddhist majority. More acceptable variants have emerged in Japan.[23]

Another point of doctrinal rigidity that can cause recruitment problems is controlled drinking. Because of its origins as a charismatic group, AA relies on received knowledge rather than experimental research. While experiments with controlled drinking have raised interest among some American social and medical scientists, they have been rejected by AA. This is not unlike battles over dogma that charismatic groups have fought—and in this case won: in the United States today, AA has set the tone for treatment across the country.

The possibility of being co-opted by other institutions within the treatment mainstream also makes AA vulnerable. Many AA members have become therapists in hospital-based rehabilitation programs for alcoholism and their commitments to the AA approach have softened. Increasingly, new AA members are being referred from professional settings; over a third of new members now come from institutional rehabilitation programs.[24] In time, AA may be seen by its members as one option among many, rather than as the definitive vehicle for their rehabilitation. Indeed, over 40% of one recent sample of AA members turned to professional help *after* joining, and most reported that such help played an "important part" in their recovery.[25]

There is a lesson in this; the fellowship struggled for years to have alcoholism find its place in the mainstream, and AA's relative influence might now decline because of its own success. Charismatic groups sometimes retain their integrity better when persecuted than when embraced by the broader society. The charismatic group may succeed on a broader scale, however, when its message becomes part of the cultural mainstream.

In conclusion, we find that AA serves as a good example of a fully evolved charismatic healing movement. Its strengths are drawn from the psychology of the charismatic group: in its proselytizing, its control over members' communications, and its Manichaean outlook. At the same time, it has the vulnerabilities of charismatic groups, and is subject to the dissipation of its founders' zeal as it achieves organizational success.

AA Offshoots and Synanon

Self-help movements vary considerably in their structure and format. Some collaborate closely with institutional caregivers, while others stand apart, making little contact with established organizations or professionals. I have studied three zealous, cohesive groups oriented toward healing in some detail. One, the Federation of Parents for Drug-Free Youth, is a national anti-drug movement that draws on parents' concern for their children's welfare.[26] The other is Recovery, a long-established self-help movement for the psychiatrically disabled.[27] And the third is a self-help program for alcoholism developed in my own hospital, closely integrated into hospital-based institutional treatment.[28] While each offers a useful perspective on the adaptability of certain aspects of the charismatic group, it will be most instructive to focus on groups that evolved most directly from AA.

Many groups have been modeled closely and successfully after AA. Over a dozen "Anonymous" groups draw specifically on the AA Twelve Step format. These deal with issues ranging from drug dependency, like Pills Anonymous and Cocaine Anonymous, to gambling and obesity. The admission of helplessness before one's problems and the bonding together with those similarly afflicted appears to work well as a self-help formula for many compulsive behaviors.

Furthest along the scale of addictive behavior lies dependence on the opiate drugs, such as heroin and morphine. For treatment of this marginally manageable problem a more profound group commitment is required, one that can take place in a residential therapeutic community. In this setting, all aspects of a member's life become engaged in the charismatic healing program, and residence is required for many months. The residential therapeutic community is used less frequently in the treatment of heroin addiction than is methadone maintenance (opiate replacement therapy), and these communities illustrate the limitations of a charismatic healing approach. Less than a fifth of all patients under treatment for opiate addiction in one state, for example, were in therapeutic communities, while the remainder were on methadone.[29] Nonetheless, certain charismatically oriented therapeutic communities such as Phoenix House and Daytop Village have gained wide acceptance because of their thoughtful use of group therapy techniques, openness to independent follow-up, and collaboration with other community agencies.

Synanon, the first of the drug-free therapeutic communities, symbolizes many of the failings of charismatic healing groups. This movement was founded in 1958 by Charles Dederich in California. A recovered alcoholic who had achieved sobriety in AA, Dederich attempted to adopt the fellowship's techniques for narcotic addicts. Principal among the changes he instituted were the shift to a residential setting and—at the outset, at least—

elimination of a religious orientation. When most successful, in the early 1970s, the movement had 1,350 members, mainly in southern California. Although the majority had entered for the treatment of drug addiction or alcoholism, about a quarter had joined to address their own problems of personal adjustment.[30] Many prominent figures, from the psychologist Abraham Maslow[31] to senior federal drug officials, were impressed by the group in its earlier days.

The Synanon experience began with inductees severing all ties with outsiders for three months, after which they lived in isolated settings and worked in Synanon-operated businesses, all designed to remove them from influences in the general community that might rekindle their craving for heroin. Strict compliance with the group's practices and standards for behavior was required from the time of entry, and enforcement was carried out by intense group encounters called "games." Members spent an average of thirty hours a month in the games, which were characterized by very harsh exchanges. The games served a number of functions, some explicit and some not. Their overt purpose was to convert the addict to a new style of living. They also acted as a safety valve for the strong feelings and animosities aroused in the communal setting. On another level, as described by Richard Ofshe,[32] they assured members' compliance with all demands of the group, and thereby secured the leaders' firm control over the community.

The group soon became increasingly self-sufficient by employing its members and monitoring them closely. By the mid-1970s members were drawn by Dederich into sexually perverse acts, defectors from the group were harassed, and critics of the movement were subjected to violence. An initially enthusiastic public and professional community wondered how the group had gone awry.

From the outset, Synanon fell victim to the inflated role of Charles Dederich, its charismatic leader. In contrast to Bill W., Dederich was arrogant and controlling, and in time even designated Synanon as a religion, granting himself a transcendent role far beyond that appropriate to the director of a drug treatment program. Unbridled power leads to feelings of grandiosity that may be difficult to withstand, so the outcome of this group depended on the establishment of a rational administrative structure. Unlike AA, however, Synanon did not develop a stable organization or a democratic community. Instead, power was concentrated in the hands of a single individual who proved ill fit to manage it.

Whereas AA addresses a highly circumscribed aspect of members' lives, alcohol use alone, Synanon impinged on all aspects of social adaptation. No doubt the magnitude of the addiction being addressed by Synanon was thought to justify such controls.

Dederich separated Synanon members from the economic life of the broader community by putting them to work in light manufacturing and retail sales in small businesses owned by the group. He thereby laid the groundwork for concentrating the group's economic assets in his hands. Dederich later acknowledged in court that his own family had received $2 million of the organization's funds over a four-year period.[33] Such pecuniary gain, of course, stands in sharp contrast to the traditional limitation on the acquisition of assets with AA, and the disavowal of all personal benefits by the founder.

In time Dederich's personal role became more bizarre, as he compelled married members to change partners at his bidding.[34] His grandiosity and increasingly unstable mental state is clear in the following statement he made in one court deposition in the later years of his rule.

> I am more famous than Santa Claus. We had enormous amounts of publicity. We had all the big ones—*Life, Look,* everything but *Reader's Digest.* More people knew about me than knew about World War II, according to various surveys we made.[35]

The splitting of good and evil and the projection of evil onto outsiders was an aspect of the aggressive paranoia of this deranged leader. When an attorney brought a case against Dederich on behalf of a disenchanted ex-member, Dederich told some of his aides:

> We're not going to mess with the old time "turn the other cheek" posture. Don't mess with us—it could get you killed dead—that's our interpretation of what a religious posture should be. I want an ear in a glass of alcohol.[36]

In response to this, three members of Dederich's armed "Imperial Guard" placed a rattlesnake in the attorney's mailbox, nearly killing him. The episode resulted in Dederich's being fined $5,000 and placed on five years' probation, with an injunction against participating further in running his cultic group.[37] Clearly, an open system of governance, as established in AA, would have militated against such a turn of events.

Recommendations

The contrast between Synanon and Alcoholics Anonymous suggests measures that would prevent abuse of power in a charismatic healing group. In particular, it is important to avoid improper concentrations of power and stifling contact with the outside world.

1. A charismatic healing group should have a broad-based administrative structure and establish written traditions for preventing the emergence of autocratic leadership. A democratic electoral process is one option.
2. Clear limits on incursions into members' social lives should be defined to avoid their being manipulated more than necessary for their own recovery.
3. Large contributions of money and other resources should be discouraged; staff functions should be carried out by volunteers.
4. Independent sources of information and open exchanges with the society at large should not be suppressed. They serve to minimize

the dangers of excessive reliance on the group's own idiosyncratic beliefs and internally generated values. They can also facilitate valuable collaboration with outside professionals.

Ironically, these very steps toward temperance can also undermine the group's charismatic zeal. Herein lies the challenge in establishing and continuing such zealous healing groups.

APPENDIX A

THE CHARISMATIC GROUP:
A SUMMARY

If there is a science to the study of the charismatic group, then the student may find it useful to refer to some operating principles. To this end, the following summary has been prepared.

The charismatic group is a close-knit community defined by the following primary characteristics: It has a strongly held belief system and a high level of social cohesiveness; its members are deeply influenced by the group's behavioral norms and impute a transcendent (or divine) role to their leader. These groups may differ among themselves in the particulars of their ideology and ritual behavior, but they do have several traits in common, some listed below. Certain groups may conform only in part to this model and to that extent they are an expression of this phenomenon in modified form.

Entry into the Group

Charismatic groups are likely to emerge at a time when the values of a society are felt to be inadequate for addressing major social issues. Individuals are more prone to join if they are unhappy because of situational problems or chronic distress and if they have limited affiliative ties to family and friends.

Groups generally engage new members by creating an atmosphere of unconditional acceptance and support and offering a worldview that promises a solution for all existential problems. Engagement (or conversion) entails experiences of intensely felt emotion or perceptual change. It also provides a relief of neurotic distress and a feeling of well-being. For the convert, these experiences serve to validate the group's mission.

The Experience of Membership

The group's leader is reputed to have the potential of bringing a resolution to the problems of humanity. In interacting with followers, the leader is also drawn into believing the grandiose role accorded him, and then justifies his behavior by referring to the transcendent mission suggested by the group's philosophy. This can cause him to make demands on his followers that outsiders would see as petulant and abusive.

The group attributes special meaning, colored by its philosophy, to everyday language and events; this meaning is usually related to dogma or written code attributed to the group's leader or progenitor.

Recruits experience a *relief effect* with membership. That is, the closer they feel to their fellow members and the group's values, the greater the relief in their emotional distress; the more they become emotionally distanced from the group, the greater their experience of distress. This relief effect serves as the basis for reinforcing compliance with the group's norms, as it implicitly rewards conformity with enhanced well-being and punishes alienation with feelings of distress. It also keeps members from leaving the group because they are conditioned to avoid the distress that results from relinquishing the benefits of the relief effect.

Group behavioral norms generally structure all areas of members' lives, their work, sexuality, socialization, and intellectual pursuits. Activities in these areas are preferentially carried out with other members, so that outsiders are generally shunned as friends and colleagues.

Membership is characterized by levels of "sanctity," so that a member is continually striving to achieve a higher level of acceptance by conforming all the more with the group's expectations. Such conformity generally results in members' experiencing considerable privation.

The Charismatic Group as a Social System

The group operates as a close-knit social system to assure its stability. It does this by manipulating the activities and views of its members. Members' activities are monitored closely, either by formally designated observers or other general members. Compliance with the group's norms is assured by the members' need to avoid estrangement and resulting dysphoria if they appear to question these values. Scapegoating of recalcitrant members helps to maintain a sense of goodness and trust among members.

Information is managed to minimize dissonance between the views of the group and the contrasting attitudes of the general society. The group may therefore engender attitudes and views that fly in the face of reality to prevent destabilization in members' commitment. Implicit "evidence" of the credibility of the group's ethos is also provided by new members, and aggressive recruitment therefore helps stabilize the entire system.

Boundary control is exercised by the group to protect it from threatening incursions from without. The group will therefore engender a suspicious attitude toward the general society to protect its members from assimilation. A clear difference is drawn between members and nonmembers, in terms of their innate value as people. Nonmembers are accorded less moral weight, and may be deceived or snubbed to assure the stability of the group as a social system.

Charismatic groups come into conflict with the surrounding society in a number of ways. They disregard the concern of the families of new converts. They behave in a defensive and paranoid way toward outsiders suspected of being hostile to the group. They aggressively maintain ideologic positions at variance with those of the general culture.

After their initial most zealous phase, charismatic groups may follow any of these courses: They may become bureaucratized with the charisma of the original leader ascribed to the group's leadership hierarchy. They may assimilate into the broader society if the group's self-protectiveness and isolation are not sustained by the leadership. They may come into direct conflict with the surrounding society because of differences in ideology and defensiveness on both sides, potentially leading to violence. To escape a negative outcome, these groups may also migrate to an isolated setting.

Spiritual Recovery Movements

These are modified forms of the charismatic groups in that they are not as intensely cohesive and do not assert the same degree of control over all aspects of their adherents' lives. They espouse belief systems that typically give an existential or transcendent meaning to illness, and they expect certain behaviors of their adherents to relieve the consequences of disease or even avert the threat of mortality. The benefits experienced by their adherents may result from the relief of anxiety, from greater social support for health-promoting behaviors, and even from the physiologic consequences of affiliation.

APPENDIX B
THE CHARISMATIC GROUP:
EXAMPLES

The following grid is a complement to Appendix A, which defines the overall psychology of charismatic groups. This grid gives an additional perspective on these groups. It includes many of the movements discussed in the book, past or contemporary, benign or malignant, and illustrates how some of their characteristics can be defined to help in understanding the differences among them. While all charismatic groups have a characteristic pattern of cohesiveness and ideology, this pattern does not carry with it an obligate moral character or a necessary pattern of overt behaviors. Each group, instead, is a very real social entity with its own mores; and like each nation, corporation, or primitive tribe, it is unique unto itself.

Type of Ideology	Charismatic leader	Gained public attention	Notable behaviors	Leadership structure
Neo-Christian				
Latter-Day Saints	Joseph Smith	mid-1800s	Corporate, missionaries	Elders determine dogma
Christian Science	Mary Baker Eddy	1870s	Avoid medical care	Complex organization
Unification Church	Reverend Moon	1970s	Arranged marriages	Leader's hierarchy
Branch Davidians	David Koresh	1993	Sexual control and weapons	Leader controls
Eastern				
Transcendental meditation	Maharishi Mahesh Yogi	1970s	Meditation and relaxation	Guru and lay organization
Rajneeshees	Bhagwan Shree Rajneesh	1970s	Saffron clothing, murder plots	Guru and appointees
Divine Light Mission	Guru Maharaj Ji	1970s	Flashes at conversion, meditation	Loosely led by leader

Aum Shinrikyu	Shoko Asahara	1995	Plots and murder	Paranoid leadership
Science Fiction				
Scientology	L. Ron Hubbard	1950s	Mercantile religion	Closed hierarchy
Heaven's Gate	Marshall Applewhite	1997	Millennial, suicide	Leader controlled
Idiosyncratic				
Oneida Colony	John Noyes	1840	Seclusive, sexual management	Leader's hierarchy
Manson Family	Charles Manson	1969	LSD, murder	Leader controlled
Peoples Temple	Rev. Jim Jones	1978	Paranoid escape, mass suicide	Leader's hierarchy
Solar Temple	Luc Jouret	1994	Armageddon, suicide-murder	Loose-knit charismatic leadership
Spiritual Recovery				
Alcoholics Anonymous	Bill W.	1940s	Alcoholics only, abstinence	Democratic electoral
EST	Werner Erhard	1970s	Self-realization as business	Tightly held hierarchy
"Special" patients	Bernie Siegel, M.D.	1980s	Cancer patients, spiritual	By books and seminars
Rational Recovery	Jack Trimpey	1980s	Substance abusers	Private, certification

APPENDIX C

CHRONOLOGY OF THE STUDIES

Findings from several of my studies are discussed at different points. To clarify the sequence of this work, the actual research projects are listed here in chronological order.

Year Conducted	Research Project, Site, and Subjects	Principal References
1970–72	Marijuana: physiology, psychology, and social behavior. National Institute of Mental Health (12 volunteers; 36 volunteers)	Galanter et al., 1973 Galanter et al., 1973 Galanter et al., 1974
1974	Divine Light Mission, active members. New York, Orlando, Florida (119 members)	Galanter, 1978 Galanter and Buckley, 1978
1977	Unification Church, active members. New York City (237 members)	Galanter et al., 1979 Galanter, 1981
1978	Unification Church, Induction Workshops. Boston, California, Washington, D.C., New York State (104 recruits)	Galanter, 1980
1980–1981	Unification Church, study of marital engagement. New York City, Boston (321 engaged members)	Galanter, 1983(a)
1981	Unification Church, dropouts. U.S., National (66 ex-members)	Galanter, 1983(b)
1982	Federation of Parents for Drug-Free Youth. Atlanta, Georgia (135 parent members)	Galanter et al., 1984
1982–1986	Institutionally based self-help treatment for alcoholism. Bronx Municipal Hospital Center (282 experimental patients and controls)	Galanter et al., 1987

1983–1985	Unification Church, study of married couples. U.S., National (321-member follow-up)	Galanter, 1986
1983–1986	Recovery, Inc., self-help for psychiatric problems. U.S., National (one member and leader in each of 211 groups)	Galanter, 1988
1988	AA-based program for addicted physicians (100 physicians).	Galanter et al., 1989
1991–1992	Rational Recovery, nonspiritual self-help group for relief of addiction (433 subjects)	Galanter et al., 1993a
1990	"Christian Psychiatry," society for fundamentalist psychiatrists (193 subjects)	Galanter et al., 1991
1980–1991	Network Therapy, family and peers to support in addict's recovery (60 patients)	Galanter, 1993, 1993a Galanter et al., 1993
1989–1992	"Recovery" clinic for peer-led therapy for cocaine addicts (150 patients)	Galanter et al., 1993
1989–1995	Mentally ill addicts responding to peer-led care (298 patients)	Galanter et al., 1996
1995–1996	Review of the psychology of spiritual recovery movements	Galanter, 1997

NOTES

1. The Charismatic Group

1. S. Freud (1921), p. 16.
2. W. James (1902).
3. D. Hume (1779).
4. C. Darwin (1871).
5. E. O. Wilson (1975).
6. S. Wright (1945).
7. M. Galanter (1978, 1983a).
8. A. Jolly (1972).
9. S. J. Suomi (1972); S. J. Suomi et al. (1978); J. M. Smith (1964), S. Wright (1945).
10. L. von Bertalanffy (1950).
11. *U.S. News & World Report*, December 4, 1978, pp. 28–29.

2. Group Cohesiveness

1. Reference should be made here to G. H. Mead (1962), who showed that mind and self are generated in a social process. He posited a "generalized other," namely the organized community or social group that gives the individual a unity of self.
2. D. Cartwright and A. Zander (1962), p. 74.
3. M. Bowen (1978); L. Wynne et al. (1958).
4. D. Reiss (1971).
5. A. Deutsch (1980).
6. W. Bion (1959), p. 30.
7. A. K. Rice (1965). In the United States, these programs are run by the A. K. Rice Institute, with headquarters in Washington, D.C.
8. L. Coser (1974); A. L. Greil and D. R. Rudy (1984).
9. S. Freud (1921), p. 16.
10. The term *new religious movements* reflects a certain respect for these groups. It has been popularized by more sympathetic authors. The term *cult,* on the other hand, has often been used pejoratively by authors more concerned with the potential danger of these groups.

235

11. The names of individual group members and the details of their backgrounds are altered throughout to protect their identities.

12. J. G. Melton and R. L. Moore (1982).

13. J. V. Downton (1979).

14. J. V. Downton (1979); T. Pilarzyk (1978), p. 30.

15. M. Galanter and P. Buckley (1978).

16. Respondents' average age was 25. By eliminating "none" and "other" responses, the relative distribution of major religious denominations among the remaining sample prior to joining was obtained: 44% Protestant, 32% Catholic, and 21% Jewish. Comparable figures for the nation overall (*Yearbook of American Churches*, 1972, U.S. Church membership) were 57%, 38%, and 2% respectively.

17. C. Cameron (1973), p. 22.

18. T. Pilarzyk (1978), p. 38.

19. J. C. Ross (1982); D. G. Bromley and A. D. Shupe (1979).

20. M. Galanter et al. (1972).

21. Subjective symptoms not related to the group experience, however, differentiated the three experimental conditions. Thus, for symptoms such as "mouth feeling dry," "feeling dreamy," and "head feeling heavier," both marijuana and placebo are significantly different from the no drug condition, although the effect of active marijuana was stronger (Galanter et al. 1974).

22. B. J. Albaugh and P. O. Anderson (1974).

23. R. L. Bergman (1971).

24. F. Kass et al. (1980).

25. The internal reliability of the scales developed for this study and those in ensuing studies was assessed by computing the coefficient alpha, reflecting the average correlation of the test items. By this technique, the scales all had satisfactory coefficients of internal reliability. For example, for the Psychological Distress Scale, .78; group cohesiveness in relation to ten members, .75; in relation to all members, .75; in relation to nonmembers, .78; religious creed—used in the Unification Church study, .81 (Galanter, 1981). Specific points on all these scales were labeled as follows: 1—not at all; 2—a little bit; 3—moderately; 4—a lot; 5—very much.

26. Further details on symptom decline are found in Galanter (1978). Members actually had a relatively high incidence of drug use prior to joining. For example, the overwhelming majority had smoked marijuana (92%); most had used hallucinogens (68%), and a certain number used heroin (14%) too. With the exception of alcohol, the level of use for all drugs queried was two to four times that reported by a representative national sample of college students for the same period. The same number of Divine Light members (86%), though, had used alcohol, as had respondents in the national sample (National Commission on Marijuana and Drug Abuse, 1973).

27. Mean scores for the Social Cohesiveness Scale toward each of the three target groups reflected this difference: for ten members, 34.4 ± 3.4; for ten nonmembers, 26.4 ± 4.7; for all members, 32.4 ± 3.6 ($F = 214.7$, 2/116 df, $p < .01$).

28. Typical declines in symptom scores after joining were 41% for anxiety and 42% for depression. A stepwise multiple regression analysis was performed

using selected items on social cohesiveness toward sect members. These predicted 37% of the variance in scores on the Psychological Distress Scale (Galanter, 1982).

29. In one item, subjects indicated whether or not they had in the past "experienced serious emotional problems" before joining the group. Thirty-nine percent answered affirmatively.

3. Shared Beliefs

1. R. M. Kanter (1972).
2. W. M. Kephart (1976) reviews the history of this and related nineteenth-century communities.
3. R. M. Kephart (1976), p. 58.
4. P. B. Noyes (1927), pp. 126–127.
5. Oneida *Circular*, July 17, 1863.
6. R. J. Lifton (1961). R. Ofshe (1974) described Synanon games, and E. H. Schein (1956) examined inefficiencies in the Chinese brainwashing techniques.
7. A. Leighton and D. Leighton (1941).
8. B. Kaplan and D. Johnson (1964). I. Lubchansky et al. (1970) provide a similar framework for urban Hispanic faith healing in the United States.
9. R. S. Lynd and H. B. Lynd (1929); T. Caplow et al. (1981).
10. M. E. Pattison et al. (1973).
11. S. Schacter and J. E. Singer (1962).
12. M. E. Pattison and M. L. Pattison (1980).
13. J. Frank (1973).
14. L. Mosher and A. Menn (1978).
15. L. Mosher and A. Menn (1978), pp. 716–719.
16. R. J. Wendt et al. (1983).
17. R. Liberman (1973); A. Brier and J. S. Strauss (1983); W. T. Carpenter (1977).
18. L. Mosher and A. Menn (1983).
19. J. Lofland and R. Stark (1965) used the term *religious seekers* in a similar way in their early description of the new religious movements.
20. This issue is illustrated in studies on cognitive dissonance such as those by L. Festinger and J. M. Carlsmith (1959) and M. R. Lepper et al. (1973).
21. E. Barker (1974) used membership lists to generate a random sample in her study of the Moonies.
22. Typical items were, "Have you been feeling emotionally stable and sure of yourself?" and "How happy, satisfied, or pleased have you been with your personal life?" answered on a six-point scale (Dupuy, 1973). Respondents' GWB scores ($X = 74.4 \pm 17.2$) were significantly below those of the comparison group (83.4 ± 16.2, $p <. 001$). They were also highly inversely correlated ($r = -.64$, $p <. 001$) with the Psychological Distress Scale scores.
23. M. Galanter et al. (1979). Dr. John Ware of the Stanford Research Institute had not only undertaken the administration of the General Well-Being Schedule to 1,196 representative adults from Dayton, Ohio, but had also cross-

tabulated his population's scores by age and sex, making it possible to draw out a sample with very much the same demographic distribution of our own respondents.

24. Comparison responses obtained for the periods right before and after first contacts with the church (Galanter, 1981) reflected a marked increase in the intensity of religious commitment on joining.

25. Cohesiveness items accounted for 30% of the variance in GWB scores in a stepwise multiple of regression analysis ($R = .55$, $F = 2.49$, 6/230 df), but when religion items were added to the regression equation, another 6% of the variance was predicted ($R = .62$, $F = 2.52$, 8/228 df) (Galanter, 1981).

26. F. Heider (1958).

27. W. Proudfoot and P. Shaver (1975).

28. D. J. Bem (1972), p. 2.

29. H. H. Kelly (1967), p. 200.

30. M. Galanter et al. (1979); M. Galanter (1980).

31. N. J. Cameron (1943).

32. S. E. Asch (1952).

33. R. Ofshe (1976).

34. R. Lifton (1961).

4. Altered Consciousness

1. W. James (1902).

2. A. M. Ludwig (1966).

3. C. T. Tart (1975).

4. R. K. Wallace (1970).

5. M. Galanter et al. (1973); Roth et al. (1973).

6. J. V. Hardt and J. Kamiya (1978).

7. Meditation was "usually" experienced during daily activities by 72% of members with prior drug problems vs. only 47% without such problems ($X^2 = 2.43$, $p < .05$).

8. Most of these findings on transcendent experiences were reported in M. Galanter and P. Buckley (1978). These items were also used for queries regarding experiences during conversion (Buckley and Galanter, 1979).

9. In a stepwise multiple regression analysis, the significant predictors of symptom decline included the members' frequency of meditation and the occurrence of transcendental experiences during meditation. Other significant predictors in this analysis were group cohesiveness and level of participation in Divine Light activities. These variables accounted for 48% of the variance in symptom decline since conversion.

10. *The New York Times Magazine*, February 6, 1975, p. 12; it is also the source of the figures on TM.

11. H. Benson and R. K. Wallace (1972) and H. Benson (1974).

12. *The New York Times,* January 1, 1984, p. A14.

13. The term also applies to certain drugs that do not lead to addiction or abuse. Chlorpromazine, a neuroleptic, is a tranquilizer used in the treatment of

schizophrenia. One may well study the social impact on a mental ward when patients are medicated with this drug.

14. R. E. Schultes (1972); M. D. DeRios and D. E. Smith (1977); A. Paredes (1975).
15. E. M. Brecher (1972).
16. W. N. Pahnke (1966).
17. A. Deutsch (1975).
18. Parent Group members' cohesion scores toward the overall membership were tabulated. They were no different from those of Unification members' scores toward their overall membership on mean item scores (3.72 ± .96 vs. 3.66 ± 1.04). Parent group scores for nonmembers whom they knew best, however, were much higher than those of the Moonies (3.66 ± 1.14 vs. 2.62 ± 0.91; $t = 9.65$, $p <. 001$) (Galanter et al., 1984).
19. M. Orne (1969).
20. M. Galanter et al. (1978).
21. F. I. Melges et al. (1974).
22. J. G. Melton (1978).
23. R. C. Ness and R. M. Wintrob (1980).
24. W. J. Samarin (1959); E. M. Pattison (1974).
25. J. G. Melton (1978), p. 248.
26. F. D. Goodman (1972).
27. Lisa Alther, *The New York Times Magazine*, June 6, 1976, p. 18 ff.
28. R. Lane (1976) described the development of the Catholic Charismatic Movement.
29. *The New York Times*, September 8, 1974, p. A1 ff, and May 10, 1981, p. A26, among other related news items.
30. A. Greeley (1975).
31. E. Bourguignon (1974).
32. W. LaBarre (1970).
33. M. A. Kirsch and L. L. Glass (1977).
34. Irvin Yalom, a group therapy researcher, also experienced difficulties in attempts to establish a working arrangement with est (*American Journal of Psychiatry*, 134:213, 1977).
35. The membership figure and the quotation from the est trainer are from *Time* magazine, June 7, 1976, pp. 53–54.
36. E. Babbie and D. Stone (1976).
37. J. Simon (1978).

5. *Biology and Behavior*

1. C. Darwin (1889).
2. M. T. Ghiselin (1969), p. 188.
3. C. Darwin (1889), p. 402.
4. K. Z. Lorenz (1974).
5. N. Tinbergen (1951); E. Weigert (1956); J. Bowlby (1957).
6. E. O. Wilson (1975).

7. M. Ruse (1981); J. D. Baldwin and J. I. Baldwin (1981).
8. W. D. Hamilton (1975); M. J. Smith (1964).
9. R. L. Trivers (1971); B. C. R. Bertram (1982).
10. C. J. Lumsden and E. O. Wilson (1981).
11. Mean scores for the workshop registrants were 61.9 (those who joined), 67.2 (late dropouts), and 74.7 (early dropouts). Persons who were members for two years had a mean of 74.4. The comparison group drawn from the general population had a mean score of 83.4. These data and others on the inductees will be reviewed in detail in a subsequent chapter on the experience of Unification Church members.
12. A stepwise multiple regression analysis was done using items reflecting social cohesiveness as predictors, and the decline in members' scores for psychological distress after joining as the dependent variable. Cohesiveness items predicted 37% of the variance in the decline in distress.
13. In a multiple regression analysis where scores on the General Well-Being Schedule were used as the dependent variable, social cohesiveness items accounted for 30% of the variance. When items on religious belief were added to the regression equation, an additional 6% of the variance was accounted for. These data and others cited here are reviewed in M. Galanter (1981). See also National Center for Health Statistics (1977).
14. M. Galanter (1983).
15. T. H. Holmes and R. H. Rahe (1967).
16. These studies are described later. In brief, life events accounted for 15% of the variance in general well-being scores during the engagement. When affiliateness items were added to the regression equation, an additional 20% of variance was accounted for. After marriage, altogether 32% of the variance was accounted for, using a somewhat modified procedure (Galanter, 1983, 1985).
17. Point biserial correlations were obtained between the item in which respondents reported whether or not they had a history of "serious emotional problems" and their scores on each of the following two scores: (a) psychological distress and (b) social cohesiveness. There was no significant correlation in either case, among either the Moonies or the Divine Light members (Galanter, 1981).
18. The product-moment correlation (r) between this item and the decline on the psychological distress scale was .45 ($p < .01$) (Galanter, 1978).
19. M. Galanter (1984).
20. B. G. Campbell (1974), pp. 376–381.
21. W. D. Hamilton (1975).
22. A. Jolly (1972), p. 128.
23. T. Dobzhansky and O. Pavlovsky (1971).
24. D. Pilbeam (1972).
25. A. Jolly (1972), p. 126.
26. H. F. Harlow and M. K. Harlow (1969).
27. S. J. Suomi, et al. (1976); S. J. Suomi et al. (1978).
28. R. Gardner (1982).
29. J. A. Hobson and R. W. McCarley (1977).
30. A. R. Radcliffe-Brown (1939).

6. The Cult as a Social System

1. Von Bertalanffy (1968), F. Baker (1970), and J. G. Miller (1975) provide good introductions to systems theory and its relationship to social psychology.
2. American Psychiatric Association, *DSM III* (1980).
3. APA, *DSM III* (1980), p. 253.
4. J. Simon (1978).
5. L. L. Glass et al. (1977); M. A. Kirsch and L. L. Glass (1977).
6. T. Strentz (1980) provides the background on clinical interviews of hijacking.
7. D. Lang (1974).
8. A. Freud (1966).
9. A. Deutsch (1980).
10. M. Galanter (1983a).
11. M. Galanter (1983b).
12. A case reported by H. Basedow, cited by W. B. Cannon (1965).
13. R. A. DeSilva (1982).
14. J. G. Miller (1965).
15. *Newsweek*, June 14, 1976, p. 44.
16. G. Moorhouse (1981); K. Rothmyer (1984).
17. J. G. Clark (1979); M. Singer (1978).
18. J. T. Ungerleider and D. K. Wellisch (1979).
19. M. Galanter (1983b).

7. Trouble at the System's Boundary

1. J. M. Weightsman (1983), p. 47; J. P. Nugent (1979), pp. 77–78.
2. *Keesing's Contemporary Archives*, May 25, 1979, p. 29627.
3. *Time* magazine, December 4, 1978, p. 21.
4. C. Winfrey (1979).
5. J. M. Weightsman (1983), p. 98.
6. Both letters are quoted in *The New York Times*, November 29, 1978, p. A1.
7. J. R. Hall (1981), p. 188.
8. J. M. Weightsman, p. 29.
9. *Time* magazine, December 4, 1978, p. 28.
10. Gerald Parks, quoted by J. M. Weightsman (1983), p. 54.
11. Deborah L. Blakey, affidavit, quoted by J. M. Weightsman (1983), p. 57.
12. J. M. Weightsman (1983), p. 49.
13. P. Kerns and D. Wead (1979), p. 191.
14. *Time* magazine, December 4, 1978, p. 19.
15. *Keesing's Contemporary Archives*, May 25, 1979, p. 29627.
16. *Newsweek*, May 27, 1985, p. 24.
17. *Time* magazine, May 27, 1985, p. 21.
18. *The New York Times*, May 20, 1985, p. A5.
19. *Time* magazine, May 27, 1985, citation of *Philadelphia Inquirer*.
20. *Newsweek*, May 27, 1985, p. 24.
21. *Time* magazine, May 27, 1985, p. 22.

8. *A Religious Sect: The Unification Church*

1. This and the ensuing statement were quoted in *The New York Times,* January 22, 1979, p. A1 ff.
2. *The New York Times,* September 16, 1974, p. 1.
3. *The New York Times,* September 16, 1974, p. 26.
4. *Boston Globe,* May 23, 1979, pp. 37–38.
5. *The New York Times,* July 22, 1979, p. A1.
6. Berkeley Rice, The Pull of Sun Moon, *The New York Times Magazine,* May 30, 1976.
7. *The New York Times,* September 19, 1977, p. 22.
8. B. Falk, Suburbia Today, Gannett Newspapers, December 27, 1981, p. 6 ff.
9. *The New York Times,* April 2, 1984, p. C15.
10. C. Welles, *New York* magazine, September 27, 1976.
11. B. Falk, Suburbia Today, Gannett Newspapers, December 17, 1981, p. 6 ff.
12. *The New York Times,* October 16, 1981, p. A1.
13. *The New York Times,* July 5, 1985, p. B3.
14. *The New York Times,* July 27, 1985, p. A10.
15. M. Galanter (1982).
16. Models for recruitment have also been proposed by J. Lofland and R. Stark (1965); D. A. Snow and C. L. Philips (1980); and B. Kilbourne and J. T. Richardson (1984).
17. F. Conway and J. Siegelman (1978) in their popular book, *Snapping,* reflect the negative view of the induction techniques. D. Bromley and A. Shupe (1979) studied the evolution of such highly negative views in the media.
18. J. M. Carlsmith et al. (1966).
19. See M. Galanter (1980) for a full report on the methodology of this induction study.
20. E. Barker (1984), p. 146.
21. Long-standing members scored lower than a community sample on GWB (74.4 ± 17.2 vs. 83.4 ± 16.2, $t = 6.24$, $p < .001$). Those who left the workshops after the first weekend had scores that were not significantly different from the ones of long-term members. Those who stayed after the first weekend, however, did have lower scores (67.2 ± 19.2 vs. 74.7 ± 17.2, $t = 1.95$, $p < .05$), and those who actually joined had scores even lower (61.9 ± 20.1, $t = 1.89$, $p < .05$). The workshop guests who continued beyond the second day scored as high on the cohesion scales as long-standing members (mean score, 23.7 ± 3.9), even as early as day 2. The early dropouts, on the other hand, did not score as high ($t = 5.76$, $p < .001$). Early dropouts scored lower on the creed scale than those who continued (mean score, 22.3 ± 7.2 and 26.0 ± 6.0, respectively, $t = 2.39$, $p < .01$).
22. There were no significant differences at any of the test points between the two groups with regard to affiliation toward fellow group members, but significant differences existed at all points with regard to affiliative feelings toward outsiders; the early and late dropouts scored significantly higher on the outside affiliations scale than the joiners. For example, outside affiliations

scores on day 2 were 15.8 $\pm$ 6.6 and 7.4 $\pm$ 6.2, respectively; $t = 2.80$, $p <$ .01.

23. For example, if subjects were ranked according to the degree of diminished distress, the quartile who improved most showed a 128% increase in their reported religiosity scores over the course of conversion, while those who improved least showed a 76% increase ($t = 3.67$, $p < .01$). Similar results were obtained on Divine Light members, reported in a previous chapter.

24. A. S. Parsons (1984).

25. M. Galanter (1983a).

26. No doubt some of them dropped out within the year following the engagement. On these I have no data. Particulars on each of the engaged subgroups and their scores may be found in M. Galanter (1983a).

27. Their mean score on GWB items was considerably lower (53.9 ± 17.8 vs. 70.6 ± 14.1; $t = 3.48$, $p < .001$), within the range of clinically significant distress (National Center for Health Statistics, 1977).

28. B. I. Murstein (1972); W. J. Goode (1970).

29. T. H. Holmes and R. H. Rahe (1967).

30. These latter events were evaluated by each subject in relation to the amount of readjustment they required, the format originally defined for the Holmes and Rahe scale. The adaptation of the scale follows the model proposed by B. S. Dohrenwend (1978).

31. The following variables were used as predictors in the first analysis: the 15 items from Holmes and Rahe most frequently experienced by respondents and the five UC-related life changes most frequently experienced. In the second analysis 10 items reflecting affiliativeness toward the UC were added to the list of predictors. In each stage, predictors were entered into the regression equation only as long as each accounted for a portion of the variance significant at the 5% level. The percentages of variance predicted in these two analyses are reported in the text.

32. S. Milgram (1975).

33. L. Festinger et al. (1956).

34. *Life* magazine, August 1982, pp. 91–96.

35. Ibid.

36. *The New York Times,* July 2, 1982, p. B4.

37. Other life events included the issue of pregnancy, the marriage itself, assuming responsibility for rent and household bills, and adjusting to an active sexual life with one's spouse. All were rated on a five-point scale that ranged from very agreeable to very disagreeable. The methodology and results of this entire study are elaborated in M. Galanter (1986).

38. D. P. Mueller et al. (1977); I. Grant et al. (1981).

39. In the one analysis, items on the cohesiveness and religiosity scales were entered; they accounted for 21% of the variance in GWB scores. In a second analysis, maritally related life events scored for their disagreeable nature were entered as predictors; these variables themselves accounted for 14% of the variance in GWB scores. Finally, both sets of predictors (20 in all) were used for a third analysis, and in that analysis accounted for 32% of the variance in well-being.

40. *The New York Times,* January 22, 1979, p. A14.
41. Ibid.
42. T. Robbins (1979–1980); M. Galanter (1982).
43. These comparisons were made in my follow-up, M. Galanter (1986), on the engaged sample, M. Galanter (1983a).
44. In 1985, two years after the follow-up survey on married members was conducted, I was able to obtain a second follow-up on that cohort that had been engaged in 1979, with the assistance of informants in the church and with church cooperation. The results again confirmed the tenacity of commitment in this group who were now members for an average of fifteen years: 71% were still married to the spouse to whom they were originally matched. Of the total sample, 81% were documented as active. Only 10% were known to have dropped out. Of an additional 9% who could not be located, some were probably active but stationed in remote settings.
45. Specifically, active members (Galanter et al., 1979) scored lower than these dropouts (74.4 ± 17.2 vs. 81.9 ± 16.7; $t = 3.16$, $p < .01$) (Galanter, 1983b), whose scores were, in turn, not significantly different from those of a matched community group (82.3 ± 15.7). It should be noted, however, that there may be a variety of reasons for this: Members with a more benign disposition may have tended to drop out; also, members may be inclined to drop out only *after* they have improved; alternatively, members may have improved after they left. All three reasons may have played a part in this observation.
46. To corroborate these designations, participants were asked to rate the degree of force their family or its representatives had used in attempting to remove them from the sect. For clarifying the use of coercion by the Unification Church itself, respondents were also asked to use the same scale to indicate the degree to which force had been used on them by other members to retain them in the group. Those who were designated as deprogrammed reported much more coercion in a variety of ways. Nine of the ten indicated their freedom was overtly limited by their family both before the time of departure and afterward. They also reported more limitations on them by members before they left.
47. Those who were deprogrammed scored lower on cohesiveness toward the members they knew best (2.61 ± .40 vs. 3.29 ± .71; $t = 2.76$, $p < .01$), and higher on affiliative feelings toward the nonmembers they knew best (4.45 ± .25 vs. 4.01 ± .56; $t = 3.80$, $p < .001$). They also had a lower mean score on the creed scale (1.33 ± .50 vs. 2.55 ± 1.35; $t = 2.79$, $p < .01$).
48. Similar observations were made by E. Barker (1984) over the course of her contacts with the Unification Church.

9. The Millennium Approaches

1. *The New York Times,* March 3, 1993, p. 1.
2. *Newsweek,* March 15, 1993, p. 56.
3. *Time* magazine, May 3, 1993, p. 36.
4. *The New York Times,* April 21, 1993, p. A21.
5. *The New York Times,* June 18, 1994, p. 8.

6. *Time* magazine, May 1, 1995, p. 48.
7. *The New York Times*, April 23, 1995, p. A33.
8. *The New York Times*, May 1, 1995, p. 1 ff.
9. *The New York Times*, March 23, 1995, p. A14.
10. *The New York Times*, May 17, 1995, p. 8.
11. *The New York Times*, April 4, 1995, p. 4.
12. L. Festinger et al., (1956).
13. *The New York Times*, April 28, 1997, p. B8.
14. *The New York Times*, April 28, 1997, p. B9.
15. Ibid.
16. *The New York Times*, March 9, 1997, p. A1 ff.
17. *Keesing's Contemporary Archives*, May 25, 1979, p. 29627.

10. The Nature of Healing Movements

1. M. Galanter et al. (1987).
2. M. Galanter et al. (1996).
3. M. Galanter et al. (1989); M. Galanter et al. (1988, 1993).
4. R. Bezilla (1993).
5. T. A. Maugans and W. C. Wadland (1991).
6. K. K. Trier and A. Shupe (1991); M. Galanter et al. (1991); J. S. Levin et al. (1993).
7. M. Galanter et al. (1991).
8. D. M. Eisenberg et al. (1993).
9. E. Marshall (1994)
10. A. Robinson (1994); H. G. Koenig (1990); D. Doyle (1992).
11. R. D. Orr and G. Isaac (1992); D. B. Larson et al. (1986).
12. R. Bezilla (1993).
13. M. S. Peck (1985).
14. W. A. Fintel and G. R. McDermott (1993).
15. B. R. Cassileth et al. (1984).
16. M. Galanter et al. (1991).
17. H. M. Sharma et al. (1991).
18. D. Maryles (1993).
19. W. J. Kassler et al. (1991); I. J. Lerner and B. J. Kennedy (1992); A. A. Skolnick (1991).
20. D. Chopra (1991).
21. R. H. Murray and A. J. Rubel (1992).
22. J. S. Gordon (1990); A. Robinson (1994).
23. D. Chopra (1989).
24. A. Weil (1990).
25. A. Weil (1972).
26. A. Weil (1997).
27. M. Williamson (1993); B. S. Siegel (1986).
28. M. Williamson (1993); R. Shone (1988).
29. R. Shone (1988).
30. M. Beattie (1987); J. Bradshaw (1988).

31. D. R. Williams et al. (1991); H. G. Koenig (1990); H. G. Koenig et al. (1992).
32. D. M. Eisenberg et al. (1993).
33. L. F. Berkman (1978).
34. J. Richardson et al. (1990).
35. C. D. Emrick et al. (1993).
36. L. F. Berkman (1978); J. S. House et al. (1982); D. G. Blazer (1982); J. S. Goodwin et al. (1987); R. B. Shekelle et al. (1981).
37. D. Spiegel et al. (1989); D. Maryles (1993); B. S. Siegel (1990).
38. F. I. Fawzy et al. (1993).
39. S. Waldfogel and P. Root Wolpe (1993); J. W. Pennebaker et al. (1988); R. Glaser et al. (1985); D. Russell et al. (1980).
40. J. T. Cacioppo (1994).
41. S. M. Levy et al. (1990).
42. J. S. McDaniel et al. (1995); B. R. Cassileth et al. (1991).
43. B. R. Cassileth et al. (1991); F. S. Bagenal et al. (1990).
44. I. D. Yalom and M. A. Lieberman (1971); I. J. Lerner and B. J. Kennedy (1992).
45. D. M. Eisenberg et al. (1993).
46. A. A. Skolnick (1991).
47. A. Kleinman (1980).
48. A. Leighton and D. Leighton (1941); J. G. Kennedy (1967).
49. J. A. Adetunji (1992).
50. M. B. Eddy (1989).
51. R. K. Bullis (1991).
52. H. H. Kelley (1967).
53. M. Williamson (1993).
54. A. Bandura (1986).
55. V. M. Gonzalez et al. (1990).
56. A. T. Beck (1976).
57. B. S. Siegel (1986, 1990).
58. S. Milgram (1975).
59. C. K. Hofling et al. (1966).
60. E. M. Pattison et al. (1973).

11. Alternative Healing in the Medical Mainstream

1. M. Galanter et al. (1991).
2. CMDS Membership Application, undated.
3. M. Galanter et al. (1991).
4. Gallup Report 236 (1985); American Psychiatric Association (1975).
5. D. Larson et al. (1986).
6. L. Goldfarb et al. (1996).
7. H. Harwood et al. (1997).
8. M. Galanter (1984).
9. M. Galanter et al. (1987).
10. M. Galanter et al. (1993, 1993a, 1994).
11. American Psychiatric Association (1993).

12. The AA Example

1. M. Weber (1947); H. Gerth and C. W. Mills (1946).
2. Bill W.'s tale is available in a number of sources, among them E. Kurtz (1979) and R. Thomsen (1975).
3. *Alcoholics Anonymous Comes of Age* (1957).
4. Bill W. Letter to Carl Jung. *The AA Grapevine.* New York, 1963.
5. Alcohol, Drug Abuse, and Mental Health Administration. *ADAMHA News,* May 1985; M. Bean (1975).
6. H. Trice and J. M. Beyer (1983).
7. R. Lifton (1961), pp. 429–430; N. K. Denzin (1987).
8. L. A. Alibrandi (1978).
9. E. A. Bohince and A. C. Orenstein (1950).
10. Alcoholics Anonymous (1976).
11. R. Lifton (1961), p. 425.
12. Cited by R. Thompson (1975), p. 365, and the New York *Village Voice,* July 23, 1985, p. 64.
13. R. Kanter (1972), p. 113.

BIBLIOGRAPHY

The AA Way of Life. New York: Alcoholics Anonymous World Services, 1967.

Adetunji, J. A. Church-based obstetric care in a yoruba community, Nigeria. *Social Science Medicine* 35: 1171–1178, 1992.

Adler, F., et al. *A Systems Approach to Drug Treatment*. Philadelphia: Dorrance, 1974.

Albaugh, B. J., and Anderson, P. O. Peyote in the treatment of alcoholism among American Indians. *American Journal of Psychiatry* 131: 1247–1250, 1974.

Alcoholics Anonymous. New York: Alcoholics Anonymous World Services, Inc., 1939.

Alcoholics Anonymous Comes of Age. New York: Alcoholics Anonymous Publishing, 1957.

Alcoholics Anonymous (3rd ed.). New York: Alcoholics Anonymous World Services, 1976.

Alibrandi, I. A. The folk psychotherapy of Alcoholics Anonymous. In S. Zimberg, J. Wallace, and S. B. Blume (eds.): *Practical Approaches to Alcoholism Psychotherapy*. New York: Plenum, 1978, 163–180.

American Psychiatric Association. *Psychiatrists' Viewpoints on Religion and Their Services to Religious Institutions and the Ministry: A Report of a Survey Conducted by the Task Force on Religion and Psychiatry*. Washington, DC: American Psychiatric Association, 1975.

American Psychiatric Association. *Diagnostic and Statistical Manual of Mental Disorders* (3rd ed.). Washington, D.C.: American Psychiatric Association, 1980.

American Psychiatric Association. *Diagnostic and Statistical Manual IV*. Washington, DC: 1994.

American Psychiatric Association Gold Award. Comprehensive clinical services for substance abuse treatment in an inner-city general hospital. *Hospital and Community Psychiatry* 44(10): 991–994, 1993.

Asch, S. E. *Social Psychology*. New York: Prentice-Hall, 1952.

Bagenal, F. S., Easton, D. F., Harris, E., Chilvers, C. E. D., and McElwain, T. J. Survival of patients with breast cancer attending Bristol Cancer Help Centre. *Lancet* 336: 606–610, 1990.

Baker, F. General systems theory, research, and medical care. In S. A. Baker, F. McLaughlin, and C. P. McLaughlin (eds.): *Systems and Medical Care*. Cambridge: MIT Press, 1970.

249

Baldwin, J. D., and Baldwin, J. I. *Beyond Sociobiology*. New York: Elsevier, 1981.

Bandura, A. *Social Foundations of Thought and Action: A Social Cognitive Theory*. Englewood, NJ: Prentice-Hall, 1986.

Barker, E. *The Making of a Moonie: Choice or Brainwashing*. Oxford, England: Basil Blackwell, 1984.

Bean, M. Alcoholics Anonymous. *Psychiatric Annals* 5: 46–61, 1975.

Beattie, M. *Codependent No More*. New York: HarperCollins, 1987.

Beck, A. T. *Cognitive Therapy and the Emotional Disorders*. New York: International Universities Press, 1976.

Bem, D. J. Self-Perception Theory. In L. Berkowitz (ed.): *Advances in Experimental Social Psychology*, Vol. VI. New York: Academic Press, 1972, 1–62.

Benson, H. Decreased alcohol intake associated with the practice of meditation: A retrospective investigation. *Annals of the New York Academy of Sciences*, 233: 174–177, 1974.

Benson, H., and Wallace, R. K. Decreased drug abuse with transcendental meditation: A study of 1862 subjects. In C. J. D. Zarafonetis (ed.): *Drug Abuse Proceedings of the International Conference*. Philadelphia: Lea and Febiger, 1972, 369–376.

Bergman, R. L. Navajo peyote use: Its apparent safety. *American Journal of Psychiatry* 128: 695–699, 1971.

Berkman, L. F. Social networks, host resistance, and mortality: A nine-year follow-up study of Alameda County residents. *American Journal of Epidemiology* 109: 186–204, 1978.

Bertram, B. C. R. Problems with altruism. In Kings College Sociobiology Group, Cambridge (eds.): *Current Problems in Sociobiology*. Cambridge: Cambridge University Press, 1982, 260–265.

Bezilla, R. (ed). *Religion in America 1992–1993*. Princeton, NJ: Princeton Religious Center (Gallup Organization), 1993.

Bion, W. R. *Experiences in Groups*. New York: Basic Books, 1959.

Blazer, D. G. Social support and mortality in an elderly community population. *American Journal of Epidemiology* 115: 684–694, 1982.

Bohince, E. A., and Orenstein, A. C. An Evaluation of the Services and Program of the Minnesota Chapter of Alcoholics Anonymous Master's thesis (1950). Cited in C. Emrick et al., 1977.

Bourguignon, E. Cross-cultural perspectives on the religious uses of altered states of consciousness. In I. I. Zaretsky and M. P. Leone (eds.): *Religious Movements in Contemporary America*. Princeton, NJ: Princeton University Press, 1974, 228–243.

Bowen, M. *Family Therapy in Clinical Practice*. New York: Jason Aronson, 1978.

Bowlby, J. Symposium on the contribution of current theories to an understanding of child development: An ethological approach to research in child development. *British Journal of Medical Psychology* 30: 230–240, 1957.

Bradshaw, J. *John Bradshaw on the Family*. Deerfield Beach, FL: HCI Publications, 1988.

Brecher, E. M. *Licit & Illicit Drugs*. Boston and Toronto: Little, Brown, 1972.

Brier, A., and Strauss, J. S. Self-control in psychotic disorders. *Archives of General Psychiatry* 40: 1141–1145, 1983.

Bromley, D. G., and Shupe, A. D. *Moonies in America: Cult, Church, and Crusade.* Beverly Hills, CA: Sage Publications, 1979.

Bromley, D. G., Shupe, A. D., Jr., and Ventimiglia, J. C. Atrocity tales, the Unification Church and the social construction of evil. *Journal of Communication* 29: 42–53, 1979.

Buckley, P., and Galanter, M. Mystical experience, spiritual knowledge, and a contemporary ecstatic religion. *British Journal of Medicine and Psychology* 52: 281–289, 1979.

Bugliosi, V., and Gentry, C. *Helter Skelter.* New York: W. W. Norton, 1974.

Bullis, R. K. The spiritual healing "defense" in criminal prosecutions for crimes against children. *Child Welfare* 70: 541–545, 1991.

Cacioppo, J. T. Social neuroscience: autonomic, neuroendocrine, and immune responses to stress. *Psychophysiology* 31: 113–128, 1994.

Cameron, C. *Who is Guru Maharaj Ji?* New York: Bantam Books, 1973.

Cameron, N. A. The paranoid pseudo-community. *American Journal of Sociology,* 49: 32, 1943.

Campbell, B. G. *Human Evolution: Introduction to Man's Adaptations.* Chicago: Aldine, 1974.

Cannon, W. B. "Voodoo" Death. Reprinted in abridged form from *American Anthropologist* XLIV (1942), 169–181, by permission of the American Anthropological Association. In W. A. Lessa and E. Z. Vogt (eds.): *Reader in Comparative Religion: An Anthropological Approach.* New York: Harper & Row, 1965.

Caplow, T., Bahr, H. M., and Chadwick, B. A. Piety in Middletown. *Society* 18: 34–37, 1981.

Carlsmith, J. M., Collins, B. E., and Helmreich, R. L. Studies in forced compliance: I. The effect of pressure for compliance on attitude change produced by face-to-face role playing and anonymous essay writing. *Personality and Social Psychology* 4: 1–13, 1966.

Carpenter, W. T. Jr., McGlashan, T. H., and Strauss, J. S. The treatment of acute schizophrenia without drugs: an investigation of some current assumptions. *American Journal of Psychiatry* 134: 14–20, 1977.

Cartwright, D., and Zander, A. (eds.). *Group Dynamics: Research and Theory.* Evanston, IL: Row, Peterson, 1962.

Cassileth, B. R., Lusk, E. J., Guerry, D., Blake, A. D., Walsh, W. P., Kascius, L., and Schultz, D. J. Survival and quality of life among patients receiving unproven as compared with conventional cancer therapy. *New England Journal of Medicine* 324: 1180–1185, 1991.

Cassileth, B. R., Lusk, E. J., Strouse, T. B., and Bodenheimer, B. A. Contemporary unorthodox treatments in cancer medicine: A study of patients, treatments, and practitioners. *Annals of Internal Medicine* 101: 105–112, 1984.

Chopra, D. *Perfect Health: The Complete Mind/Body Guide.* New York: Harmony Books, 1989.

Clark, J. G. Cults. *Journal of the American Medical Association* 242:279–281, 1979.

Conway, F., and Siegelman, J. *Snapping.* New York: Dell, 1978.

Coser, L. *Greedy Institutions: Patterns of Undivided Commitment.* New York: Free Press, 1974.

Darwin, C. *The Descent of Man, and Selection in Relation to Sex* (1871). New York: D. Appleton, 1889.

Denzin, N. K. *The Recovering Alcoholic.* Newbury Park, CA: Sage Publications, 1987.

DeRios, M. D., and Smith, D. E. Drug use and abuse in cross-cultural perspective. *Human Organization* 36:1, 14–21, 1977.

DeSilva, R. A. Central nervous system risk factors for sudden cardiac death. In H. M. Greenberg and E. M. Dwyer (eds.): *Sudden Cardiac Death. Annals of the New York Academy of Science* 382:143–161, 1982.

Deutsch, A. Tenacity of attachment to a cult leader: A psychiatric perspective. *American Journal of Psychiatry* 137:1569–1573, 1980.

Deutsch, A. Observations on a sidewalk Ashram. *Archives of General Psychiatry* 32:166–175, 1975.

Dobzhansky, T., and Pavlovsky, O. Experimentally created incipient species of *Drosphila. Nature* 230:289–292, 1971.

Dohrenwend, B.S., et al. Exemplification of a method for scaling life events. The PERI life events scale. *Journal of Health and Social Behavior* 19:205–229, 1979.

Downton, J. V. *Sacred Journeys: The Conversion of Young Americans to the Divine Light Mission.* New York: Columbia University Press, 1979.

Doyle, D. Have we looked beyond the physical and psychosocial? *Journal of Pain Symptom Management* 7:302–311, 1992.

Dupuy, H. J. The psychological section of the current health and nutrition examination survey. In *Proceedings of the Public Health Conference on Records and Statistics* (1972). DHEW Publication (HRA) 74–1214. Rockville, MD: National Center for Health Statistics, 1973.

Eddy, M. B. *Science and Health.* Pasadena, CA: Pasadena Press, 1989.

Eisenberg, D. M., Kessler, R. C., Foster, C., Norlock, F. E., Calkins, D. R., and Delbanco, T. L. Unconventional medicine in the United States: Prevalence, cost and patterns of use. *New England Journal of Medicine* 328:246–252, 1993.

Emrick, C. D., Lassen, C. L., and Edwards, M. T. Nonprofessional peers as therapeutic agents. In A. S. Gurman and A. M. Razin (eds.): *Effective Psychotherapy.* Oxford: Pergamon Press, 1977, 120–161.

Emrick, C. D., Tonigan, J. S., Montgomery, H., and Little, L. Alcoholics Anonymous: What is currently known? In B. S. McCrady and W. R. Miller (eds.): *Research on Alcoholics Anonymous,* pp. 41–76. New Brunswick, NJ: Rutgers Center for Alcohol Studies, 1993.

Ezriel, H. A psychoanalytic approach to group treatment. *British Journal of Medical Psychology* 23:59–74, 1950.

Fawzy, F. I., Fawzy, N. W., Hyun, C. S., Elashoff, R., Guthrie, D., Fahey, J. L., and Morton, D. L. Malignant melanoma: Effects of an early structured psychiatric intervention, coping, and affective state on recurrence and survival 6 years later. *Archives of General Psychiatry* 50:681–689, 1993.

Festinger, L. *A Theory of Cognitive Dissonance.* Stanford, CA: Stanford University Press, 1957.

Festinger, L., and Carlsmith, J. M. Cognitive consequences of forced compliance. *Journal of Abnormal Social Psychology* 58:203–210, 1959.

Festinger, L., Riecken, H., and Schachter, S. *When Prophecy Fails*. Minneapolis: University of Minnesota Press, 1956.

Fintel, W. A., and McDermott, G. R. *A Medical and Spiritual Guide to Living with Cancer*. Dallas, TX: Word, 1993.

Foundation for Inner Peace. *A Course in Miracles: Combined Version*. Tiburon, CA: Viking Press, 1996 (orig. publ. 1975).

Frank, J. *Persuasion and Healing*. New York: Schocken, 1973.

Freud, A. *The Ego and the Mechanisms of Defense*. New York: International Universities Press, 1966.

Freud, S. Group Psychology and the Analysis of the Ego (1921). In J. Strachey (ed.): *The Standard Edition of the Complete Psychological Works of Sigmund Freud*, Vol XVIII. London: Hogarth Press, 1955.

Freud, S. *Group psychology and the analysis of the ego*. London: Hogarth Press, 1948.

Galanter, M. The "relief effect": A sociobiological model for neurotic distress and large-group therapy. *American Journal of Psychiatry* 135:588–591, 1978.

Galanter, M. Psychological induction into the large-group: Findings from a contemporary religious sect. *American Journal of Psychiatry* 137:1574–1579, 1980.

Galanter, M. Sociobiology and informal social controls of drinking. *Journal of Studies on Alcohol* 42:64–79, 1981.

Galanter, M. Charismatic religious sects and psychiatry: An overview. *American Journal of Psychiatry* 139:1539–1548, 1982.

Galanter, M. Engaged members of the Unification Church. *Archives of General Psychiatry* 40:1197–1202, 1983(a).

Galanter, M. Unification Church ("Moonie") dropouts: Psychological readjustment after leaving a charismatic religious group. *American Journal of Psychiatry* 140:984–988, 1983(b).

Galanter, M. Self-help large-group therapy for alcoholism: A controlled study. *Alcoholism: Clinical and Experimental Research* 8:16–23, 1984.

Galanter, M. Moonies get married: A psychiatric follow-up study of a charismatic religious sect. *American Journal of Psychiatry* 143:1245–1249, 1986.

Galanter, M. Recovery: Self-help groups for the mentally ill. *American Journal of Psychiatry* 143:1245–1249, 1986.

Galanter, M. Zealous self-help groups as an adjunct to psychiatric treatment: A study of Recovery, Inc. *American Journal of Psychiatry* 145:1248–1253, 1988.

Galanter, M. Cults and zealous self-help movements: A psychiatric perspective. *American Journal of Psychiatry* 147:543–551, 1990.

Galanter, M. Network therapy for addiction: A model for office practice. *American Journal of Psychiatry* 150:28–36, 1993.

Galanter, M. Network therapy for substance abuse: A clinical trial. *Psychotherapy* (American Psychological Association) 30:251–258, 1993a.

Galanter, M. Spiritual recovery movements and contemporary medical care. *Psychiatry: Interpersonal and Biological Processes* 60(3): 1997.

Galanter, M., and Buckley, P. Evangelical religion and meditation: Psychotherapeutic effects. *Journal of Nervous and Mental Disease* 166:685–691, 1978.

Galanter, M., Castaneda, R., and Salamon, I. Institutional self-help for alcoholism: Clinical outcome. *Alcoholism: Clinical and Experimental Research* 11: 424–429, 1987.

Galanter, M., Egelko, S., De Leon, G., and Rohrs, C. A general hospital day program combining peer-led and professional treatment of cocaine abusers. *Hospital and Community Psychiatry* 144:644–649, 1993(b).

Galanter, M., Egelko, S., and Edwards, H. Rational Recovery: Alternative to AA for addiction? *American Journal of Drug and Alcohol Abuse* 19:499–510, 1993(a).

Galanter, M., Egelko, S., Edwards, H., and Vergaray, M. A treatment system for combined psychiatric and addictive illness. *Addiction* 89:1227–1235, 1994.

Galanter, M., Franco, H., Kim, A., Metzger, E., and De Leon, G. Inpatient treatment for the dually diagnosed: A peer-led model. In J. Solomon, S. Zimberg, and E. Shollar (eds.): *Dual Diagnosis: Evaluation, Treatment, and Training.* New York: Plenum, 1993, 171–193.

Galanter, M., Gleaton, T. J., Marcus, C. E., and McMillin, J. Parent self-help groups for young drug and alcohol abusers. *American Journal of Psychiatry* 141:889–891, 1984.

Galanter, M., Larson, D., and Rubenstone, E. Christian psychiatry: The impact of evangelical belief on clinical practice. *American Journal of Psychiatry* 148:90–95, 1991.

Galanter, M., Rabkin, R., Rabkin, J., and Deutsch, A. The "Moonies": A psychological study. *American Journal of Psychiatry* 136:165–170, 1979.

Galanter, M., Stillman, R., Wyatt, R. J., Vaughan, T. B., Weingartner, H., and Nurnberg, F. L. Marihuana and social behavior. *Archives of General Psychiatry* 30:518–521, 1974.

Galanter, M., Talbott, D., Gallegos, K., and Rubenstone, E. AA and professional care for addicted physicians. Presented at the annual meeting of the American Medical Society for Alcoholism and other Drug Dependencies. Atlanta, GA, April 1989.

Galanter, M., Talbott, D., Gallegos, K., and Rubenstone, E. Combined Alcoholics Anonymous and professional care for addicted physicians. *American Journal of Psychiatry* 147:46–48, 1990.

Galanter, M., Weingartner, H., Vaughan, T. B., Roth, W. T., and Wyatt, R. J. Delta-9 tetrahydrocannabinol and natural marihuana: A controlled comparison. *Archives of General Psychiatry* 28:278–281, 1973.

Galanter, M., Wyatt, R. J., Lemberger, L., Weingartner, H., Vaughan, T. B., and Roth, W. T. Effects on humans of delta^9-tetrahydrocannabinol administered by smoking. *Science* 175: 934–936, 1972.

Gallup Organization. *Religion in America.* Gallup Report 236: Princeton, NJ, 1985.

Gardner, R. Mechanisms in manic-depressive disorder: An evolutionary model. *Archives of General Psychiatry* 39: 1436–1441, 1982.

Gerth, H., and Mills, C. W. *From Max Weber.* New York: Oxford University Press, 1946.

Ghiselin, M. T. *The Triumph of the Darwinian Method.* Berkeley and Los Angeles: University of California Press, 1969.

Glaser, R., Kiecolt-Glaser, J. K., Stout, J. C., Tarr, K. L., Speicher, C. E., and Holliday, J. E. Stress-related impairments in cellular immunity. *Psychiatry Research* 16:233–239, 1985.

Glass, L. L., Kirsch, M. A., and Parris, F. N. Psychiatric disturbances associated with Erhard Seminars Training: I. Report of cases. *American Journal of Psychiatry* 134:245–247, 1977.

Goldfarb, L., Galanter, M., McDowell, D., Lifshutz, H., and Dermatis, H. Medical student and patient attitudes toward religion and spirituality in the recovery process. *American Journal of Drug and Alcohol Abuse* 22:549–561, 1996.

Gonzalez, V. M., Goeppinger, J., and Loring, K. Four psychosocial theories and their application to patient education and clinical practice. *Arthritis Care Research* 3:132–143, 1990.

Goode, W. J. *World Revolution and Family Patterns.* New York: Macmillan, 1970.

Goodman, F. D. *Speaking in Tongues.* Chicago: University of Chicago Press, 1972.

Goodwin, J. S., Hunt, W. C., Key, C. R., and Samet, J. M. The effect of marital status on stage, treatment, and survival of cancer patients. *Journal of the American Medical Association* 258:3125–3130, 1987.

Gordon, J. S. Holistic medicine and mental health practice: Toward a new synthesis. *American Journal of Orthopsychiatry* 60:359–370, 1990.

Grant, I., Sweetwood, H. L., Yager, J., and Gerst, M. Quality of life events in relation to psychiatric symptoms. *Archives of General Psychiatry* 38:335–339, 1981.

Greeley, A. M. *The Sociology of the Paranormal: A Reconnaissance.* Beverly Hills, CA and London: Sage Publications, 1975.

Greil, A. R., and Rudy, D. R. Social cocoons: Encapsulation and identity transformation organizations. *Social Inquiry* 54:260–278.

Hall, J. R. The Apocalypse at Jonestown. In T. Robbins and D. Anthony (eds.): *In Gods We Trust: New Patterns of Religious Pluralism in America.* New Brunswick, NJ: Transaction Books, 1981.

Hamilton, W. D. Innate social aptitudes of man: An approach from evolutionary genetics. In R. Fox (ed.): *Biosocial Anthropology.* New York: John Wiley & Sons, 1975, 133–155.

Hardt, J. V., and Kamiya, J. G. Anxiety change through electroencephalographic alpha feedback seen only in high anxiety subjects. *Science* 201: 79–81, 1978.

Harlow, H. F., and Harlow, M. K. Effects of various mother-infant relations on Rhesus monkey behaviors. In B. M. Foss (ed.): *Determinants of Infant Behavior* IV. London: Methuen, 1969, 15–36.

Harwood, H., Fountain, D., Livermore, G., et al. *Economic Costs of Drug and Alcohol Abuse in the United States: 1991.* Fairfax, VA: NIDA/NIAAA; The Lewin Group, 1997.

Heider, F. *The Psychology of Interpersonal Relations.* New York: Wiley, 1958.

Hobson, J. A., and McCarley, R. W. The brain as a dream state generator: An activation-synthesis hypothesis of the dream process. *American Journal of Psychiatry* 134:1335–1348, 1977.

Hofling, C. K., Brotzman, S. C., Graves, N., and Pierce, C. M. An experimental study in nurse-physician relationships. *Journal of Nervous and Mental Disease* 143:171–180, 1966.

Holmes, T. H., and Rahe, R. H. The social readjustment rating scale. *Journal of Psychosomatic Research* 11:213–218, 1967.

House, J. S., Robbins, C., and Metzner, H. L. The association of social relationships and activities with mortality: Prospective evidence from the Tecumseh Community Health Study. *American Journal of Epidemiology* 116:123–140, 1982.

Hume, D. *An Enquiry Concerning the Human Understanding* (1779). Oxford: Clarendon Press, 1894.

James, W. *The Varieties of Religious Experience* (1902). New York: Modern Library, 1929.

Jellinek, E. M. *The Disease Concept of Alcoholism*. New Haven: College and University Press, 1960.

Jolly, A. *The Evolution of Primate Behavior*. New York: Macmillan, 1972.

Kanter, R. M. *Commitment and Community: Communes and Utopias in Sociological Perspective*. Cambridge: Harvard University Press, 1972.

Kaplan, B., and Johnson, D. The Social Meaning of Navajo Psychopathology and Psychotherapy. In A. Kiev (ed.): *Magic Faith in Healing*. New York: Free Press, 1964, 203–229.

Kass, F., Skodol, A., and Charles, E. Therapists' recognition of psychopathology: A model for quality review of psychotherapy. *American Journal of Psychiatry* 137:87–90, 1980.

Kassler, W. J., Blanc, P., and Greenblatt, R. The use of medicinal herbs by human immunodeficiency virus-infected patients. *Archives of Internal Medicine* 151:2281–2288, 1991.

Kelley, H. H. Attribution Theory in Social Psychology. In D. Levine (ed.): *Nebraska Symposium on Motivation*, Vol XV. Lincoln: University of Nebraska Press, 1967, 192–238.

Kennedy, J. G. Nubian Zar ceremonies and psychotherapy. *Human Organization* 4:185–192, 1967.

Kephart, W. M. *Extraordinary Groups: The Sociology of Unconventional Life-Styles*. New York: St. Martin's Press, 1976.

Kerns, P., and Wead, D. *Peoples Temple: Peoples Tomb*. Plainfield, NJ: Logos, 1979.

Kilbourne, B., and Richardson, J. T. Psychotherapy and new religions in a pluralistic society. *American Psychologist* 39:237–251, 1984.

Kirsch, M. A., and Glass, L. L. Psychiatric disturbances associated with Erhard Seminars Training: II. Additional cases and theoretical considerations. *American Journal of Psychiatry* 134:1254–1258, 1977.

Kleinman, A. *Patients and Healers in the Context of Culture*. Berkeley, CA: University of California Press, 1980.

Koenig, H. G. Research on religion and mental health in later life: A review and commentary. *Journal of Geriatric Psychiatry* 23:23–53, 1990.

Kolata, G. B. Human evolution: Life-styles and lineages of early hominids. *Science* 187:940–942, 1975.

Kroll, J., and Sheehan, W. Religious beliefs and practices among 52 psychiatric in patients in Minnesota. *American Journal of Psychiatry* 146: 67–72, 1989.

Kurtz, E. *Not God: A History of Alcoholics Anonymous.* Garden City, MN: Hareldon Educational Services, 1979.

LaBarre, W. *The Ghost Dance.* New York: Doubleday, 1970.

Lane, R., Jr. Catholic charismatic renewal. In C. Y. Glock and N. Bellah (eds.): *The New Religious Consciousness.* Los Angeles: University of California Press, 1976.

Lang, D. A reporter at large. *New Yorker*, November 1974, 56–126.

Larson, D. B., Pattison, E. M., Blazer, D. G., Omran, A. R., and Kaplan, B. H. Systematic analysis of research on religious variables in four major psychiatric journals, 1978–1982. *American Journal of Psychiatry* 143: 329–334, 1986.

Leighton, A., and Leighton, D. Elements of psychotherapy in Navajo religion. *Psychiatry* 4: 515–523, 1941.

Lepper, M. R., Greene, D., and Nesbitt, R. E. Undermining children's intrinsic interest with extrinsic reward: A test of the "over-justification" hypothesis. *Journal of Personality and Social Psychology* 28: 129–137, 1973.

Lerner, I. J., and Kennedy, B. J. The prevalence of questionable methods of cancer treatment in the United States. *CA-Cancer Journal Clinical* 42: 181–191, 1992.

Levin, J. S., Lyons, J. S., and Larson, D. B. Prayer and health during pregnancy: Findings from the Galveston low birthweight survey. *Southern Medical Journal* 86: 1022–1027, 1993.

Levy, S. M., Herberman, R. B., Whitside, T., Sanzo, K., Lee, J., and Kirkwood, J. Perceived social support and tumor estrogen/progesterone receptor status as predictors of natural killer cell activity in breast cancer patients. *Psychosomatic Medicine* 42: 73–85, 1990.

Lewin, K. *A Dynamic Theory of Personality.* New York: McGraw-Hill, 1935.

Liberman, R. P., Teigen, J., Patterson, R., et al. Reducing delusional speech in chronic paranoid schizophrenics. *Journal of Applied Behavioral Analysis* 6: 57–64, 1973.

Lifton, R. J. *Thought Reform and the Psychology of Totalism.* New York: W. W. Norton, 1961.

Lockard, J. S., McDonald, L. L., Clifford, D. A., and Martinez, R. Panhandling: Sharing of resources. *Science* 191: 406–408, 1976.

Lofland, J., and Stark, R. Becoming a world-saver: A theory of conversion to a deviant perspective. *American Sociology Review* 30: 862–875, 1965.

Lorenz, K. Analogy as a source of knowledge. *Science* 185: 229–234, 1974.

Lorenz, K. *On Aggression.* New York: Harcourt Brace, 1966.

Lubchansky, I., Egri, G., and Stokes, J. Puerto Rican spiritualists view mental illness: The faith healer as a paraprofessional. *American Journal of Psychiatry* 127: 312–321, 1970.

Ludwig, A. M. Altered states of consciousness. *Archives of General Psychiatry* 15: 225–234, 1966.

Lumsden, C. J., and Wilson, E. O. *Genes, Mind, and Culture.* Cambridge: Harvard University Press, 1981.

Lynd, R. S., and Lynd, H. M. *Middletown: A Study in American Culture*. New York: Harcourt and Brace, 1929.

Manatt, M. *Parents, Peers and Pot*. US DHEW Publication (ADM) 79–812, 1979.

Marshall, E. The politics of alternative medicine. *Science* 265: 2000–2002, 1994.

Maryles, D. Behind the best-sellers. *Publishers Weekly*, July 26, 1993, p. 20.

Maslow, A. H. Synanon and eupsychia. *Journal of Humanistic Psychology* 7: 28–35, 1967.

Maslow, A. H. *Religions, Values, and Peak Experiences*. New York: Viking Press, 1964.

Maugans, T. A., and Wadland, W. C. Religion and family medicine: A survey of physicians and patients. *Journal of Family Practice* 32: 210–213, 1991.

Maxwell, M. A. *The Alcoholics Anonymous Experience*. New York: McGraw-Hill, 1984.

Maynard Smith, J. Group selection and kin selection. *Nature* 201: 1145–1147, 1964.

McDaniel, J. S., Musselman, D. L., Porter, M. R., Reed, D. A., and Nemeroff, C. B. Depression in patients with cancer. Diagnosis, biology and treatment. *Archives of General Psychiatry* 52: 89–99, 1995.

McDowell, D., Galanter, M., Goldfarb, L., and Lifshutz, H. Spirituality and the treatment of the dually diagnosed: An investigation of patient and staff attitudes. *Journal of Addictive Disease* 15: 55–68, 1996.

Mead, G. H. *Mind, Self, and Society from the Standpoint of a Social Behaviorist*. Chicago: University of Chicago Press, 1962.

Melges, F. T., Tinklenberg, J. R., Deardorff, C. M., Davies, N. H., Anderson, R. E., and Owen, C. A. Temporal disorganization and delusional-like ideation. *Archives of General Psychiatry* 30: 855–861, 1974.

Melton, J. G. *The Encyclopedia of American Religions*, Vol. II. Wilmington, NC: McGarth, 1978.

Melton, J. G., and Moore, R. L. *The Cult Experience: Responding to the New Religious Pluralism*. New York: Pilgrim Press, 1982.

Menninger, K. *The Vital Balance*. New York: Viking Press, 1963.

Milgram, S. *Obedience to Authority*. New York: Harper Colophon Books, 1975.

Miller, J. G., Freedman, A. M., Kaplan, H. I., and Saddock, B. K. (eds.). *Comprehensive Textbook of Psychiatry* II. Baltimore, MD: Williams and Wilkins, 74–88, 1975.

Miller, J. G. Living systems: Basic concepts. *Behavioral Science* 10: 193–237, 1965.

Miner, H. Body ritual among the Nacirema. *American Anthropologist* 58: 503–507, 1956.

Mitchell, E. Father of the child within. *Time*, November 25, 1991, p. 82.

Moorhouse, G. The Moonies invade Gloucester. *Harper's*, January 1981, pp. 46–52.

Mosher, L. R., and Menn, A. Z. Community residential treatment for schizophrenia: A two-year follow-up. *Hospital and Community Psychiatry* 29: 715–723, 1978.

Mosher, L. R., and Menn, A. Z. Scientific evidence and system change: The Soteria experience. In H. Stierlin et al. (eds.): *Psychosocial Interventions in Schizophrenia*. Heidelberg: Springer-Verlag, 1983, 93–108.

Mosher, L. R., Menn, A., and Matthews, S. M. Soteria: Evaluation of a home-based treatment for schizophrenia. *American Journal of Orthopsychiatry* 45: 455–467, 1975.

Mueller, D. P., Edwards, D. W., and Yarvis, R. M. Stressful life events and psychiatric symptomatology: Change or undesirability? *Journal of Health and Social Behavior* 18: 307–317, 1977.

Murray, R. H., and Rubel, A. J. Physicians and healers—unwitting partners in health care. *New England Journal of Medicine* 326: 641–642, 1992.

Murstein, B. I. Physical attractiveness and marital choice. *Journal of Personality and Social Psychology* 22: 8–12, 1972.

National Center for Health Statistics. *A Concurrent Validational Study of the NCHS General Well-Being Schedule*. Vital and Health Statistics Series 2, No. 73. Hyattsville, MD: DHEW Publication No. (HRA) 78-1347, 1977.

Ness, R. C., and Wintrob, R. M. The emotional impact of fundamentalist religious participation: An empirical study of intragroup variation. *American Journal of Orthopsychiatry* 50: 302–315, 1980.

Noyes, P. B. *My Father's House: An Oneida Boyhood* (1927). Gloucester, MA: Peter Smith, 1966.

Nugent, J. P. *White Night: The Untold Story of What Happened Before—and Beyond—Jonestown*. New York: Rawson and Wade, 1979.

Ofshe, R. Synanon: The People Business. In C. Y. Glock and R. N. Bellah (eds.): *The New Religious Consciousness*. Berkeley: University of California Press, 1976, 116–137.

Ofshe, R., Eisenberg, N., Coughlin, R., Dolinajec, G., Gerson, K., and Johnson, A. Social structure and social control in Synanon. *Voluntary Action Research* 3: 67–76, 1974.

Orne, M. Demand characteristics and the concept of quasi-controls. In R. Rosenthal and L. Rosnow (eds.): *Artifact in Behavioral Research*. New York: Academic Press, 1969, 143–179.

Orr, R. D., and Isaac, G. Religious variables are infrequently reported in clinical research. *Family Medicine* 24: 602–606, 1992.

Pahnke, W. N. Drugs and mysticism. *International Journal of Parapsychology*, Vol. VIII, 2:295–314, 1966.

Paredes, A. Social control of drinking among the Aztec Indians of Mesoamerica. *Journal of Studies on Alcohol* 36:9, 1139–1153, 1975.

Parsons, A. S. The Moonies: The triumph of family. *Smith Alumnae Quarterly*, Summer 1984, pp. 8–13.

Pattison, E. M. Nonabstinent drinking goals in the treatment of alcoholism. *Archives of General Psychiatry* 33:923–930, 1976.

Pattison, E. M. Ideological support for the marginal middle class: Faith healing and glossolalia. In I. I. Zaretsky and M. P. Leone (eds.): *Religious Movements in Contemporary America*. Princeton, NJ: Princeton University Press, 1974, 418–455.

Pattison, E. M., Labins, N. A., and Doerr, H. A. Faith healing: A study of personality and function. *Journal of Nervous and Mental Disease* 157:367–409, 1973.

Pattison, E. M., and Pattison, M. L. "Ex-gays": Religiously-mediated change in homosexuals. *American Journal of Psychiatry* 137:1553–1562, 1980.

Peck, M. *The Road Less Traveled.* New York: Simon and Schuster, 1985.

Penfield, W. *The Mystery of the Mind.* Princeton, NJ: Princeton University Press, 1975.

Pennebaker, J. W., Kiecolt-Glaser, J. K., and Glaser, R. Disclosure of traumas and immune function: Health implications for psychotherapy. *Journal of Consulting Clinical Psychology* 56:239–245, 1988.

Pilarzyk, T. The origin, development, and decline of a youth culture religion: An application of sectarianization theory. *Review of Religious Research* 20 (Fall 1978).

Pilbeam, D. *The Ascent of Man: An Introduction to Human Evolution.* New York: Macmillan, 1972.

Proudfoot, W., and Shaver, P. Attribution theory and the psychology of religion. *Journal for the Scientific Study of Religion* 14:317–330, 1975.

Radcliffe-Brown, A. R. *Taboo.* Cambridge: Cambridge University Press, 1939.

Reiss, D. Varieties of consensual experience. *Family Process* 10:1–35, 1971.

Rice, A. K. *Learning for Leadership.* London: Tavistock Publications, 1965.

Richardson, J., Sheldon, D., Krailo, M., and Levine, A. The effect of compliance with treatment on survival among patients with hematologic malignancies. *Journal of Clinical Oncology* 8:356–364, 1990.

Robbins, T. Religious movements, the state, and the law: Reconceptualizing "the cult problem." *New York University Review of Law and Social Change* 19: 33–49, 1979–1980.

Robinson, A. Spirituality and risk: Toward an understanding. *Holistic Nurse Practitioner* 8:1–7, 1994.

Robinson, D. *Talking Out of Alcoholism.* The Self-Help Process of Alcoholics Anonymous. Baltimore, MD: University Park Press, 1979.

Ross, J. C. Errors on "Moonies." *American Journal of Psychiatry* 140: 643–644, 1983.

Roth, W. T., Galanter, M., Weingartner, H., Vaughan, T. B., and Wyatt, R. J. Marijuana and synthetic delta-9-trans-tetrahydrocannabinol: Some effects on the auditory evoked response and background EEG in humans. *Biological Psychiatry* 6:221–223, 1973.

Rothmyer, K. Mapping out Moon's media empire. *Columbia Journalism Review,* November–December, 1984, 23–31.

Rudy, D. R. *Becoming Alcoholic: Alcoholics Anonymous and the Reality of Alcoholism.* Carbondale: Southern Illinois University Press, 1986.

Ruse, M. Sociobiology: Sound science or muddled metaphysics. In *Is Science Sexist? and Other Problems in the Biomedical Sciences.* Boston: D. Reidel, 1981.

Russell, D., Peplau, L. A., and Cutrona, C. E. The revised UCLA Loneliness Scale: Concurrent and discriminant validity evidence. *Journal of Personality and Social Psychology* 39:472–480, 1980.

Samarin, W. J. Glossolalia as learned behaviour. *Canadian Journal of Theology* 15: 60–64, 1959.

Schacter, S., and Singer, J. E. Cognitive, social, and physiological determinants of emotional state. *Psychology Review* 69:379–399, 1962.

Schein, E. The Chinese indoctrination program for prisoners of war. *Psychiatry* 19:149–172, 1956.

Schultes, R. E. An overview of hallucinogens in the Western Hemisphere. In P. Furst (ed.): *Flesh of the Gods.* New York: Praeger, 1972.

Sharma, H. M., Triguna, B. D., and Chopra, D. Maharishi Ayur-Veda: Modern insights into ancient medicine. *Journal of the American Medical Association* (letter from New Delhi) 265:2633–2637, 1991.

Shekelle, R. B., Raynor, W. J., Ostfeld, A. M., Garron, D. C., Bieliauskas, L. A., Liu, S. C., Maliza, C., and Paul, O. Psychological depression and 17-year risk of death from cancer. *Psychosomatic Medicine* 43:117–125, 1981.

Shone, R. *Creative Visualization.* Rochester, VT: Destiny Books, 1988.

Siegel, B. S. *Love, Medicine & Miracles: Lessons Learned about Self-healing from a Surgeon's Experience with Exceptional Patients.* New York: Harper & Row, 1986.

Siegel, B. S. Exceptional patients live long and live well. *Maryland Medical Journal* 39:181–182, 1990.

Simon, J. Observations on 67 patients who took Erhard Seminars Training. *American Journal of Psychiatry* 135:686–691, 1978.

Singer, M. Therapy with ex-cult members. *National Association of Private Psychiatric Hospitals Journal* 9(4):14–18, 1978.

Singer, M., and Borrero, M. G. Indigenous treatment for alcoholism: The case of Puerto Rican spiritualism. *Medical Anthropology: Cross-Cultural Studies in Health and Illness* 8:246–273, 1984.

Skolnick, A. A. Maharishi Ayur-Veda: Guru's marketing scheme promises the world eternal "perfect health." *Journal of the American Medical Association* 226:1741–1750, 1991.

Smith, M. J. Group selection and kin selection. *Nature* 201:1145–1147, 1964.

Snow, D. A., and Phillips, C. L. The Lofland-Stark conversion model. *Social Problems* 27:430–447, 1980.

Spiegel, D., Kraemer, H. C., Bloom, J. R., and Gottheil, E. Effect of psychosocial treatment on survival of patients with metastatic breast cancer. *Lancet* 2: 888–891, 1989.

Stark, R., and Bainbridge, W. S. Networks of faith: Interpersonal bonds and recruitment to cults and sects. *American Journal of Sociology* 85:1376–1395, 1980.

Sterling, C. *The Terror Network.* New York: Holt Rinehart, 1981.

Suomi, S. J., DeLizio, R., and Harlow, H. F. Social rehabilitation of separation-induced depressive disorders in monkeys. *American Journal of Psychiatry* 133:1279–1285, 1976.

Suomi, S. J., Harlow, H. F., and McKinney, W. T., Jr. Monkey psychiatrists. *American Journal of Psychiatry* 128:927–932, 1972.

Suomi, S. J., Seaman, S. F., Lewis, J. K., DeLizio, R. D., and McKinney, W. T. Effects of imipramine treatment of separation-induced social disorders in Rhesus monkeys. *Archives of General Psychiatry* 35:321–325, 1978.

Suwaki, H. "Naikan" and Danshukai for the treatment of Japanese alcoholic patients. *British Journal of Addictions* 74:15–19, 1979.

Tart, C. T. *States of Consciousness*. New York: E. P. Dutton, 1975.

Thomsen, R. *Bill W*. New York: Harper & Row, 1975.

Tinbergen, N. *The Study of Instinct*. London: Oxford University Press, 1951.

Trice, H., and Beyer, J. M. The routinization of charisma in two social movement organizations. Paper presented at the Academy of Management Meetings, Dallas, TX, 1983.

Trier, K. K., and Shupe, A. Prayer, religiosity, and healing in the heartland, USA: A research note. *Review of Religious Research* 32:351–358, 1991.

Trivers, R. L. The evaluation of reciprocal altruism. *Quarterly Review Biology* 46: 35–37, 1971.

Ungerleider, J. M., and Wellisch, D. K. Coercive persuasion (brainwashing), religious cults, and deprogramming. *American Journal of Psychiatry* 136:279–282, 1979.

Vaillant, G. E., and Milofsky, E. S. Natural history of male alcoholism. *Archives of General Psychiatry* 39:127–133, 1982.

von Bertalanffy, L. *General Systems Theory*. New York: George Braziller, 1968.

Waldfogel, S., and Root Wolpe, P. Using awareness of religious factors to enhance interventions in consultation-liaison psychiatry. *Hospital and Community Psychiatry* 44:473–477, 1993.

Wallace, R. K. Physiological effects of transcendental meditation. *Science* 167: 1751–1754, 1970.

Weber, M. *The Theory of Social and Economic Organization*. New York: Macmillan, 1947.

Weigert, E. Human ego functions in the light of animal behavior. *Psychiatry* 19: 325–332, 1956.

Weightsman, J. M. *Making Sense of the Jonestown Suicides*. Lewiston, NY: Edwin Mellon Press, 1983.

Weil, A. *8 Weeks to Optimum Health: A Proven Program for Taking Full Advantage of Your Body's Natural Healing Power*, New York: Knopf, 1997.

Weil, A. *Natural Health, Natural Medicine*. Boston: Houghton Mifflin, 1990.

Weil, A. *The Natural Mind*. Boston: Houghton Mifflin, 1972.

Weiner, N. *Cybernetics*. New York: Wiley, 1948.

Wendt, R. J., Mosher, L. R., Matthews, S. M., and Menn, A. Z. Comparison of Two Treatment Environments for Schizophrenia. In J. G. Gunderson, O. A. Will, Jr., and L. R. Mosher (eds.): *Principles and Practices of Milieu Therapy*. New York: Jason Aronson, 1983.

Williams, D. R., Larson, D. B., Buckler, R. E., Heckmann, R. C., and Pyle, C. M. Religion and psychological distress in a community sample. *Social Science Medicine* 32:1257–1262, 1991.

Williamson, M. *A Return to Love: Reflections on the Principles of a Course in Miracles*. New York: Harper Perennial, 1993.

Wilson, E. O. *Sociobiology: The New Synthesis*. Cambridge: Harvard (The Belknap Press), 1975.

Winfrey, C. Why 900 Died in Guyana. *New York Times Magazine*, February 26, 1979, p. 45.

Wolin, S. T., and Steinglass, P. Interactional behavior in an alcoholic community. *Medical Annals of the District of Columbia* 43:183–187, 1974.

Wright, S. Tempo and mode in evolution—a critical review. *Ecology* 26:415–419, 1945.

Wynne, L. C., Ryckoff, I. M., Day, J., and Hirsch, S. Pseudomutuality in the family relations of schizophrenics. *Psychiatry* 21:205–222, 1958.

Yalom, I. D., and Lieberman, M. A. A study of encounter group casualties. *Archives of General Psychiatry* 25:16–30, 1971.

INDEX